TEACHING
NUMBER SENSE

GRADE 2

2

SUSAN SCHARTON

Math Solutions
Sausalito, California, USA

Math Solutions
150 Gate 5 Road
Sausalito, CA 94965
www.mathsolutions.com

Library of Congress Cataloging-in-Publication Data
Scharton, Susan.
  Teaching number sense, grade 2 / Susan Scharton.
    p. cm.
  Includes index.
  ISBN 0-941355-60-8 (acid-free paper)
  1. Mathematics—Study and teaching (Primary) 2. Numeration. 3. Counting. 4. Arithmetic. I. Title.
  QA135.6.S415 2005
  372.7—dc22

                                    2005010702

ISBN-13: 978-0-941355-60-5

Editor: Toby Gordon
Production: Melissa L. Inglis
Cover & interior design: Catherine Hawkes/Cat and Mouse
Composition: Interactive Composition Corporation

Printed in the United States of America on acid-free paper
09   ML   3   4   5

A Message from Math Solutions

We at Math Solutions believe that teaching math well calls for increasing our understanding of the math we teach, seeking deeper insights into how children learn mathematics, and refining our lessons to best promote students' learning.

Math Solutions shares classroom-tested lessons and teaching expertise from our faculty of professional development instructors as well as from other respected math educators. Our publications are part of the nationwide effort we've made since 1984 that now includes

- more than five hundred face-to-face professional development programs each year for teachers and administrators in districts across the country;
- annually publishing professional development books, now totaling more than seventy titles and spanning the teaching of all math topics in kindergarten through grade 8;
- four series of videos for teachers, plus a video for parents, that show math lessons taught in actual classrooms;
- on-site visits to schools to help refine teaching strategies and assess student learning; and
- free online support, including grade-level lessons, book reviews, inservice information, and district feedback, all in our *Math Solutions Online Newsletter*.

For information about all of the products and services we have available, please visit our website at *www.mathsolutions.com*. You can also contact us to discuss math professional development needs by calling (800) 868-9092 or by sending an email to *info@mathsolutions.com*.

We're always eager for your feedback and interested in learning about your particular needs. We look forward to hearing from you.

mathsolutions.com

Contents

Computational Fluency

Blackline Masters

Acknowledgments

Thank you to the students and teachers who generously opened up their classrooms and participated in the lessons that became part of this book: Carin Ong, Laurel Elementary School, Oceanside, California; Beth Mahony, Santa Margarita Elementary School, Oceanside, California; Kristin Garrison, McAuliffe Elementary School, Oceanside, California.

Thank you to Paula Snowdy for the suggestions and ideas that turned into successful lessons.

Thank you to Rusty Bresser for being a constant source of support and wisdom.

Thank you to Sally Renouf and Michael Scharton for your love and encouragement.

Thank you to Randy Baker for encouraging me to follow my aspirations.

Introduction

In learning mathematics, second graders regularly demonstrate fragile number sense. As classroom teachers, we witness their developing understandings and are curious about their misconceptions. The following stories will no doubt sound familiar.

At regular intervals throughout the school year, a class of twenty-five second-grade students first estimates, then counts, the total number of pockets on students' clothing on a particular day. Their first pocket-counting experience is in the fall. It is a cool day and many students are wearing pants with pockets. The teacher introduces the activity, then asks, "I want you to look around the room at what your classmates are wearing. Think about the number of children in our classroom, as well as any other important information you could use. How many total pockets do you think students in our classroom are wearing today?" The first student responds with great confidence: "Nine!"

Students in another second-grade classroom keep track of the total number of days that school has been in session, by numbering the days consecutively and working daily with the new number. On the first day of school, the teacher records a *1* on a number chart, and students are asked to collaboratively generate a list of equations equal to "today's number," then "build" that number with various mathematics manipulatives. On the thirty-first day of school, a child yells out, "It's Halloween!"

A group of second graders is introduced to the game *Guess My Number*. The teacher explains the goal of the game: to guess the number he has "hidden" in his head in the fewest number of guesses. He tells students the range of numbers they can consider, writing this range on the board: *1–20*. He asks students to raise their hands to guess possible numbers. He will let them know if the secret number is greater or less than the number guessed and record this information on the board as well. The first student called on says, "I know! Thirty-five!"

Midway through the school year, second-grade students at Lincoln Elementary take their annual trip to the local fire station. They learn about fire prevention, home-evacuation procedures, and what to do in case of fire emergencies. They receive plastic fire helmets, book covers, stickers, and pencils. After practicing how to "Stop, drop, and roll," a recommended action in fire emergencies, they tour the fire station and are invited to hop aboard the ladder truck. The 100-foot-long ladder—clearly labeled with a tag stating *100 feet*— is extended for all to marvel at. One child says to another, "Wow . . . that thing is *really* long! How long do you think it is?" Her friend responds, "Long! At *least* ninety inches!"

The above anecdotes suggest that it is sometimes easier to identify what number sense *isn't* than to identify what it *is*. As teachers of small children, we all share similar stories about our students' struggles with number. We also share the difficult task of addressing their misconceptions and inconsistencies with appropriate, meaningful, and engaging experiences.

What Is "Number Sense"?

This book contains lessons that address aspects of number sense important to consider when teaching second-grade students.

Counting and Estimation

Counting experiences help students to understand that numbers represent quantity. Place-value understanding depends on counting experiences. It is through counting and grouping objects that students come to know the relationship between the placement of a digit and groups of things.

Estimation experiences enable students to consider reasonableness and appropriateness while also creating situations in which students have a stake in the outcome.

Composing and Decomposing Numbers

Number sense includes understanding how numbers relate to each other as well as knowing that numbers can be broken into meaningful chunks. Without explicit experiences that focus on separating quantities into two or more parts, students continue to count to determine quantity. When students have experiences in composing and decomposing numbers, they learn that numbers can be broken apart and put back together in lots of different ways. They develop and use benchmark numbers and show flexibility with numbers and number relationships. The realization that numbers have component parts—including but going beyond groupings of ones, tens, hundreds, and so on—is important for students to develop if they are to operate on numbers in efficient and meaningful ways.

Numbers in Our World

While adults encounter number and computation daily, it can be difficult to convince young children that numbers have purpose and usefulness outside of the four walls of the classroom. Numbers are necessary to locate, quantify, label, and measure. As adults, we are required to interpret and use numbers in a variety of real-world contexts. To prepare them for the world, it is important for our students to become aware of how numbers are used in various contexts as well.

Developing Computation Strategies

The types of numbers we choose, the problems we pose, and the procedures we value have an effect on students' developing number sense. Different people reason in different ways. Rather than memorizing a teacher-demonstrated procedure for computing with numbers, students with number sense are able to understand the procedures they construct and use. They understand and use relationships among operations, as well as knowledge of the base ten system, in order to solve problems. They can explain the procedures they use to others.

Place Value

Place-value understanding grows from experience with counting. When students have frequent opportunities to count objects in many different ways, they come to realize the connections between quantity and the position of a digit. Students that have place-value understanding know that the 6 in 63 refers to sixty, as well as six groups of ten. Until students understand place value, they solve problems based on counting and "one more than" relationships. Understanding that each digit in a multidigit number represents a quantity as well as groups of a specific size is critical for students if they are to solve problems efficiently and flexibly.

Computational Fluency

Students with number sense can transfer their understandings to new situations. They know which methods are appropriate in various problem-solving situations and become more efficient with the methods they choose and use. If students are to develop computational fluency, they need experience with calculating mentally, with paper and pencil, and with a calculator. They also benefit and learn from hearing other students explain their solution strategies.

The Structure of the Lessons

The lessons in this book differ in a variety of ways. Some lessons last one day and others continue over three or more days. Some are one-shot activities, while others are intended to be repeated at regular junctures throughout the school year. To assist you with planning and implementing the lessons in this book, they are organized in the following ways:

Overview   This is a brief description of the lesson, and includes the mathematical focus of the lesson.

Materials   This section lists the special materials used in the lesson, as well as their quantities. Regular classroom supplies, such as paper, pencils, and scissors, are not listed. Overheads and worksheets are provided in the Blackline Masters section at the back of the book.

Time   The estimated length of the lesson, as well as the suggested number of times to repeat the lesson, is included here.

Teaching Directions   Directions for the lesson are given in a step-by-step lesson plan.

Teaching Notes   Information about the mathematics underlying the lesson is given in this section. It also contains information regarding the type of experiences or prior knowledge students need in order to be most successful with the lesson.

The Lesson   This is a vignette describing what happened when the lesson was taught over a period of one to three days. It follows the sequence of the teaching directions, but contains details that are important to consider when planning for the lesson. It also includes samples of student work.

Linking Assessment and Instruction   This section contains questions to consider when observing students work. These questions help uncover the degree to which students are connecting with the mathematical focus of the lesson.

How to Use This Book

The seventeen lessons in this book are grouped into sections. The sections are organized by those features of number sense most central to the lessons included, even though these lessons easily share multiple aspects of number sense.

While estimated length and suggested number of class periods are provided for each lesson, it is appropriate that many of these lessons be repeated throughout the school year. This repetition is especially beneficial with respect to lessons that involve playing games. It takes several class periods for students to feel comfortable with the rules for and steps in playing a game. Once students become experienced with these issues, they can begin to focus on the mathematics concepts inherent in the game. Thus, it is beneficial to play games many times, as the purpose for playing them evolves.

Teaching the lessons in this book requires thirty-five to fifty instructional days. However, it is not recommended that these lessons be taught in a continuous manner for seven to ten weeks. After exposure to the experiences and content in a particular lesson, students benefit from time between lessons to reflect upon and take in presented concepts. Lessons within each section are ordered by level of difficulty. It is suggested that lessons that come first in a section are taught earlier in the school year and those that occur last are taught later.

Having students communicate about what they know and can do is an important aspect of this book. Students are asked to regularly explain their thinking aloud and in writing. These explanations serve a number of purposes, important to students and teachers alike. They provide the teacher with valuable assessment information about current conceptual understanding, helping teachers to judge the effectiveness of recent instruction and plan for future instruction. Students deepen their understanding when they explain their thinking to others. Listening to the thinking of others allows students insight into ways of thinking they may not have considered on their own.

Requiring students to explain their thinking through discussion and in writing is not a trivial task. Students benefit from explicit classroom time devoted to modeling effective communication. These lessons provide examples in which students demonstrate what they know and can do both verbally and in writing. Classroom discussions initially focus on the value of listening to and learning from their classmates, as well as helping students recognize the types of behaviors associated with good listening. Students have many opportunities to engage in meaningful talk, in pairs, small groups, and whole-class discussions. Students learn that their thinking processes are valued, and that their contributions are expected, honored, and respected.

Representation is another way that students share their understanding with others. Many lessons detail ways to chart student thinking through the use of words, numbers, pictures, and equations. Recording their ideas not only validates the contributions of individual students but also serves as support: students consider these models as ways to represent their ideas independently.

Lengths of Yarn

OVERVIEW

Measurement experiences provide real-world opportunities for students to use and compare numbers. In this activity, students first estimate the length of pieces of yarn and then determine the measurement using familiar counters as non-standard units. Students discuss the differences between yarn pieces of different lengths, as well as the differences between their estimates and the actual measurements.

MATERIALS

- pieces of thick yarn of different colors, varying in length from 10 to 30 inches, 4–5 pieces per group of 4 students
- Unifix cubes in various colors, approximately 200 per group of students
- *Yarn Lengths* recording sheet, 1 per student (see Blackline Masters)

Yarn Name	Estimate	Measurement	Difference

TIME

- one class period

Teaching Directions

1. Have each student choose a piece of yarn and record its "name" on the recording sheet.
2. Ask the students to estimate the number of cubes that equals the length of the yarn and add this estimate to their recording sheet.
3. Have students determine the actual number of cubes equal to the length of the yarn and add this "measurement" to their recording sheet.
4. Ask the students to compare the difference between their estimate and the actual measurement and add this to their recording sheet.
5. Invite the students to repeat the exercise with another piece(s) of yarn.

Teaching Notes

This measurement activity provides students with real, hands-on, meaningful experience with numbers. Estimating, then measuring, the yarn lengths makes children invested in the result. It also provides an opportunity for students to compare the estimate and the actual measurement. As students continue measuring yarn pieces of varying lengths, they acquire referents to which they can compare successive lengths of yarn. Knowing the number of cubes it will take to equal the length of a piece of yarn makes it possible for students to use this knowledge when estimating and measuring lengths of yarn that are longer and shorter. These repeated experiences allow students to acquire an understanding of how these numbers relate to each other.

The Lesson

Before beginning the lesson, I had cut different lengths of various colors of yarn and attached a masking tape label to the end of each. Each label had a different capital letter written on it, so that students could differentiate one length of yarn from another. I then assembled baskets of materials for each group of four students. Inside each basket were four or five lengths of yarn, recording sheets, and cubes.

To begin, I invited the students to join me in a seated circle on the rug. I placed one of the baskets in front of me, then laid out the basket's contents so that all of the children could see the materials.

"What are those?" Daniel asked.

"It's yarn," answered Maria.

"They are all different sizes!" Valerie noticed. "Why do they have tape on the end?"

"There's letters on the tape!" said Todd.

"You noticed many things about the materials in front of me," I acknowledged. "Some of us noticed that these are pieces of yarn and that they are all different sizes, or 'lengths.' Others saw that there is a tape label on the end of each piece of yarn and that this tape label has a letter on it. So we've noticed some important details."

Because the students were going to be estimating and measuring different pieces of yarn, it was important for them to realize that these pieces were indeed of different lengths. I asked them, "If I wanted to know if these pieces really were all different lengths, what could I do to be sure?"

"Lay them all out!" Juan said.

"Put them next to each other . . . then you could see!" Kelly suggested.

"What if you put them side by side? But you have to make the ends all the same," Jonathon offered.

I encouraged him to clarify this idea. "Jonathon, you told me that I would have to make the ends all 'the same.' I am not sure what you mean. Could you tell me in a different way?"

Jonathon got up from his place in the circle and came to the center of the rug. He carefully began ordering all of the pieces of yarn, laying one above the other, matching the left end of each piece so that it was even with the piece below it. "See?" he said. "You can't tell if they're all different unless you make the ends the same." He pointed to the right ends of the yarn pieces. "See how they all stick out different? That means all the yarns are different sizes." The students nodded in agreement.

"Let's find out about their sizes, or 'lengths,'" I said. I pulled out a medium-size piece of yarn from the pile. "See this tape label? This label helps me remember the 'name' of this piece of yarn," I explained. "It helps me remember which piece I have already used." I showed them the recording sheet for the activity. It had four columns, labeled *Yarn Name*, *Estimate*, *Measurement*, and *Difference*. "I am going to write the name of this piece, D, in this column." As

I said this I pointed to the *Yarn Name* column and wrote down the letter *D*. "I am going to use cubes to measure the yarn. But first, I wonder how many it would take to go from one end of the yarn to the other?" Many hands went up to assist me with making an estimate.

I called on students one at a time. They gave different estimates, ranging from twelve to twenty-nine. "Mathematicians have a word for these types of 'wonderings,' or 'smart guesses,'" I said. Since the students had been exposed to prior experiences with estimation, I was not surprised to hear them offer, "Estimates!" and "Estimation!" and "Prediction!"

"I am going to do something a little different than 'predict,'" I said. "A prediction is a smart guess about what you think is going to happen. An estimate is a little different. When you make a smart guess about the size of something, or how big it is, that is called an 'estimate.' It isn't a 'wild guess,' because you use what you already know. I have a lot of experience with cubes. I am going to use that experience to make a 'smart guess,' or estimate about how many it will take to equal the length of yarn D. I estimate that it will take twenty-nine cubes, snapped together, to equal the length of this yarn." I showed them how to record the estimate in the appropriate column on the recording sheet.

"Now I need to use the snap cubes to measure. I am interested in finding out how close my estimate is to the actual measurement. First, I am trying to remember some important things about using cubes as measuring tools. Can you help remind me of some things to think about?"

Several students raised their hands. "You have to put them next to each other," one student commented.

"No spaces between the cubes," said another.

"They have to go in a line," suggested a third.

"Your suggestions are quite helpful," I said. "I am going to remember them as I measure the yarn. There is something else you will do when measuring the pieces of yarn with cubes. I want you to take one color of cubes at a time and only ten of that color."

"What if you need more than ten cubes?" John asked.

"After you use ten cubes of one color, use ten cubes of a different color. If you still need more cubes, continue to use different colors, each time taking a group of ten. Can someone help me get started with my measurement using this first group of cubes?" I continued.

When Maria raised her hand, I asked her to come to the center of the rug. "I am going to start with red," Maria said. She counted out ten red cubes and locked them into a continuous "train," placing the train underneath the straightened piece of yarn. "You still need more!" Maria said as she sat back in her place in the circle.

"I wonder how *many* more we need?" I said. Many students whispered their estimates to the students seated near them in the circle. I called on Shannon to assist me. Shannon counted out ten yellow cubes and added them, one at a time, to the train that Maria had begun. She put the completed train of twenty below the yarn. Various students added their ideas. "You *still* need more!" "I think you need five!" "No, she needs more than that!" "I think it will take ten more." The students seemed very interested in finding out how many cubes it would take to equal the length of yarn.

I was interested to see if students would use their place-value understanding to determine the quantity of cubes in front of them, or if they would resort to counting. "How many cubes have we used so far?" I asked.

Some students extended their index fingers toward the trains, pointing to individual cubes and silently counting by ones, while others immediately saw the two groups of ten and raised their hands, saying, "I know! I know!" I asked students to explain how many there were and how they figured out the total. Juan got up from his place on the rug and came to the center of the circle. He counted each cube by ones and said, "There's twenty." After he sat down, Jonathon added, "But, there are two colors of cubes and ten in each group, so it has to be twenty! Ten . . . twenty!" he said, first pointing to the red cubes, then to the yellow.

We still needed more cubes to equal the length of the yarn. Bradley volunteered. He came to the center of the rug, shaking his head and saying, "I don't think it's going to take ten!" He counted out ten green cubes into a pile and added them one by one to the red/yellow train that had already been made. He added six more cubes and said, "I think that's it! I only needed six." He put the remaining four cubes back into the cube pile and took his place in the circle.

"How many cubes did it take to equal the length of the yarn?" I asked. "And how did you figure that out?" Students began pointing at the cubes from their places. Some counted by ones, while other students put their hands up immediately. I gave students the opportunity to again explain how they figured out the total number of cubes. Some of the students explained how they counted the cubes by ones while others reported that they'd counted the two groups of ten and knew that six more would make twenty-six.

"Some of you counted the cubes by ones and some of you counted the groups by tens," I said. "Is there a different way to count the cubes? Carolyn?"

"We could count them by fives!" Carolyn said.

"If we *did* count the cubes by fives," I answered, "would there be more than twenty-six, less than twenty-six, or twenty-six? How many think more than twenty-six?"

Several students raised their hands.

"Less than twenty-six?" I asked. Again, a number of the students' hands went up.

"How many think the number will still be twenty-six?" I asked, and the rest of the students raised their hands.

I asked Carolyn to come to the center of the rug and count the cubes by fives. She picked up the red/yellow/green train and laid it in front of her. She counted five red cubes, snapped off a train of five, counted five more, snapped off the train of five cubes, and continued until she had five trains that were five cubes long and one leftover cube. She counted aloud while touching each train: "Five, ten, fifteen, twenty, twenty-five, twenty-six! I *knew* there would be twenty-six!"

Juan called out, "We could count by twos!" Again, I asked the students if there would be more, less, or the same number of cubes if we counted by twos. This time, fewer students thought there would be a quantity different from twenty-six, but there were still students who thought there would be a different quantity using this new counting method. Juan came up, separating the trains into individual cubes. He gathered the cubes into sets of two and counted aloud, "Two, four, six, eight, ten," all the way to twenty-six. "Yep! There's twenty-six!" he said.

At this point, the students seemed convinced that it did, indeed, take twenty-six cubes to equal the length of the yarn. I showed them where to record 26 on the recording sheet, pointing to the column titled *Measurement*. I pointed to my estimate and said, "You know, I estimated that it would take twenty-nine cubes to equal the length of yarn, but the measurement was twenty-six. Was I close? How close? And how do I know?"

"You were pretty close," Jonathon stated. "You were only . . ." He counted from twenty-six to twenty-nine quietly, extending one finger as he said each number, "three off!"

When I asked him to explain his thinking, Jonathon touched his forehead and said, "I started with twenty-six in my head, and I counted to twenty-nine." He used his fingers again to keep track: "Twenty-seven, twenty-eight, twenty-nine. It was three more."

"Is there another way to figure out the difference between my estimate and the actual measurement?" I asked.

Carolyn had a suggestion. "You could do it the same way, but go back."

"What do you mean?" I asked.

"You could start with twenty-nine and go to twenty-six, like this: twenty-eight, twenty-seven, twenty-six. It still takes three to go from twenty-nine to twenty-six." Like Jonathon, Carolyn used her fingers to keep track of the difference.

"Jonathon and Carolyn used two different ways to find the difference between my estimate and the actual measurement. Jonathon started with the actual measurement, twenty-six, and counted on to get to my estimate, twenty-nine. Carolyn started with my estimate and counted back to get to the actual measurement. Both used their fingers and both got a difference of three. I am going to record that number in the column labeled *Difference*. This is the last piece of information for your recording sheet before you try a different length of yarn."

The students were getting fidgety; they were anxious to try the activity on their own. Before they did so, I wanted to be sure they were clear about what the activity entailed. "Who can remind us what we should do with our baskets of yarn?" I asked.

"You choose a yarn and write down the letter that's on the tape," one student said.

"You predict—I mean *estimate*—how many cubes long it is. You write that down, too," another offered.

"Then you use the cubes and measure the yarn," another said.

"But don't forget to use different colors!" another stressed. "And you can only take ten of each color!"

"Then you have to figure out how many cubes you were wrong," another explained, "how many cubes between your estimate and the real thing . . . the difference."

"Good! One last thing," I said. "Please count your cubes in at least two different ways." I then had the students go back to their tables, and asked one student from each table to come up front to get a basket containing the lengths of yarn, recording sheets, cubes, and pencils.

As the children began to work I slowly circulated around the classroom, making sure that they were following the proper steps, and also to see how they would approach the task. I was curious about students' counting strategies: would they be able to easily count by twos, fives, and tens? I also wondered how they would find the difference between their estimates and the actual measurement: would they count on from the lesser number or back from the greater number, or would they have sufficient experience with number combinations to "just know" the difference? I was also interested to see if students would build on their earlier findings: would they use their measurement of one piece of yarn to make a reasonable estimate about the length of a subsequent piece of yarn?

Students were eager to get started. Most immediately got a recording sheet, a pencil, and a piece of yarn from the basket. Some students began working as partners. I had initially conceived of this activity as something they would be doing alone, but I realized that by working together students could help each other remember the steps involved and discuss with each other their number choices.

"I think it's going to be twenty-eight. It's almost the same size as the one Ms. Scharton picked," Danielle said.

Her table partner, Aaron, disagreed. "I think it's less. I think it's going to be twenty-four."

Both students wrote down their estimates in the appropriate column of their recording sheets and proceeded to measure with the cubes. Aaron began placing random colored cubes on the desk in a line next to the piece of yarn. This caught the attention of Maria, a tablemate. "Hey, you guys! You have to take all one color!"

"Oops!" Aaron said, and he began removing all of the cubes except the blue ones, gathering more to make a complete set of ten. "You get blue and I'll get green ones," Danielle suggested, and she began bringing together a group of ten green cubes.

When they had connected first the blue and then the green cubes, I asked, "How many cubes have you used so far?" Aaron began touching each cube, one by one, and counting, while Danielle said, "I know!"

"Wait until Aaron is done and see if your idea matches his," I instructed.

Danielle patiently waited until Aaron touched the last cube, stating, "Twenty!"

"I knew it!" Danielle said.

"How did you know?" I inquired.

Danielle touched the blue cubes and said, "See . . . ten." Then she touched the green cubes and said, "Twenty!"

"So you counted by . . ." I prompted.

"Tens," she said, "and Aaron counted by ones. My way's quicker!"

"That could be," I responded, "but if it doesn't make sense to Aaron, he needs to count in a way he understands. Are you done? Or do you still need more cubes to find out how long the string is?"

Both students looked at me as if I had asked them a very silly question. "Ms. Scharton, we're not done! Look!" and Aaron pointed to a length of the piece of yarn that had no cubes lined up next to it.

"Why don't you think about how many more cubes you'll need to get the right measure," I said, and I left as Danielle and Aaron began to talk about their estimates.

I stopped by Shannon's table. She had just finished measuring her yarn length, and she had a train of five different colors, ten red, ten yellow, ten blue, ten green, and six brown cubes. She had written *38 cubes* as her estimate but she was erasing her number.

"Hi, Shannon. How's it going?"

Shannon looked up at me a bit sheepishly. "Hi, Ms. Scharton."

"It looks like you finished measuring. Good for you! How many cubes equaled the length of your yarn?" I asked.

"Forty-six," she said.

"You know, I should have known that! You wrote *forty-six* right here!" I pointed to the *Measurement* column. She continued to look a little guilty.

"Why are you erasing your estimate?" I asked gently. When she didn't answer, I continued. "You know Shannon, most of the time, when I measure, my estimate is not the same as what I find out by measuring. Remember when I showed the class how to do *Lengths of Yarn*? When I measured my yarn, I didn't get the same answer as my estimate. But you know what? I do my very best job of making a careful estimate. Sometimes I really want to erase my estimate after I do my measuring, but that would be silly. Then it would be a 'matching the numbers' job and not an 'estimating and measuring job.' This activity is an 'estimating and measuring' job. Could you do me a big favor? Could you leave your estimate so I remember what a really careful estimate you made before you measured?"

Shannon rewrote the part of her estimate that she had erased and then began breaking the train into five-cube sections, counting aloud as she snapped them off, "Five, ten . . ."

Kelly and Daniel had just finished measuring a length of yarn they were sharing and were putting their yarn back in the basket.

"You look like you are done measuring," I stated. "Tell me what you noticed."

Kelly began, "We counted by twos and fives and tens and each time we got thirty-two!" Daniel chimed in, "Kelly estimated thirty-six, but I estimated thirty-two! I won!"

"Your estimate *did* match your measuring, Daniel. I bet Kelly put good thinking into her estimate, though. How close is Kelly's estimate to yours?" Daniel looked puzzled, but Kelly started counting aloud, using her fingers: "Thirty-three, thirty-four, thirty-five, thirty-six! Four. Our guesses are four apart!"

"That was fast thinking," I said. "Could you explain how you figured that out?"

"I went 'thirty-two'"—and she put up fingers one by one and said, "'thirty-three, thirty-four, thirty-five, thirty-six.' It took four fingers. It's four!"

"You could also go, thirty-six," Daniel added, putting up fingers one at a time and saying, "thirty-five, thirty-four, thirty-three, thirty-two! It's still four!" He then reached for another yarn piece that was longer than the one he and Kelly had just measured.

"What do you think about that yarn length? Is it longer, shorter, or the same length as the one you just measured?"

"Longer!" they sang out together.

"The last yarn was thirty-six cubes long. How much longer do you think this one is?"

"Oh, Ms. Scharton," said Daniel, "you ask too many questions!"

Linking Assessment and Instruction

As the students work, think about the following:

- Are the students comfortable with "committing" to an estimate? Or do they feel compelled to change their estimate once they have counted the actual number of cubes?
- Do the students become more comfortable estimating as they work through the activity? Does the difference between their estimates and the actual measurements decrease with experience?
- Are they able to count by twos, fives, and tens? How high can they count using each of these ways?

- Do the students use the information about the number of cubes it takes to equal the length of one piece of yarn to make estimates about the number of cubes it will take to equal the length of another piece of yarn?
- What methods do they use to find the difference between their estimate and the actual number of cubes it takes to equal the length of a piece of yarn? Do they need to build each quantity to compare the difference? Or do they count on or back from one quantity to another? Do they use their knowledge of number combinations to determine the difference between two quantities?
- Do the students realize that the total number of cubes for a particular measurement will not change when the counting method changes?

Estimation Jars

CHAPTER 2

OVERVIEW

Numbers express quantity. Children need many experiences with counting in order to develop an understanding of this concept. Estimation activities involving familiar objects provide children with contexts that enable them to attach meaning to a quantity. Making reasonable estimates requires children to think about what they already know about a quantity.

In this series of activities, students learn how to make reasonable estimates and then test those estimates by counting in a variety of ways. Place-value concepts, based on an understanding of groups of ten, develop as students have practice counting groups of objects in different ways.

MATERIALS

- clear quart-size jar with lid
- Unifix cubes, enough to fill the jar (about 50)
- chart paper, several sheets

TIME

- four class periods over a three- to four-week period, with subsequent lessons repeated about twice a month

Teaching Directions

1. Prior to the lesson, fill a quart jar halfway with Unifix cubes and prepare a class chart on which students can record their names and estimates.

2. Gather the students to discuss the definition of *estimate*. Show the students the jar and explain that you would like them to estimate how many cubes are in the jar.

3. Introduce the chart to the class.

4. Have students estimate the number of cubes they think are in the jar and then record their name and estimate on the chart.

5. Conduct a class discussion about the estimation chart. Ask students to explain what they notice about the compiled information. Have them explain how they came up with their estimates.

6. Ask the students how the class might figure out how many cubes are in the jar. Elicit suggestions for counting the items in different ways (by ones, twos, fives, and tens).

7. Have individual students count the jar contents in various ways (by ones, twos, fives, and tens) while the rest of the class watches.

8. Discuss the relationship between students' estimates and the actual quantity of cubes in the jar.

9. Repeat the process on subsequent days, using the same jar but altering the contents or the number of objects. Encourage the students to use the information on charts from previous lessons to make reasonable estimates.

Teaching Notes

Making reasonable estimates involves using known information and applying it to a new situation. Students gain information about how much a jar can hold by repeatedly estimating and then counting different objects and different amounts inside of it. In this activity, certain features remain constant—the size of the jar—while other features change—the type of objects used to fill the jar and the number of those objects—forcing students to attend carefully to the features that are changing.

In this series of lessons, students consider the number of objects in the same jar on different occasions, based on how many objects filled it in previous lessons. Initially, the type of object used to fill the jar remains the same, while the number of objects changes. Knowing how many objects fill *half* a jar allows students to begin to use what they know about halving and doubling to determine how many of the same objects *fill* the same jar. Once students are familiar with the jar and the contents used to fill it, the type of object is changed. Students then consider the relationship between the size of the objects used in previous lessons and the size of the objects used in the current one. Using posted information from previous estimation experiences, they begin to make estimates that are more informed.

This activity also gives students experience with counting objects in different ways. Grouping and counting objects by twos, fives, and tens helps children understand an important aspect of number sense: that the number of a particular set of objects remains unchanged no matter how the items are counted. Grouping and counting objects by tens helps students understand place value: the placement of digits directly relates to groups of ten. Counting groups of objects provides opportunities for students to see number patterns and practice skip-counting in preparation for later work in multiplication.

The Lesson

Day 1

"I have a difficult question for you," I announced to my second-grade students in September of a new school year. I showed them a quart-size jar half-filled with Unifix cubes. "I have filled this jar partway with Unifix cubes. I didn't count the cubes that I put in the jar and I am wondering how many cubes there are. I want to make a 'smart guess' about how many cubes I think are in the jar. When mathematicians make smart guesses, they are making 'estimates.' They look at the size of the jar and its contents. They use what they know to make an estimate of the size, worth, or value of something. I want to know your estimate for how many cubes are in the jar, but I would also like to know the reason you chose that number. Please pay careful attention to your thinking as you make your

estimate. We're going to be recording our estimates on a class chart."

I showed the students the large chart I had posted on the board, and I set the jar on the tray beneath the board. I read them the words at the top of the chart: *Estimation Jar 1*. Next to the title, I had drawn the jar with cubes filling it halfway. I had drawn Unifix cubes to decorate the chart, to remind the students of the size and shape of the objects that were in the jar. I also explained the chart's two labeled columns: *Name* and *Estimate*.

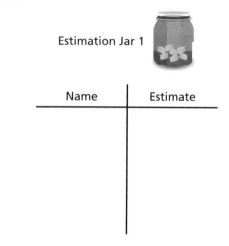

"When I call your table," I said, "please come to the front of the room and write your name and your estimate in the proper column on the chart. Then take a seat in a circle on the rug." I stationed myself close to the chart and jar, so that I could observe the students as they recorded their estimates and offer any assistance they might need.

As they came up to contribute to the chart, some students first picked up the jar and examined it closely, and then recorded their names and estimates. Others took a quick glance at the jar or the information already recorded on the chart and then added their own name and estimate. One by one, each student wrote on the chart and took a seat on the rug in front of the room.

When everyone had contributed, the chart showed estimates ranging from twelve to sixty-two. Some estimates were the same, but most students had written estimates that were different from those their classmates had chosen. With the students now seated in their circle on the rug, I said, "Let's take a look at the information we have just recorded. What do you notice about our chart?"

Few students raised their hands, perhaps because it was their first experience with the activity. I gave them some time to observe the chart before I called on individual students.

"Some people wrote really neat," said Jason.

"There's a lot of numbers and names on the chart," added Tania.

Jose offered, "Everyone wrote their name and a number."

I wanted them to focus on the numbers on the chart, so I narrowed my question. "Let's take a look at the numbers that people wrote. What do you notice about them?"

"Some people wrote really big numbers. Some people wrote really small numbers," said Elena.

"Can you tell us more about what you mean when you say 'big' number?" I inquired.

Elena explained. "Like, sixty-two is a big number and twelve is a small number."

"Oh, I see. Can someone say that a different way?"

"Yeah. Sixty-two is more than twelve," Daniel said.

"I think I get it. I'm wondering if you mean that some people think there is a larger, or greater, number of cubes and some people think that there is a smaller, or lesser, number of cubes."

"Yeah. Sixty-two is greater than twelve. Twelve is less than sixty-two," Jose said.

"OK. What else do you notice about the numbers on the chart?" I wanted both to further assess what number features students were attending to and to give as many students as possible an opportunity to broaden the perspectives of their classmates.

"Some people wrote the same number. Dennis and Katie both wrote thirty-seven," Jose said.

Katie added, "Some numbers go in order."

"What do you mean?" I asked.

"Like when you count 'thirty-six, thirty-seven.' They go in order," Katie explained.

I was curious about their thought processes in coming up with an estimate. "You know," I said, "I am wondering something else. How did you figure out what estimate to give? What were you thinking when you wrote your number? How did you come up with your estimate for how many cubes you think are in the jar?"

"I looked at the jar. I thought there were twenty-three," stated Jason.

"It looked like thirty. That's why I wrote *thirty*," Daniel said.

Tania added, "Forty-one is my favorite number."

Such answers are typical of beginning second-grade students. Verbalizing the reasoning behind their estimates was challenging for them. It would be important to provide them with many more experiences with estimating the number of objects in the jar. Repeated opportunities to estimate would help them to develop a visual appreciation of size and quantity, helping them establish benchmarks that they could use in future activities of this kind. We moved on to discussing how to determine exactly how many cubes were in the jar. "We made our estimates," I said. "Now, how might we find out the number of cubes that are really in the jar?"

"Count them!" was the overwhelming response.

"OK. How might we count them?" Several hands went up in the air. "Jason, what do you think?"

"By ones!"

I asked Jason to come to the center of the rug to demonstrate this approach. He dumped the cubes out of the jar and proceeded to count aloud using one-to-one correspondence. "It seems as though Jason is keeping track of what he has already counted by moving each cube aside as he counts it." Jason finished counting the cubes and found that twenty-five were in the jar. I recorded these words on the bottom of our chart, then read aloud what I'd written: *We counted by 1s. We got 25.*

"How else might we count the cubes?" I asked. Again, several students raised their hands eagerly.

"Patty?"

"By fives!" she stated.

"I wonder what we will get if we count by fives. I wonder if we will get more than twenty-five, less than twenty-five, or exactly twenty-five. Does anyone think we will get more than twenty-five?" Five or six hands went up. "Does anyone think we will have less than twenty-five?" Three or four students raised their hands. "Does anyone think we will get exactly twenty-five?" About half of the students raised their hands. It is not unusual for students at this age to think that the quantity of a certain number of items will change if the method used to count them changes. I asked Patty to come to the center of the rug to demonstrate her approach.

She first put the cubes in scattered groups of five. Rather than counting out each group by ones, it seemed as though Patty was able to visualize five and group the cubes accordingly. She quickly counted aloud as she touched each group: "Five, ten, fifteen, twenty, twenty-five."

I told the students, "I am going to write down what Patty just helped us do." Again, I read as I wrote underneath the previous sentence: *We counted by 5s. We got 25.*

"Hmm," I said. "We got the same number when counting by fives as we got when counting by ones."

Some students looked surprised; others looked at me as if I had said something that was blatantly obvious; others looked puzzled.

As a challenge, I asked for a volunteer to count the cubes by tens. Derek came to the middle of the rug.

Before he began, I said, "I am wondering again. I am wondering how many there will be if we count them by tens. Do you remember what happened when we counted by ones and fives?"

"We got the same number!" exclaimed Carl.

"You are right. We did!" I said. "This time, I wonder how many cubes Derek will count. I wonder if there will be more than twenty-five, less than twenty-five, or exactly twenty-five." Again, I asked students to raise their hands when I called out each option. A few students thought there would be more, a few thought there would be less, and about half of the students thought the number of cubes would stay constant.

"If we count by tens, can you tell me how many groups of ten there would be? Hold up that many fingers, but don't show us yet, hide your number in your lap." I gave the students time to think and then said, "Now show me." Students held up a range of fingers, from one to five.

I asked Derek to go ahead and count the cubes. He put two groups of five together and immediately said, "Ten." I quickly interjected to have him explain why he had combined groups. He said, "I know that five and five make ten. I don't need to count the cubes. I can just put two groups together!" Derek continued. He put another two groups together and said, "Twenty." He finished counting the rest by ones, touching them individually and saying, "Twenty-one, twenty-two, twenty-three, twenty-four, twenty-five."

"Before Derek counted, I asked you to show me how many groups of ten you thought Derek would make. Some of you thought one, some of you thought two, some thought three, some four, and some five. How many groups of ten did Derek make?"

The students answered, "Two."

"How many cubes were left?"

"Five!"

"So, what should I record on our chart?"

In unison, the students responded, "We counted by tens. We got twenty-five!" I recorded what they had said. I ended the session by asking the students, "So, what did we find out by doing the estimation jars today?"

"It took twenty-five cubes," Derek stated.

"We counted by ones and fives and tens," added Tania.

Sonia said, "We got the same number each time."

"It didn't matter how we counted. We still got the same number," Patty said.

"Today was our first day working with estimation jars," I explained. "We will have a new estimation activity each week. Tomorrow, I will put out the same jar with a different number of objects. You will have a few days to look at the jar, think about the estimates you and your classmates gave, and remember the ways we counted to figure out the number of objects in the jar. Mathematicians use what they already know to learn new things. Your job will be to use what you already know about today's jar to figure out how many objects are in tomorrow's jar. I will put our chart on the wall, so that you can use that information to help you with your next estimate."

I wanted to give the students a few days to look at, think about, and discuss the possibilities for the next jar. I also wanted the activity to become a classroom routine that the students would come to expect on a weekly basis, so I waited a week before discussing the new one. The next day, I completely filled the same jar with Unifix cubes and placed it on the ledge of the board at the front of the room. I posted the first class chart on the wall to the side of the board and made another class chart, again drawing a picture of the jar and surrounding it with drawings of Unifix cubes. Underneath the title *Estimation Jar 2*, I wrote, *25 Unifix cubes filled the jar halfway. How many will fill the jar?* I posted the chart on the board above the jar. I asked the students to look carefully at the jar, look at the class chart from the first lesson, and discuss their estimates with their classmates for the next few days. At different times of the day during the week, I noticed students picking up the jar and looking at the contents. Sometimes students discussed estimates with a student nearby; other times, they silently replaced the jar on the ledge and went on to do something else.

Day 2

The following week, I brought the children's attention back to the estimation activity. "Last week, we did our first estimation jar activity. You have had several days to look at the second jar and think about how the number of cubes in this jar compares with the number of cubes in the first jar. I posted the first chart on the wall next to the board, so you could use that information to help you. What might you think about when coming up with an estimate?"

Several students raised their hands.

"You used Unifix cubes again," said Jason.

"This time the jar is filled up to the top. Last time it was only filled up halfway," Sonia said.

"It has to be more than last time. Last time, there were twenty-five cubes, but this time there are more cubes," Patty surmised.

"You have many things to think about when making your estimates," I explained. "Your classmates have offered several ideas. You can also use the estimation chart we worked on last week. Think about all of those things as you come up with an estimate to record on the class chart today. Pay close attention to the thinking that you do in deciding what your estimate will be. After you have written down your name and your estimate, take a seat in a circle on the rug." I invited the students to come up, table by table, to write down their estimate on the chart.

Some students picked up the jar and looked at the contents and some walked over to the class chart made during the first activity. Others looked at what students had already recorded, while the rest quickly wrote down their name and estimate before taking a seat on the rug. This time, the smallest estimate was twenty-one, even after Patty's observation that the new number had to be higher than twenty-five. The highest estimate was eighty.

When all the students had recorded their estimates and were seated in a circle on the rug, I began. "I see that you have all recorded your estimates for the number of cubes that fill our estimation jar. When you wrote down your estimate, I asked you to pay attention to the thinking that you did to figure out the number of cubes you thought were in the jar. Would anyone like to share their estimate and why they chose that number?"

"I think sixty cubes are in the jar. It looks like sixty," offered Tania.

Derek was next to contribute. "I think that there are eighty in the jar because it looks like a lot and eighty is a lot."

The students were able to locate the numbers they had recorded on the chart and read them back, but it was difficult for them to articulate the reasoning behind their estimates.

"What number *couldn't* be the number of cubes in the jar and why do you think so?" I asked.

Carl said, "It couldn't be one hundred because one hundred is too many."

"It couldn't be eighty-two because that's too many, too!" added Patty.

Finally, Sonia connected the number of cubes in the previous week's jar to the new number. "It couldn't be less than twenty-five, because twenty-five cubes fill the jar partway, so it can't be smaller than twenty-five. This time, there are more cubes."

"It can't be less than twenty-five because we counted twenty-five cubes when the jar went up to here." Patty came up and pointed to the halfway point on the jar. "There has to be like sixty or eighty this time."

While to adults doubling the number is an obvious strategy in this case, second graders need repeated exposure to the relationship between "half-full" and "full" in order for this concept to develop.

When I asked how we could find out how many cubes were in the full jar, the immediate reply was counting by groups of ones, twos, fives, and tens. One by one, a different student came up to count in a way that was different from the previous way. Each time, we discussed whether the total would change, depending on the method used for counting. I asked the students how to record the way in which the cubes were counted and the total number of cubes. Each time, we counted fifty-one cubes. When we finished counting, we had recorded the following at the bottom of the class chart:

We counted by 1s and we got 51.
We counted by 2s and we got 51.
We counted by 5s and we got 51.
We counted by 10s and we got 51.

Before the class session ended, I wanted students to see the relationship between these two estimation jar experiences. I moved the chart from the first session and posted it next to the new chart.

"Before we end our math time today," I said, "I want to remind you of something that is important to think about when estimating. A mathematician makes a good estimate by carefully thinking about all the information he or she has. The size of the jar and the size of what is in the jar are two important pieces of information. When we partly filled the jar with cubes and counted what was inside, we had a third piece of information. All of this information helped us when making estimates the second time. Tomorrow, I will put new contents in the same jar. We will have this jar on display for a few days so that you can think about a new estimate and discuss it with your classmates. It will be very important to use the information from the last two experiences to help you make a good estimate the next time. Good luck!"

The next day, I used the same jar and chose wooden cubes similar in size to the Unifix cubes that filled the first two jars. I filled the jar about half full. I wanted students to apply the information from these prior experiences to this new one. Once again, I placed the jar up in the front of the room on the chalkboard ledge. When the day began, I reminded students that the jar would be there for a few days so that they could observe it and estimate the quantity inside. I encouraged them to use the posted charts from the first two *Estimation Jars* activities and to discuss their thinking with their classmates. The jar was on display for five days. During that time, students looked at the jar on their own and in small groups throughout the day, and I observed them pointing to the posted charts and discussing their estimates.

Day 3

I was curious about how the students would handle this third estimation experience. The size of the jar was the same as the previous two experiences. While the type of object used to fill the jar had changed, the size of the object was nearly identical to what we'd used before. I filled the jar about halfway, just as I had the first time we had estimated.

As our math period began, I asked students to come up to the front of the room and sit in a circle on the rug. I said to them, "For the last week, the estimation jar has been on display, and I've noticed that you've all been making observations about it, and you've been looking at our two charts and talking among yourselves about estimates. I am very impressed by all of the thinking and observing and discussing I have seen. Today, we are going to be doing something a little different from what we did for the first two estimation jars. This time, I'd like you to again pay close attention to your thinking when you come up with your estimate. I want you to 'think about your thinking,' but this time, I want you to write down what you did to come up with your estimate. Please tell me all of the information you used to figure out how many cubes you think are in this third estimation jar. I will give you some suggestions about the words you might want to use."

I wrote the following on the board:

I think there are _____ cubes in the jar.

I came up with this number by _____.

"What could you use to help you with your estimate?" I asked. Several students raised their hands.

Terry said, "You could use the other charts. They could help."

"How would the other charts help you?" I asked.

Sonia said, "Each time, we used the same jar and we counted what was in the jar. We wrote the numbers that we counted. The numbers can help you."

Carl wanted to contribute. "You can use the numbers on the other charts. Like, you know it can't be fifty-one," he said.

"What makes you say so?" I asked.

"Fifty-one cubes were in a *whole* jar. This jar is only filled up half!" he explained.

"The cubes in the jar can help you!" Derek offered.

"What do you mean?" I asked.

"Look! The Unifix cubes and the wooden cubes are the same size! The first jar was filled up halfway and so is this one. I think this one will have the same number of cubes as the first one."

I wondered if Derek's explanation would greatly influence the estimates of his classmates. I would have to wait and see. "You have some great ideas about what you could use to help you with your estimate. Read your paper to a classmate when you finish writing. Can someone remind us why reading your paper to a friend is a smart thing to do?"

"Sometimes your brain is moving so fast when you write and you make mistakes," Sonia explained. "When you read it to someone, you see your mistakes and then you can fix them."

"Thanks, Sonia," I said. "After you have read your paper to someone, turn it over and illustrate some of the information you used to come up with your estimate." In addition to offering students another way to represent their thinking, asking them to illustrate their responses addressed the situation of students finishing at different rates. "Any questions?" I asked.

Jason spoke up. "What if we didn't get a chance to come up and look at the jar?"

"Feel free to take a look at the jar and any other information that might help you on your way back to your seat."

"What if I don't know how to spell a word?" Tania inquired.

"Who can help Tania with her question?" I countered.

Carl reminded us about some of the classroom resources we had learned to use. "Use the Mathematics Vocabulary chart and Word Wall. Then do your best!"

Patty added, "Circle the word if you are still not sure about the spelling."

"Any other questions?" No other hands went up, so I began dismissing students to write about their estimates. As I called out names, some students took one last look at the jar. A few walked over to the charts from the previous two times. The rest of the students stopped by the paper tray, took a sheet of paper, and went to their seats.

While several students quickly began writing, some students got up to view the estimation charts before returning to their seats. I circulated the room as an observer; my role during this time was more to assess rather than teach.

Students were divided in how they approached the task. Some wrote down information that was seemingly unconnected to their previous *Estimation Jars* experience. Terry wrote, *I like 21 because it is more than 10,* and Tania's paper read, *I yoosd my hans and I thingt in my hed.* Some students made a reference to what they observed: Jason wrote, *I look-itd at it and I got 13 and I gestid it and thats how I got 13,* while Patty's paper stated, *I looked at the jar and I thougt that there were twenty things in the jar.*

However, most students used the previous experiences to make their estimate. Some used the estimation chart for the jar filled with Unifix cubes but most made reference to the half-filled jar. Ashley wrote, *The old estimation charts kind of helped me. I looked at the old estimation chart and I think it is 25.* Alexandra recorded, *The reason I estimated 17 because if 25 cubes were in $\frac{1}{2}$ jar and 51 cubes were in a hole jar, I think that it will be 17.* Only one child used the wrong information in determining a number: *My estimate was 52. I picked that number because last time it was 51* (51 was the number for the filled jar).

I gave students about fifteen minutes to write down their new estimate and explain what information they used. They were then expected to read their paper to a classmate. Several students had time left over to illustrate the information they'd used. Some students drew jars and labeled these jars with numbers. Derek drew three jars and labeled the first *25,* the second *51,* and the third, *25 of course!* Tania drew lots of Unifix and wooden cubes and Sonia attempted to reproduce the first chart, adding her own conclusion: *It has to be the sam as the younifix cubs!* After fifteen minutes, I let the students know that we would be meeting for a whole-class discussion in two minutes. Some gasped and quickly finished their writing, while others began putting their crayons away.

I posted the new chart on the board at the front of the room. I wrote *Estimation Jar 3* at the top of the chart; underneath were the two columns headed *Name* and *Estimate.* I had drawn a half-full jar, as well as small wooden cubes, at the top of the chart. I announced to the class, "I am going to call your table to the rug. As you come, please quickly record your name and your estimate on the estimation chart. Then take a seat in a circle on the rug." I called tables, one by one. Students recorded their information and then gathered in a circle.

I asked if any of the students wanted to share their work with the class, and a few volunteers showed their papers and explained their estimates. I asked the rest of the students to briefly turn to a partner on the rug, read their writing, and then give me their attention. We then counted the wooden cubes in the jar in the ways we had previously (by ones, twos, fives, and tens), and found that, this time, twenty-six cubes filled the jar halfway. We recorded the ways in which we counted, as well as the final count, on the bottom of the class chart. The estimates ranged from thirteen to fifty-two, although most clustered in the twenties. The range of estimates was decreasing!

Before ending the day's session, I called the students' attention to the three completed class charts. "When you look at these charts from our three *Estimation Jar* activities, what do you notice?" I asked.

Some students called attention to the chart features that were similar: the number of columns, the titles, and the illustrations. Other students were beginning to realize that the number of cubes in the first and third jars were "close to each other," to which Derek responded, "I *told* you that!" We ended the day's session by discussing how the charts were related to each other, how the information was similar and different, and how we might use the information from these charts in later *Estimation Jar* experiences.

Day 4

For the fourth session, I decided to once again use the wooden cubes. I had filled the same jar with cubes and posted a new chart next to the three previous ones. The students observed the jar for several days, just as they had before. I reminded them to use the charts for information as well. On the day of the activity, I explained to the students that sometime during the morning, I wanted them to write their name and estimate on new the chart, titled *Estimation Jar 4.* Most students wrote estimates between forty-five and fifty-five; the lowest estimate was forty and the highest was fifty-eight.

This time, when I asked students to share the reasoning behind their estimates, at least half the class volunteered to do so. Most referred to the previous chart that listed numbers from the filled jar.

Patty said, "The last time the jar was filled with cubes, we got fifty-one. The wood cubes are the same size, so I think there will be the same number of cubes."

Tania offered, "I think it will be fifty-two. I think that because the first time we filled half the jar it took twenty-five cubes. The next time it took twenty-six. The first time we filled the jar it took fifty-one, and fifty-two is close to fifty-one." Students paired up with a classmate to share their estimates and explain how they came up with them. We ended this session by counting the cubes by various groupings and recording what we found on the class chart. There were fifty-two wooden cubes in the jar.

Subsequent Days

The class continued to have a new estimation jar about twice a month. While the quantity changed each session, the materials used to fill the jar changed approximately every three sessions. Sometimes the jar was half-filled, sometimes it was filled to the top, and sometimes it was filled three-quarters of the way. The type of objects changed from time to time. We discussed the range of estimates, often representing the range by building the lowest and highest estimate and comparing the difference between the two. Each time we used the estimation jars, I prompted students to draw on previous information. I wanted to support them in seeing that they could base new estimates on previous ones. Students either discussed how they came up with their estimates or used writing to explain their reasoning. Fundamental to each lesson was the transfer of information from a previous experience to a new and related one, to inform students' thinking and reasoning.

Linking Assessment and Instruction

As you observe students work, think about the following:

- How does the range of estimates change with repeated experience?
- Are students able to count by twos, fives, and tens? How high can individual students count? When do students understand that the number of objects will not change when the counting method changes?
- How do students find the difference between their estimates and the actual number of objects it takes to fill the jar? Do they build each number and count the difference? Do they count on from the lesser number to the greater one, or back from the greater number to the lesser one? Or do they use their understanding of number combinations to figure the difference?
- How do students apply information from previous estimation experiences? Do they use information about the quantity used to *partially fill* a jar when considering the quantity used to *fill* a jar? Do students begin to consider that the size of objects is related to the number it takes to fill a jar? When do students realize that more small objects and less large objects will fill a jar?

Beans in the Jar

CHAPTER 3

OVERVIEW

Beans in the Jar is a series of estimation, data collection, and computation activities in which students estimate the number of scoops of beans it will take to fill a jar. While engaged in these activities, students use number sense in a variety of ways. They use mental computation when they form their estimate. When given a benchmark, they compare quantities and use their understanding of number relationships to adjust their estimates and narrow the range of possibilities. Estimate data is then collected, organized, analyzed, and interpreted. Beans in the Jar gives students an opportunity to use their number sense in an engaging and meaningful context, one that simulates the way we use numbers in the "real world."

MATERIALS

- 3-by-3-inch sticky notes, 1 per student
- 8-ounce jar
- 2 cups dried large lima beans
- 2-tablespoon coffee scoop

TIME

- two class periods

Teaching Directions

1. Prepare a number line from 1 to 20, ending with >20. Numbers are spaced 4 inches apart.

2. Pass out a blank sheet of paper and one 3-by-3-inch sticky note to each student. Students observe the size of the scoop, beans, and jar. Ask students to estimate how many scoops of beans will fill the jar, then have them record their estimate on their paper.

3. Ask students to write their name on their sticky note, then position their note in the column of the graph that corresponds to their estimate.

4. Discuss the graph data with the class.

5. Ask them to watch and count aloud as you partially fill the jar with scoops of beans.

6. Explain to the students that you want them to use their observation of the partially filled jar to adjust their estimates of how many scoops it would take to fill the jar, then invite them to repost their sticky notes on the graph.

7. Discuss the new graph data with the class, noting any changes.

8. As the students watch, completely fill the jar with scoops of beans. Students count each scoop of beans as it is emptied into the jar.

9. Discuss with the class how they might be able to find the difference between their estimates and the actual number of scoops it took to fill the jar.

10. Encourage them to use the information about the number of scoops of beans it took to fill the jar to determine the total number of beans in the jar.

11. Have them find the number of beans in each scoop, and ask them to use this information to compute the total number of beans in the jar.

12. Discuss with the class ways of counting the total number of beans in the jar, then have them use these various ways to count the beans.

13. As a class, compare this total to the total obtained in Step 10.

Teaching Notes

Estimation experiences naturally engage students' developing number sense. In this activity, students are able to observe and handle the materials—a scoop, a jar, and the beans used to fill the jar—to make an informed estimate of how many scoops of beans it would take to fill the jar as well as the total number of beans in would take to fill the jar. Observation of the partially filled jar and knowledge of the number of scoops used to fill it to that level allow students to adjust their estimates based on important benchmark information. Students display, analyze, and interpret estimate data in graphical form; this data is meaningful to the students because, having each contributed to the graph, they have a stake in it. When the jar is filled, students have an authentic context in which to compare their estimates to the actual number of scoops it took to fill the jar. They are able to see how their estimates are based on important information as opposed to being random "guesses."

Students think about and then discuss various ways to find the total number of beans in the jar. This independent problem-solving time and subsequent sharing helps students develop confidence in their problem-solving ability and competence with calculation. They are expected to explain their methods in written form and/or in class discussion, thus ensuring that these methods are fully understood by them. They come to find that there are several ways to calculate an answer and that all of these ways are both valid and valued. Students find the total number of beans, using a method they understand, and then share their method with their classmates. Class discussions focus on various problem-solving methods while accomplishing several important goals. They allow students to deepen their own understanding by communicating their strategies and listening to those of others, and by considering methods they may not have otherwise considered, and they give teachers important assessment information about students' developing number sense.

The Lesson

Day 1

Before the lesson began, I selected an 8-ounce jar, which was large enough for students to easily view the contents and would accommodate between 120 and 200 beans, a number that was appropriate for these second-grade students at the middle of the school year. On the bottom of the board, I drew a number line from 1 to 20 and >20 to serve as the basis for a bar graph. This would be the range for student estimates of how many level scoops of beans would fill the jar. I placed a recording sheet and a sticky note on each student's desk. As they came in from morning recess, they seemed quite curious about the materials I had set out and about the upcoming lesson.

"Good morning!" I began. "I can see that you're all interested in the paper and sticky note on your desk, but please leave these things alone while I explain what we'll be doing with them. We are going to be doing an activity today called *Beans in the Jar*, but first, there are some words we need to talk about, to make sure that we all understand what they mean."

I began a vocabulary list, writing *estimate* on the board. "What do you know about this word?" I asked.

Several students offered ideas. "It's a guess for how many you have of something," one said.

"It's like *prediction*," said another.

"Sometimes it's right, but sometimes it isn't," another added.

"You think of a number, and that's your estimate," another explained.

It was clear that these students had encountered the word *estimate* before. "You know a lot about the meaning of this word," I said. "I estimate all the time, trying to make an educated guess about how many things I have, or how long they are, or how heavy something might be. When, in the real word, do you estimate?" I asked.

"When your mom or dad is cooking, they estimate. They guess how much of something they need," was one response.

"In first grade, we guessed how many jelly beans were in the jar. We had to estimate," said another.

I wanted to push their understanding of contexts in which estimation can be used, beyond mere volume. "I had to estimate when wrapping a present for my niece," I said. "I was using ribbon to decorate the box and I had to estimate how much I needed. How might using ribbon involve estimation?"

"You don't want too much, because you would be wasting it!" one student answered.

"If you didn't estimate, you might not buy enough and then the present wouldn't be so pretty," another offered.

"I had to estimate when driving here today," I continued. "I wanted to stop at the vet to buy some medicine for my dog, but I wasn't sure if I had time. How might thinking about time involve estimation?"

"You had to think if you had enough time, so you wouldn't be late!" one student said.

"Yeah, we would be sad if you didn't have time to do math with us!" one added.

I smiled and continued. "Today we are going to use estimation. An estimation is something like a guess, but also different. A guess is something you make without having information. But I am going to give you some information. You will use that information to make an estimate. Otherwise, you would be making a 'wild guess.'"

I took out the scoop, a bag of lima beans, and a jar and showed them to the class, walking around to each table so that the students could take some time to observe all three items. "Here is the information that will help you estimate," I said. "And here is the estimation question: If I make level scoops of lima beans, how many scoops will it take to fill this jar level with the top of the jar?" Before I had even finished my question, several hands shot up into the air.

"Wow! Fast thinkers! Please write *First Estimate* on your paper. Here is what I am going to ask you to do: think hard about the number of level scoops it will take to fill the jar. Write that number on your paper for your first estimate. Write your name—just your name—on the sticky note and listen for the next direction." I walked around the room with the jar, scoop, and beans and observed as the students recorded their estimates on their papers and their names on the sticky notes.

"I am going to call a table at a time," I said when they had all finished. "When you come up, remember the number you wrote on your paper. Whisper the number to me. You are going to place your sticky note on the board, above the number that matches the number you wrote on your paper. Put it as close to the number as you can. If there is another sticky note over your number, put your sticky note right above it." As I spoke, I demonstrated to the students where, on the board, they would place their sticky notes.

"Let's pretend that I estimate it will take two scoops of beans to fill the jar," I said. "I am going to place my sticky note right above the number two on the number line." With this, I pointed to the correct position on the board. "Let's pretend that Rosa also estimates that two scoops will fill the jar. She is going to position her sticky note right above mine, without any spaces in between our two sticky notes."

I was not sure that students knew what the symbol ">" meant, so I walked to the right side of the board and pointed to the symbol on the number line.

"I used a symbol at this end of the number line. I wonder if you know what this symbol means," I said.

"It looks like an arrow," one student said.

"It means 'greater,'" said another.

"If the number is more, that's where it goes," another student contributed.

"If your number is bigger than twenty, it goes there," offered yet another.

"Look at the number you've written on your recording sheet and then memorize it—remember it, keep it in your head. You've all written your names on your sticky notes. When your table is called, I want you to whisper your number to me, place your sticky note above that number on the graph, and take a seat on the rug." Students wriggled in their seats, anxious to contribute to the graph.

I called on one table at a time. Individual students whispered to me their estimates. "Telling" the teacher their estimates allows the students both to "commit" to their numbers and to gain assistance, if needed, in placing their notes on the graph. After all had contributed a sticky note to the graph and had taken a seat on the rug, I began the class discussion.

"Take a look at the estimates you have placed on the board," I said. "I am wondering if you know what we call the information—data—you have arranged in this way." The data on the board looked like this:

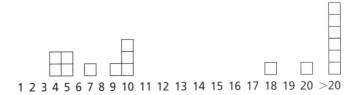

"It's a graph!" said one of the students.

"You are right. It is a graph, a 'bar' graph, because the data is arranged in columns, or 'bars.'" I wrote *bar graph* under *estimate* on the board. "When you look at our bar graph, what do you notice?"

"Twenty and over has the most," said one student.

"Four numbers have one sticky: seven, nine, eighteen, and twenty," said another.

"One, two, three, six, eight, eleven, twelve, thirteen, fourteen, fifteen, sixteen, seventeen, and nineteen don't have any stickies," was yet another observation.

"Four and five have two stickies," one student noticed.

"Greater than twenty won," said another.

It is important that students remember what the sticky notes represent. "Remind me what this sticky note stands for," I requested, touching the tag above the number 7.

"That person thinks 'seven,'" Randy offered.

"He means that person thinks seven scoops will fill the jar," added Rosa.

I took the opportunity to have the students compare data in preparation for a task to follow. "Take a look at these two columns, or 'bars,'" I said, pointing to the bars above the numbers 9 and 10. "What could you say about them?"

"Ten has more than nine," said Cindy.

"How many more, and how can you tell?" I asked.

"Two," she added, coming up to the graph. "If they both had one, there would be a tie, but these two," she said, touching the top two sticky notes in the column above the number 10, "are the two more."

I added *difference* to the word list. "Nine has one sticky note and ten has three sticky notes." I wrote *1* and *3* on the board. "We can say the 'difference' between one and three is two. How about these two columns," I asked, walking to the 20 and >20 columns. "What is the difference in the number of sticky notes in these columns?"

"Five," said Erin. "More than twenty has six and twenty has one. Six has five more than the other."

"Oh! Six minus one is five!" said Joshua.

"Look! It's like how far apart the numbers are," began Peter. "One," and then he counted on his fingers, putting one up for each number he said: "two, three, four, five, six! I have five fingers up!"

"So, we can compare the number of sticky notes in different columns of our bar graph. Someone noticed that 'greater than twenty' had the most sticky notes. On a graph, that is called the *mode*," I explained.

"The mode?" Randy said.

"Yes, the mode is the number that most people picked." I added this word to the vocabulary list. "The lowest number picked was . . ."

"Four scoops!"

"Yes, and the greatest number picked was . . ."

"Greater than twenty!"

My need to limit the length of the bar graph made it difficult for students to see the range of estimates. The first sticky note was placed above the 4 and the last above the >20. It would be challenging to discuss the range of estimates. I would need to ask the students what the sticky notes in this part of the graph represented.

"Raise your hand if you placed a sticky note in the last column. How many scoops of beans do you estimate will fill the jar?" I asked.

"Twenty-five," said Rose.

"Any estimates greater than twenty-five?" I asked.

"Thirty-six!" answered Darrell.

"I think forty," said Sarah.

"Any estimates higher than forty?" I asked. No hand remained in the air and those whose hands had just been up shook their heads.

"Another way we can speak about the graph is to discuss the range of estimates. The fewest number of scoops estimated to fill the jar was four and the greatest was forty. We can say the range is four to forty. I wonder if anyone can find the difference between four and forty."

"How far apart they are?" asked Randy.

"Or we can do forty minus four," said Cindy.

"If I look at the one-to-one-hundred chart, I can start at forty. I can go up ten, twenty, thirty. That puts me on ten. I can go back one, two, three, four, five, six to get to four. That's . . . thirty-six!" said Rosa.

Cindy wanted to check out this new strategy. "If I start at forty and count back four, that's thirty-nine, thirty-eight, thirty-seven, thirty-six. I get thirty-six, too!"

"So, we can say the range is thirty-six, or four to forty." I wrote *range* on the board. "We can look at the shape of the data as well," I said, as I traced a line up and over the sticky notes, making the horizontal flat line where there were no stickies. "These flat parts, where there are no sticky notes, are holes in the data." I added *shape* to the word list.

"You had some information to make your first estimate, so that you were not making a wild guess. You were able to look at the scoop, the jar, and the beans to help you make your estimate for how many level scoops of beans it would take to fill the jar. Now I am going to give you some more information: I am going to put some scoops of beans in the jar. See if this information will help you to make a new estimate." I put four level scoops of lima beans into the jar. Each time, students carefully watched, counting out loud as each scoop went into the jar and glancing excitedly from the jar to the graph.

"If you want," I said, "you can make a new estimate. Maybe your estimate will stay the same and maybe it will change. When I call your name, come up to the board and get your sticky note and take it back to your desk. Write your second estimate and wait for directions. How many people will change their estimate, after seeing what four scoops of lima beans looks like?" I asked. About two-thirds of the students raised their hands.

After the students had retrieved their sticky notes and made their second estimate, I said, "We will go through the same process. When I call your name, please bring your sticky note, whisper your new estimate to me, and place your sticky above that number, just like we did with our first estimate."

Once students had repeated the process, the graph looked markedly different:

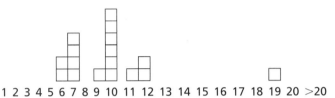

I asked the students to observe the graph again and note the changes that had taken place.

"Ten has the most," one student observed.

"Ten had the same number of stickies this time that 'greater than twenty' had last time," another said.

"Nine, eleven, and nineteen only have one sticky note," said a third.

"Seven is the second to the most. It has four stickies," was another comment.

"Twelve and six have the same. They both have two," one student noticed.

"There is a hole from thirteen, fourteen, fifteen, sixteen, seventeen, and eighteen," said another.

"One, two, three, four, five, thirteen, fourteen, fifteen, sixteen, seventeen, and eighteen don't have any sticky notes," was still another observation.

"The hole got shorter," one student observed.

We discussed the changes in the shape of the data, the mode, and the range. The students noticed that the sticky notes were more "squished together" this time. We discussed how the mode changed from *greater than twenty* on the first graph to *ten* on the second. They figured out that the new estimates ranged from six to nineteen, a range of thirteen, quite a change from the previous range of thirty-six!

"Are you ready to see how many scoops fill the jar?" I asked. Students were clearly eager to see how closely their estimate reflected the actual number of scoops. As I filled each level scoop and emptied it into the jar, students counted aloud from four, the benchmark I had provided for their refined estimate. It took twelve level scoops to fill the jar.

Before ending today's lesson, I wanted the students to have the opportunity to compare their estimates to the actual number of scoops it took to fill the jar with lima beans, so that they could see that the use

of a benchmark provided more information to help them make a better estimate. "Before we finish today, I would like you to take a moment to look at the numbers you used. I would like you to find the difference between your first estimate and your second estimate. I would also like you to find the difference between your second estimate and the actual number of beans." I decided an example would be helpful, so I wrote some numbers on the board. "Pretend that my first estimate was fifteen scoops and my second estimate was eleven scoops. I know the actual number of scoops was twelve." I wrote the following on the board:

1st estimate: 15
2nd estimate: 11
actual: 12

"How could I find the difference between my first estimate and my second estimate?" I asked.

Peter helped out. "Well, if you count from eleven to fifteen, it's four. See?" He demonstrated by counting on his fingers. "I start with eleven and I go, twelve, thirteen, fourteen, fifteen!" He showed his four extended fingers.

Rose explained her way, saying, "You could do the same thing, except backwards: fifteen, fourteen, thirteen, twelve, eleven. See? It's four that way, too!"

"So, the difference between my first estimate and my second estimate is four. What is the difference between my second estimate and the actual number of scoops it took to fill the jar?" I asked.

"Easy! One!" most students called out.

"Interesting . . ." I said. "I wonder why the difference went from four to one?"

"You got better!" one of the students said.

"Seeing the four scoops really helped!" said another.

"When you knew what four looked like, you could just look and see!" said a third.

"Having more information was really helpful in making a second estimate. I'd like you to find the difference between your first and second estimate and the difference between your second estimate and the actual number of scoops it took. Then I'd like you spend a few minutes writing about what you learned by doing this activity."

Students began writing as soon as they got to their seats. For some students, finding the difference was not an easy task. Some perceived it as a literal, rather than a mathematical, question and wrote about how answers differed: *40 is way too high to be the answer, but the answer 7 is not*. Others knew that computation was involved but performed a different operation, adding the numbers used for different estimates. Some students were able to compare the number of scoops estimated and found the actual difference.

Students' ideas about what they learned varied as well. Some students pulled numbers from the activity; Rose wrote, *I learned that 12 scoops could fill a little jar*, and Lizzy wrote, *I figured out that 12 was the actual number not 10*. Other students wrote about their acquisition of new skills; Pablo wrote, *I learned how to use a graph*, and Miguel explained, *I learned how to measure really good*. Peter wrote about what qualifies as an estimate (*I learned that an estimate is not a guess because a guess has no information and an estimate has a little information*) and Veronica wrote about vocabulary she learned (*I learned that estimate means to guess and actual means the real number*). Students' positive attitude toward mathematics was something expressed in writing as well. Robert mentioned, *I have a good time doing mathematics*, and Andrea wrote, *If I keep on practicing to estimate, I will get better and better*.

Day 2

Before the students came in from recess, I assembled the materials from the previous day's lesson. Students took a seat on the rug, looking quite excited to see the jar, the bag of beans, and the scoop.

"Good morning," I said. "I am glad to see that you are excited to see the materials from yesterday's math lesson. In that lesson, we did a lot of thinking about estimation. What important ideas about estimation did you think about yesterday?"

The students had many ideas. One remarked, "I wonder how many beans would fill up the jar."

"Ah!" I said. "Today we are going to think about just that idea. Yesterday we thought about a question: How many scoops will it take to fill up the jar? First we estimated and then we found the actual number of scoops. Today I have a new question for you: how many beans do you think it will take to fill up the jar? I want you to think about what you could do to find the total number of beans. Here's the catch: you don't get to spill the beans out and count them all, one at a time." Students feigned disappointment. I smiled and went on. "I'd like you to take a silent moment to think: What might you do to figure out the total number of beans if you had to do it another way?"

After students had some silent thinking time, I asked them to share their ideas with their classmates. Students looked a little puzzled. "You do have *some* information already," I explained. "What is it that you *do* know?"

"We know the number of scoops!" said one student.

"We know it took twelve of them of them to fill the jar," said another.

"I know! If we know how many are in a scoop, we can add that . . . twelve times! That will tell us!" said Miguel.

"Yeah! Can we count the beans in a scoop, Ms. Scharton?" asked one of his classmates.

"Will that work? Or not? Is there someone who can talk a little bit about how or why it would make sense to count the beans in one scoop, then add that number twelve times?" I asked.

After a few moments, several students raised their hands tentatively.

"You said we couldn't count the beans in the jar. But we could count the beans in one scoop!" one student said.

"We know there are twelve scoops. So we could add that number twelve times because that's how many scoops there are," said another.

"So, should we try that and see if it works?" I asked.

"Yeah!" the students chorused.

Pursuing this approach would result in an estimate for the total number of beans it would take to fill the jar, using a sample of one scoop. Instead of using a sample of one scoop to find the number of beans in the jar, students would need to know the number of beans in *each and every scoop* . . . and this number would vary from scoop to scoop. If we looked at the different numbers of beans that actually filled each scoop, students could begin thinking about a range of numbers that were reasonable, a beginning step in understanding the concept of an "average" scoop.

"Here is what I will do," I said. "I will scoop out the beans and place twelve scoops around the room. Please count the number of beans in the scoops placed at your group. Keep the scoops separate from each other. After you have counted, I will ask you for the numbers you got and I will write the numbers on the board." I walked around the room, placing scoops of beans throughout the classroom until all twelve were distributed. I dismissed the students to their groups and they got busy counting. It only took a few minutes before students began stating the numbers of beans in their table scoops.

"I am going to call a group at a time," I said. "As I do, please state the total number of beans in each of your scoops."

As each table reported their numbers, I recorded them on the board:

12   13   14   13   16   14   13   13   15

The last group to report numbers admitted to having some difficulty.

"Ms. Scharton, we don't have all our numbers," said Veronica.

Robert added, "We got two of our numbers, but then our beans got all mixed up."

"Now we just have one big pile of beans," said Veronica. "We counted all of the beans in that big pile, though! And we got forty-one beans!"

Classroom mishaps can often turn into learning opportunities. This incident offered us an authentic problem to solve and several options for where the lesson could go next.

"So, we seem to have a 'mystery scoop,'" I said. "I wonder if we have enough information to figure out the number of beans that are in the mystery scoop. You said you counted the number of beans in two of the scoops. What numbers did you get?"

I then recorded what the students told me, adding a question to represent the mystery scoop. The array of numbers now looked like this:

12   13   14   13   16   14   13   13   15   12   15   ?

"Here are the numbers that match the number of beans in the twelve scoops," I said. "Take a look at the numbers and talk about what you notice with someone next to you." A soft hum of observations issued from the group as they spoke among themselves. After a minute or two, I asked them to share some of their observations with the rest of their classmates.

"There are four thirteens," said one student.

"It goes in order at the beginning: twelve, thirteen, fourteen," said another.

"There are two fourteens," said a third.

"There are two twelves, two fourteens, and two fifteens," was yet another observation.

"There's only one sixteen," observed a student.

To focus the students' attention on the subject of our investigation, I asked, "Remind me: what do these numbers represent?"

"How many beans in a scoop," said one student.

"What we counted," said another.

"Each scoop is a number," said a third.

"So, we have lots of information—eleven different numbers—about the number of beans in the scoops I placed at your tables. But we don't know the amount of beans in our mystery scoop. I wonder if we can use these numbers to help us make a good guess about the number of beans that are likely to be in our mystery scoop. What numbers are likely, which are unlikely, and why do you think so?" Previous discussions about basic probability concepts gave the students access to the concepts of *likely* and *unlikely*.

"Six is unlikely. It's way too small a number," said one student.

"Fifty is unlikely. It's way too big," said another.

"It could be thirteen because thirteen came up already . . . four times!" was another comment.

"Sixteen is sort of likely and sort of unlikely. It only came up once," said yet another.

"Twelve and thirteen and fourteen and fifteen are likely because they came up two or three times," one student said.

"It sounds like we could make a pretty good guess about the number of beans in the 'mystery scoop,' based on the data from the other eleven scoops," I said. I wanted to gear students' thinking toward figuring out the actual number of beans in the mystery scoop. I realized they would probably come up with the idea of taking the forty-one beans, separating out the scoop of twelve and the scoop of fifteen and counting what remained. However, I wanted to see how they might use mental calculations to figure out the quantity. If we initially used a counting strategy, the mental calculations might not prove so challenging.

"We have some other information about the mystery scoop," I said. "We know the total number of beans at Robert, Veronica, and Andrea's group is forty-one. We know that twelve beans were in one scoop and fifteen were in the other. How might we use that information to figure out the number of beans in the third scoop?"

"We could start with forty-one and take away twelve, then take away fifteen. That would give us the rest of the beans," said Rosa.

Darrell used what Rosa had provided. "Forty-one minus twelve is . . . you take the ten from the twelve away . . . and you get thirty-one. You take the two away and you get . . . twenty-nine. You have twenty-nine . . ."

"Darrell, you are giving us lots of good information," I interrupted. "I want to make sure that I put your thinking on the board." I wrote on the board:

$$41 - 10 = 31$$
$$31 - 2 = 29$$

Darrell continued. "You have twenty-nine and you got to take away fifteen. You take away the ten and you get nineteen."

"Where did the ten come from?" I asked.

"The ten comes from the fifteen . . . the fifteen in the second scoop," he explained.

I wrote what he said:

$$41 - 10 = 31$$
$$31 - 2 = 29$$
$$29 - 10 = 19$$

"And there's a five to take away," Darrell continued. "And you get . . ." Darrell counted back on his fingers. "Fourteen."

I continued writing:

$$41 - 10 = 31$$
$$31 - 2 = 29$$
$$29 - 10 = 19$$
$$19 - 5 = 14$$

It was important for students to recall what the numbers had to with our math lesson. "Thanks, Darrell." I addressed the class, "What did we find out?"

"The answer is fourteen!" Cindy called out.

"It is, isn't it? What does fourteen have to do with what we are thinking about?" I asked.

"That's how many beans are in the mystery scoop!" Joshua called out.

Veronica said, "Yeah! There's twelve and fifteen and now we found out there's fourteen in the last scoop."

I erased the question mark on the board and added our new number:

12   13   14   13   16   14   13   13   15   12   15   14

I wanted to make sure that the students realized that this row of numbers represented the number of beans in each scoop. We also needed to consider Miguel's original idea for finding the total number of beans: take the number of beans in one scoop and add that number twelve times. I said, "Now we have a row of numbers. Remind us what this row of numbers is all about."

"Scoops!" said several children.

"Those are the numbers we got when we counted," one student explained.

"When we counted each scoop, we got those numbers," another added.

"Some scoops had twelve beans, some had thirteen, some had fourteen, some had fifteen, and one had sixteen beans," said another.

"There's twelve numbers for the twelve scoops," one student said.

It seemed as though the students had a clear idea about the numbers written on the board. I decided to return to the idea about how to find the total number of lima beans to fill the jar. "Miguel had an idea about how to find the number of beans in the jar. He told us that you could find the number of beans by finding the number of beans in a scoop of beans and adding that number twelve times. What do you think of that method? Would it work?"

Miguel was the first to answer. "No!" he began. "*Some* of the scoops had twelve beans. They didn't all have twelve."

"It wouldn't work. There were different numbers, not just twelve," added Joshua.

Rosa continued, "You'd have to add all the numbers, like the twelve plus the thirteen, and then add the fourteen to that number, then add the thirteen to that number, like that, until you added all the numbers."

"Why would that make sense as a way to find the total?" I asked.

"You have to use all the numbers, not just the twelves," said Randy. "You have to use the thirteens and fourteens and the rest. You have to add them all."

"Anyone else?" I asked.

"You told us we couldn't count the beans in the jar, right? But you said we could count the beans in the scoop. We got all those numbers. If we add them, we'll know how many there are!" said Cindy.

"I'd go ten, twenty, thirty . . . all the way to the end," began Steven. "Then I'd go back and add the two and the three, and that would be the number."

Steven was offering a strategy for finding the total number of beans. He was splitting each scoop total into tens and ones, first combining the tens and then adding up the ones. I wanted to make sure that his classmates understood where he was getting these numbers. "I'm not sure I understand," I said. "Tell us about the ten, twenty, thirty part."

Steven said, "Easy . . . see? The twelve is a ten and a two and the thirteen is a ten and a three and the fourteen is a ten and a four . . . like that. So I took all of the tens and counted them up. Then I did the same thing with the ones."

"We have heard some ideas about finding the total number of lima beans in the jar using the numbers that are posted on the board," I said. "Rosa explained how she would add two numbers at a time, find a total, add the next number, find the next total, and so on. Steven split the tens and the ones, adding the tens first and then adding the ones. One of these ways might make sense to you, or maybe you would use another way. What I would like you to do next is, using a way that you understand, find the total number of beans in the jar. Before you do, write down an estimate for how many beans you think will fill the jar. Then go ahead and do some figuring. I will ask a few students to share their thinking with the rest of us, then we will count the beans to find out how many beans are in the jar. Please do all of your writing on a sheet of paper. Don't throw anything away because I am really interested in seeing what kind of thinking you do to figure out the answer. Any questions?"

"What if our answer is not the same as our guess?" one student said.

It can be difficult for students to appreciate the validity of an estimate once they have found the actual number. I was glad that this question was raised, so that I could address what I had observed was a familiar practice among young math learners: erasing an estimate and changing it to match the actual number. "That's OK," I said. "Once you write down your estimate, don't erase it! It hardly ever is exactly the same as the actual number. You will want to see how close you got."

Since I knew that the students would take varying amounts of time to finish the activity, I also needed to head off questions of the "Now what do we do?" type. "If you finish before your classmates," I said, "I'd like you to see if you can find another way to figure out the number of beans in the jar, using the information on the board. You can try Rosa's or Steven's way, or you can use another way." With that, I asked the students to get to work.

After a few minutes of circulating among the students, I stopped by Rose's desk. She had written down her estimate and was looking somewhat frustrated.

"Hi, Rose. I see you have an estimate! How are you doing?" I asked.

"OK . . . I don't know what to do," she admitted.

"Tell me what you *do* know," I suggested, to gain an understanding of the difficulty she was having.

"I am trying to use Steven's way, but I don't know what to write down," she explained.

"Tell me a little about Steven's way," I said.

"I want to take the tens out of those numbers," she went on. "Ten, twenty, thirty, forty . . . like that, but I don't know what to put on my paper."

"What if you put down the numbers you just said out loud?" I asked.

"That's it?" she asked.

"Well, that sounds like what you are doing," I answered. "When you finish with the tens, then what will you do?"

"I'll add the ones," she said. "I'll go, 'one hundred and twenty-two, one hundred and twenty-five,'" Rose continued, showing how she would add the ones from each number. She seemed to have regained her confidence, so I moved on.

Randy was busy at work. He was using a common method for totaling a long list of numbers: repeatedly finding sums for a pair of numbers, then using these sums as addend pairs and again finding the sum. He drew lines to pull the addends together; this was an effective way to demonstrate his method and it made it easy for me to see that he had used a number as an addend more than once (see below).

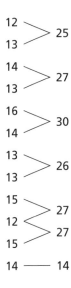

"Hi, Randy. You are busy. Can you tell me a little about what you are doing?" I asked.

"Yeah. I am putting two numbers together, see?" He showed me the lines he had drawn and the sums that resulted from adding these pairs of numbers.

"Can you show me the numbers you put together and what you got each time you did?" I asked.

"I added twelve and thirteen and got twenty-five. I added fourteen and thirteen and got twenty-seven. I added sixteen and fourteen and got thirty. I added thirteen and thirteen and got twenty-six. I added fifteen and twelve and got twenty-seven. I added . . . uh oh." Randy had realized his error.

"Uh oh? What happened?" I asked.

"I used the twelve two times," he admitted.

"I see," I said. Randy quickly moved to correct his mistake. He erased the lines showing that he added the final twelve and fifteen, then drew new lines connecting the fifteen and fourteen and wrote the sum.

"What will you do now?" I asked.

"I am going to do the same thing," Randy explained. "I will put the twenty-five with the twenty-seven and get the answer, then the thirty and the twenty-six, like that!" (See below.)

$$
\begin{array}{c}
12 \\
13
\end{array} \Big\rangle\ 25
$$

$$
\begin{array}{c}
14 \\
13
\end{array} \Big\rangle\ 27
$$

$$
\begin{array}{c}
16 \\
14
\end{array} \Big\rangle\ 30
$$

$$
\begin{array}{c}
13 \\
13
\end{array} \Big\rangle\ 26
$$

$$
\begin{array}{c}
15 \\
12
\end{array} \Big\rangle\ 27
$$

$$
\begin{array}{c}
15 \\
14
\end{array} \Big\rangle\ 29
$$

When I stopped by Veronica, I saw that she had arranged all of the scoop totals in a vertical list and drawn a line through the numbers, separating the tens and ones column. She had used a method that merged Randy's and Steven's ways, but she had omitted one of the numbers:

$$
\begin{array}{c|c}
1 & 2 \\
1 & 3
\end{array} \Big\rangle\ 5
$$

$$
\begin{array}{c|c}
1 & 4 \\
1 & 3
\end{array} \Big\rangle\ 7
$$

$$
\begin{array}{c|c}
1 & 6 \\
1 & 4
\end{array} \Big\rangle\ 10
$$

$$
\begin{array}{c|c}
1 & 3 \\
1 & 5
\end{array} \Big\rangle\ 8
$$

$$
\begin{array}{c|c}
1 & 2 \\
1 & 5
\end{array} \Big\rangle\ 7
$$

$$
\begin{array}{c|cc}
1 & 4 & 4
\end{array}
$$

"How are you doing, Veronica?" I asked.

"Good. I am using Steven's way!" she announced.

"Terrific! Tell me a little about why his method makes sense," I asked.

"I drew a line through the numbers. These are the tens," she said, pointing to the digits to the left of the line, "and these are the ones," she said, pointing to the digits on the right side of the line. "I added the ones, see?" she explained, pointing to the lines she had drawn to pull the pairs of ones digits into sums.

"You seem like you know what you are doing!" I said. "How many numbers do you need to have in your list?" I asked.

"Twelve," she answered. "For the twelve scoops."

"Could you count to make sure that you have all the numbers you need?" I asked.

Veronica counted the numbers in her list and got eleven. "Oops! I missed one!" she said.

"Let's head to the board," I suggested. "I'll read the numbers and you check to see which ones you have."

Veronica followed me to the board. I read the numbers to her and she realized that she had left out the thirteen. She readily inserted it into her list and continued with the process that worked for her.

After about thirty minutes of independent work time, I called students to the rug. I had asked Steven and Rosa if they would be willing to share their work with their classmates. Rosa went first. She showed her paper to her classmates as she explained how she added the first two numbers, found the total, added the next number, and continued on, keeping a "running total." (See Figure 3–1.)

Since several students had made mathematical errors based on difficulty with organizing their ideas on paper, I pointed out Rosa's method for keeping track of the numbers she had used: by drawing a line through them as she used them.

"Who used Rosa's way?" I asked, and a handful of students raised their hands.

Steven went next. He had organized his paper very clearly, by writing twelve columns of numbers with four numbers in each column: a scoop number, a line of tens, the number of ones in the corresponding scoop number, and the running total:

12	13	14	13	16	14	13	13	15	12	15	14
10	10	10	10	10	10	10	10	10	10	10	10
2	3	4	3	6	4	3	3	5	2	5	4
122	125	129	132	138	142	145	148	153	155	160	164

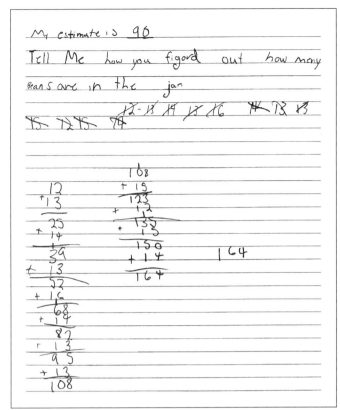

FIGURE 3–1 Rosa kept a "running total."

Steven explained what he had written on his paper. "First I put the numbers that were on the top, then the numbers that are down. I took them away from the greatest numbers then the least numbers, they were left. I added them to the greatest numbers. I got one hundred and sixty-four, because I counted the tens and it was one hundred and twenty, then I added the last numbers to the one-twenty, so I went like this: one twenty-two, one twenty-five, one twenty-nine."

We spent some time discussing the way Steven had organized his information. His method of vertically separating the tens and the ones made sense to many students. Steven explained the bottom row of numbers. Heads nodded in understanding as students heard him count by tens to 120 and explain the running total he kept as he added the ones from the numbers obtained from the twelve scoops. When I asked students, "Who used Steven's way to find the total number of beans?" about ten students raised their hands. I told students, "Rosa got one hundred and sixty-four beans as her total and so did Steven. Did anyone else get an answer of one hundred and sixty-four beans?" Most students raised their hands.

The students were now anxious to count the beans to verify the number reached through computation. They'd had many experiences with counting

objects by ones, twos, fives, and tens and they quickly suggested these methods for counting the lima beans. Four students were chosen to count the beans in these different ways. After each counting method was used, I recorded the results on the board:

> We counted by 1s and got 166.
> We counted by 2s and got 166.
> We counted by 5s and got 166.
> We counted by 10s and got 166.

I used to become nervous when data "conflicted." I now see such irregularity as an opportunity for students to discuss what might have happened and experience a situation familiar to adults: exposure to data that might be skewed. I told the students, "When Rosa and Steven shared their ways of finding the total number of lima beans used to fill the jar, they got one hundred and sixty-four. I asked you to raise your hands if you also got one hundred sixty-four and most of you raised your hands. Then we counted the beans four different ways. Each time, we got one hundred and sixty-six. What might have happened?"

"There are some beans that are really half a bean," one student said. "I wonder how people counted them."

"When we counted the scoops, I bet some people found some extra beans they forgot to count. Like on the floor or in their desk or something!" said another.

"Maybe some accidentally got in the jar after," said a third.

"Let's think about one hundred and sixty-six and one hundred and sixty-four. Those numbers are pretty big. We were pretty close, don't you think?" I asked.

"They were only two apart."

"Yeah, if you count up, one sixty-six is only two more!"

"We did pretty good, huh, Ms. Scharton?"

I smiled. "Good? I think you were an incredible group of mathematicians! You did a lot of mathematics with a jar, a scoop, and some beans! You estimated, you graphed, and you discussed the graph observations. You got some information—what four scoops of beans in the jar looked like—and you made some adjustments to your estimates, then discussed a new graph that you made. You did a lot of problem solving, discussing how many beans would fit in a scoop, counting the beans in each scoop, and figuring out how to find the number of beans that could be—and actually were—in the 'mystery scoop.' Then you listened to some ideas about how you might find the total number

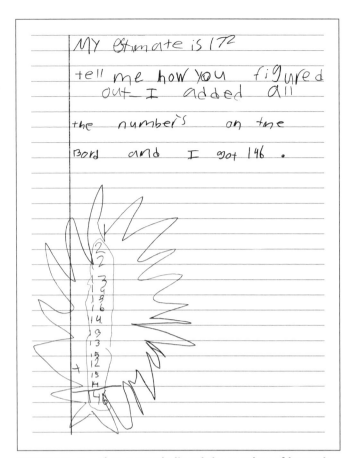

FIGURE 3–2 **Alan correctly listed the number of beans in each scoop but made an error in calculation.**

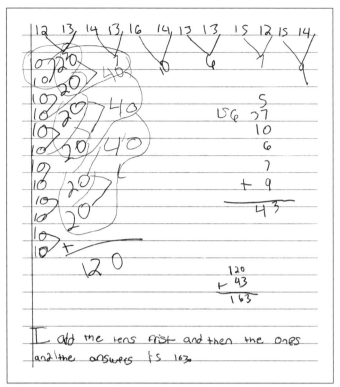

FIGURE 3–3 **Erin added all the tens correctly. She made a minor error adding the ones, resulting in a computation error.**

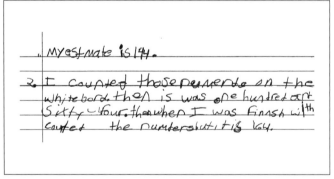

FIGURE 3–4 **Joshua's brief explanation makes his method difficult to understand.**

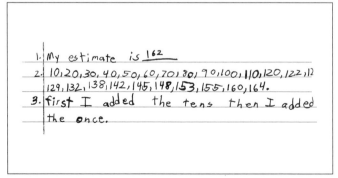

FIGURE 3–5 **Rose used Steven's method, adding first the tens, then the ones.**

of beans and you used a way that made sense to you to figure out the total. Lastly, you helped to count the beans in the jar and participated in discussing why the numbers from the mathematics and the numbers from the counting didn't match. I say that is pretty impressive." The students responded to my praise with big smiles.

After the close of the lesson, I reviewed the students' work. Alan accurately listed the scoop numbers but made an error in calculation. His explanation for how he found the sum was unclear, so it was hard to determine where his error occurred. (See Figure 3–2.)

Erin's method was clear. She added the tens to get twenties and the twenties to get forties and the forties to get 120. She then added the ones and made an error. (See Figure 3–3.)

Joshua got a correct answer, but it was difficult to figure out what method he actually used. (See Figure 3–4.)

Many students were able to use a reliable and accurate method to find the total number of beans. A popular method was Steven's. Rose used his way and explained it well. (See Figure 3–5.) While Rose used a minimum amount of information, it was easy to see

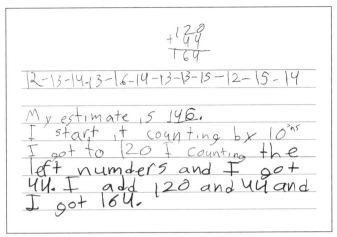

FIGURE 3–6 Carlos also used Steven's method. He found two subtotals, then the total.

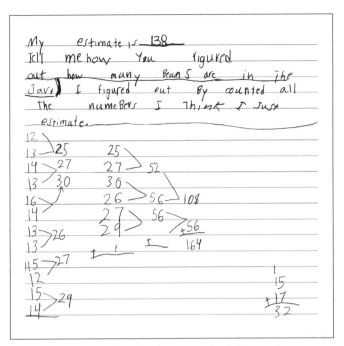

FIGURE 3–7 Randy paired sums to find the total.

how she counted first the tens and then added on the ones.

Carlos also used this method. He provided no evidence of counting but explained how he got two "subtotals." (See Figure 3–6.)

Randy finished a well-organized paper that showed his pairing of sums, from six to three to two. (See Figure 3–7.)

This series of activities proved to be rich and complex. Students had opportunities to estimate, adjust estimates, and represent estimates in a graph. They'd analyzed the data they displayed and learned some statistical vocabulary and concepts. After the jar was filled with scoops of beans, students compared their original and adjusted estimates to the actual number of scoops it took to fill the jar. This information was used in determining a method for finding the total number of beans. The class used one student's idea: each table got two or three scoops to quantify. When a table accidentally made one larger pile out of their separate "scoops," the class looked at the range of numbers generated from tables counting the number of beans in each of their scoops to consider what was a reasonable number of beans in the "mystery scoop." The class collaborated on some methods for determining how many were in the unknown scoop. After students were given some independent work time to calculate the total number of beans, their answers were confirmed by having student volunteers count the actual number of beans by ones, twos, fives, and tens.

Linking Assessment and Instruction

As you observe students work, think about the following:

- Do students understand how the graph represents real data? What statements do they make to inform you of their understanding?
- Can students make reasonable estimates? How does the range of student estimates change when they are given a "benchmark number" by which to judge their new estimates?
- What methods do students use to find the difference between their estimates and the actual number of scoops of beans it takes to fill the jar?
- Are students able to count the total number of beans by twos, fives, and tens? How high can they count? Do they understand that the total number of beans does not change when the method of counting changes?
- When given the number of beans in each scoop, what methods do students use to find the total number of beans that fill the jar? Do students use a standard addition algorithm or alternative algorithms?

CHAPTER 4

The Missing Piece

OVERVIEW

The Missing Piece *is an activity that helps students understand how numbers can be decomposed and recombined in various ways. In this activity, students use a given number of counters. Working in pairs, one student "hides" some counters and displays the rest to a partner. The partner determines the hidden quantity and explains the strategy used to determine the number of hidden counters. Students with strong number sense understand how numbers can be "broken apart" and "put back together" in lots of different ways. Experiences that require students to consider "wholes" and "parts of a whole" help them to develop this understanding, while also helping them to formulate a variety of computation strategies. An extension activity,* What's in the Bag?, *can be done as a follow-up to* The Missing Piece.

MATERIALS

- small counters, such as beans or cubes, 10–20 per pair of students
- file folder, 1 per pair of students
- *The Missing Piece* recording sheet, 1 per pair of students (see Blackline Masters)
- chart paper

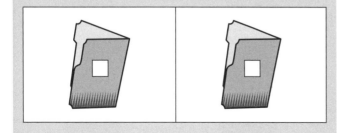

TIME

- three to five class periods

Teaching Directions

1. Determine a total quantity of counters to use (e.g., between ten and twenty), and count out that number. Explain to the class that this is the number you will be investigating.

2. Tell the class that you will be hiding a portion of the counters, and that you want them to figure out how many are hidden.

3. Hide a portion of the counters behind a file folder.

4. Ask the students to determine the unknown, hidden quantity.

5. Have the students explain the method they used to determine the unknown.

6. Write/draw the students' method on chart paper.

7. Discuss the similarities between methods with the class.

8. Have the students play *The Missing Piece* independently with a partner.

Teaching Notes

The ability to think of numbers in terms of part–whole relationships is one of many landmarks in developing more complex understanding about number. Understanding that a quantity can be decomposed into different-size parts is fundamental to grasping the concept of place value. The ability to deal with part–whole relationships allows students to go beyond simple counting to solve problems.

This activity helps students practice determining an unknown quantity in a part–whole situation. It also develops students' understanding of the relationship between addition and subtraction, as well as the commutative property.

Students practice different strategies to determine the hidden quantity and communicate that strategy to their partner. Communication through both writing and speaking allows students to better understand the methods they are using. Hearing about the methods used by their classmates gives students an opportunity to acquire addition and subtraction strategies they may have not considered on their own.

The Lesson

The students settled into a circle on the rug as they came into the classroom. I sat on the floor with them, a bag of lima beans and a file folder in front of me. I began by saying, "We have had many opportunities to break numbers apart and put them back together. You have become experts at breaking numbers into 'pieces.' Today we are going to do an activity in which you will see a piece of a larger quantity. You have to figure out the 'missing piece': the quantity that is hiding. It is kind of like a guessing game. I am going to choose a total number of beans between ten and twenty. I will use the same number throughout our guessing time. For this lesson, I choose eleven."

I put a handful of beans on the rug in front of me. I counted aloud, moving each bean aside as I counted, until I had eleven beans in a pile. My choice of eleven beans was a deliberate one. For some time, the students had been working on learning combinations of numbers that made ten. I was interested in seeing if they could use what they knew about ten and transfer that knowledge to a quantity that was very close to that quantity. I also wanted to minimize the challenge somewhat, so that students could focus their attention on learning the directions.

"You know that I am using eleven beans. I am going to hide some of them behind this file folder and put the rest of them in front of the folder. Look at how many beans are in front of the folder and then figure out how many beans are 'missing' from the eleven. We will repeat these steps many times, each

time using a total of eleven beans; I will hide some beans and you will guess the number of beans that are hidden. Pay close attention to how you figured out the 'missing piece,' the part of eleven that you cannot see. I would like you to explain your way of finding the missing piece of eleven that is hiding behind the folder. Any questions?"

"What if we are wrong?" Brad inquired.

"What is most important is the thinking involved in figuring out the missing part of eleven. Being 'right' is not as important as having a way of figuring out the number of beans you cannot see and explaining that to the rest of us," I said encouragingly.

Kyle looked concerned. "What if we don't know how to figure out how many you are hiding?"

"Listen to what your classmates tell you," I advised. "They will explain their methods for figuring out the missing piece. Maybe one of their ways will make sense to you and you can use it to figure out the missing part."

No more hands were in the air. I scooted backward a bit, placing the folder on its side to provide a barrier, and continued. "Here I go. I am going to put some of the eleven beans in front of the folder." As I said this, I placed eight beans in front of the folder. "The rest I am putting behind the folder. When you have figured out how many beans are hiding, put your hands on your knees." I placed the three beans near the folded edge of the folder so that no one could see them. I purposely chose to keep a larger number of the beans visible to the students, because I wanted them to be successful at determining the unknown quantity. The closer the known quantity was to the actual number of beans, the easier it would be to determine the unknown quantity that was hidden from sight. Some students began counting on their fingers while others immediately put their hands on their knees. I waited until all students had finished solving the problem before speaking.

"I see you have finished figuring out eleven's 'missing piece.' If you are willing to explain how you figured out the number of beans behind the folder, please raise your hand." Many children were willing to do so. I stood up and got ready to record their ideas on chart paper. This record of student thinking would later enable me to address the various strategies that students were using, help them make comparisons about the different methods, and encourage them to develop a repertoire of strategies that would prepare them for later work with larger numbers. I also wanted to model for them some ways of recording their ideas. I called on a few volunteers.

"It's three," Kyle said. "I counted."

I prodded him to elaborate. "How did you start?" I asked.

"With eight," he replied.

"Why eight?" I continued.

"That's how many beans were showing," Kyle answered.

"I am going to write down what you said," I responded. On the chart paper, I wrote:

Kyle

I started with 8. That's how many beans were showing.

"What did you do next?" I asked.

"I counted. I used my fingers," he answered.

Again, I prodded Kyle to elaborate. He may have represented "eight" on eight fingers, counting on three more until he got to eleven. Or he may have begun with eight "in his head" and counted on to eleven. I wanted to encourage the students to be as specific as possible. "Can you show us?" I asked.

Kyle held up a fist. "I went eight," he said, and then he unfolded one finger at a time as he said, "nine, ten, eleven. That's three."

I went back to the chart, reading back the words I had already written. "Here's what we have so far: *I started with eight.* What should I write next?"

Kyle added, "I counted on my fingers."

"How far did you count?" I pressed.

"To eleven!" Kyle looked at me as though I had asked a very silly question.

"Why did you stop at eleven?" I asked.

"That's how many beans you used altogether," he said.

"That is a lot of valuable information," I stated. "You told us what tool you used: your fingers. And you told us that you counted to the number of beans we used altogether. Let me write that down." I added the words *I counted to the number of beans we used altogether* to the chart.

"What did you say as you counted?" I wanted to get as complete a record as possible to show what Kyle did.

"Nine, ten, eleven," said Kyle, again demonstrating by unfolding one finger at a time until three fingers were extended.

Again, I let the students know what I was doing. "I am going to write down what you just said,"

I told them. The chart now looked like this:

Kyle

I started with 8. That's how many beans were showing. I counted on my fingers. I counted to the number of beans we used altogether. I said, "9, 10, 11."

To make sure that students were remembering that these words had a relationship to the method Kyle used, I asked him, "What did we find out?"

"Three beans are hiding," he said.

I added, *3 beans are hiding* to the chart. Now came the time to connect the words to another representation of Kyle's method: a picture. "I am going to draw a picture of what Kyle did," I explained to the class. "Since he used his fingers, I am going to draw a hand. But he held up only three fingers on his hand, so I am only going to draw three fingers. Each time he put up a finger, he said a number. So, for each finger, I am going to write the number Kyle said." I added the following illustration to the chart:

Finally, I wanted the students to see that a number sentence could be connected to what Kyle had done. Since Kyle's expertise had been tapped already and I was concerned about involving more students, I asked the students as a group, "What number did Kyle start with?"

"Eight!" was the unanimous response.

"And Kyle counted up to what number?" I asked.

"Eleven!" they chorused.

"Because?" I inquired.

"That's how many beans you used altogether," said one student.

"That's how many there were showing," said another.

"That's the number of beans you used," said a third.

"That's the total," another student stated.

"What was Kyle trying to figure out?" I asked.

"How many beans were hiding," offered one student.

"How many he couldn't see," suggested another.

"The missing piece," said a third.

I explained the number sentence as I wrote it. "So, Kyle started with the number of beans he could see: eight." I wrote *8* on the chart beneath Kyle's strategy. "And he counted to, or added on to get, the total number of beans." I added a plus sign next to the 8 on the chart. "He was trying to figure out how many beans were hiding. This was the unknown, missing part. He found that there were . . ."

"Three!" the class responded.

"I am going to put this number, the unknown that Kyle figured out, in a box." I added a boxed *3* to the chart.

"He started with eight, counted on three, to get to . . . ?" I prompted.

"Eleven!" said several students.

"The number of beans we are using," said another.

"The total," said yet another.

I finished writing the equation on the chart (see below).

$$8 + \boxed{3} = 11$$

"Kyle used a particular way, a method or a strategy, to solve the problem. Do you know the name of that method or strategy?" I asked.

Kyle attempted a response. "Counting on?" he said.

"Exactly," I said. "I am going to add the name of that strategy to the chart." Under Kyle's strategy, I wrote *Counting On*.

It is important for students to see that equations represent a problem-solving context. The way that Kyle solved this problem could be represented using his words, a picture, and an equation. I was curious to see if other students had different ways that could be represented. But first I needed to demonstrate for the students how to record this combination on their *Missing Piece* recording sheet. I showed students the sheet that they would be using when independently completing this activity. Because the features of the sheet were not easily seen, I drew an enlarged version of the folder on the board, saying, "This recording sheet has eight pictures of a folder, just like this one. Pretend that this is a space on your recording sheet. You want to record what Kyle saw in front of the folder. I want to record the number that matches the quantity of beans he could see in front."

"Eight!" many called out.

"That is the number I need to write in front of the folder." I added an *8* to the drawing on the board.

"And the number that Kyle figured out was hidden behind the folder?" I asked.

"Three!" many students said.

"So I am going to record that in back of the folder. Again, it was a number he did not know, so I am going to put that in a box." The recording looked like this:

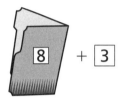

I continued. "Those two sets of beans—the ones in front of the folder and the ones that were hiding . . ." I began.

"Make eleven!" Kyle reported.

"So I need to write that as well," I continued, adding to what I had already drawn and written:

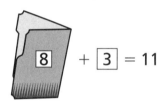

"Each time you find the missing piece for a quantity of beans—the number of beans that is hiding behind the folder—you will record an equation in a spot on the recording sheet, just like I have shown you," I explained.

"Do you always keep the same number of beans?" Michael asked.

"Yes. I want you to keep the number of beans the same for the entire recording sheet. You and a partner will repeat the activity with the same number of beans. Take turns hiding some behind the folder and putting some in front of the folder. You will try and figure out the number of beans that is hiding behind your partner's folder. You will then explain the way in which you figured out the missing piece, just like Kyle explained to us. Record the equations for you and your partner's turn. You will each record both sets of equations."

Troy asked, "Do we have to write down the words that they used, and the pictures and stuff, like you did on the chart?"

"Some of you might really want to push yourselves today. You can do that if you would like, but I don't expect you to. I wanted to show you how you can record a person's thinking in many ways. You can write down their words, a picture that matches their method, and a number sentence as well. It is only the number sentence—the equation—that you need to record. If you would like to practice recording your way, or your partner's way, you can turn over your paper and give it a try. You can try words, numbers, and pictures, or all three," I explained.

I wanted to give the students another example of how to record a person's thinking in words, numbers, and pictures. I wanted them to see that there was more than one way to determine the number of hidden beans. By listening to other methods, perhaps they would begin to use other ways that they had not previously considered. Flexibility in how they use and represent numbers is an important goal I have for my students.

We had taken some time to write down Kyle's method and I was concerned that his classmates may have lost track of the method they had used to solve this first problem. For this reason, I decided to give them a new one to solve. I said, "I am going to use eleven beans again. This time, I am going to put a different number of beans in front of the folder. Again, figure out how many beans are hiding, the 'missing piece' of eleven. When you have figured out the missing piece, put your hands on your knees." I placed six beans in front of the folder this time, hiding five behind. Students quickly put their hands on their knees. I asked, "Who used Kyle's method?" Many students raised their hands. I asked, "Who used a different method?" and several students put their hands up. I called on Jessica to share what she had done.

"I didn't use my fingers," she began. "I just used my head. My brain told me."

It is important to make students aware of their thinking so that they can express their problem-solving process to others. By verbalizing their thinking, they develop an understanding of the effectiveness of their own method while also helping others to acquire new ways of approaching a problem. "Sometimes our brains work so fast, it isn't easy to slow them down and see the steps they went through in figuring something out," I said. "Did your brain tell you with numbers or pictures?"

"No, I just knew the numbers," she replied.

I suspected that Jessica had used her knowledge of number combinations to arrive at her answer. I pressed her to more fully articulate her strategy.

"That is really interesting," I said. "What numbers did you know?"

"There's six beans in front, right? I know that six and four is ten. So, it's one more. It's five," she explained.

Jessica had used what she knew about combinations of numbers that made ten. She adjusted this information to fit a similar context: eleven. Her explanation still had some gaps, however. I wanted Jessica's classmates to thoroughly understand her method of determining the number of missing beans.

"I think I understand. I need to ask some questions to make sure, though. Maybe if I start writing down your way, it will help me. The first thing you said was 'I know six and four is ten.' Let me start with that information." On the chart, under where I had recorded Kyle's strategy, I wrote:

Jessica

I know 6 and 4 is 10.

"Then you said 'I know it's one more.' What do you mean?" I asked.

"Well, six and four is ten. But we have eleven. So it's one more. It's eleven," Jessica explained.

"Maybe it would help if we reminded each other where these numbers came from. How about the six? Where did that number come from?" I asked.

"Six beans are in front of the folder . . . I can see them," she said. "If we had ten beans, then four would be hiding. But we have eleven beans and it's one more," she added.

"One more than . . . ?" I prodded.

"Than ten!" Jessica said.

"Let me go back to the chart and see if I have the words I need. 'I know six and four is ten,' it says. Help me add some more words, Jessica," I said.

"We have eleven beans. Eleven is one more than ten."

I added this to Jessica's strategy. The chart now read:

Jessica

I know 6 and 4 is 10. 11 is 1 more than 10.

"OK . . . this is tricky," I said. "So you know that eleven is one more than ten. How does that help you to know what is hiding behind the folder?"

"If we had ten, and six showing, there would be four hiding, because six and four is ten," Jessica explained. "But we're using eleven beans. But six is showing, see? So, instead of six showing and four hiding, it's six showing and five hiding! You give that one to the four to make five!"

"You did a lot of explaining. Let me make sure that I have recorded what you have said," I said. I added words a few at a time, reading aloud as I wrote and pausing for Jessica to tell me what to write next, omitting any repetition. The chart now read as follows:

Jessica

I know 6 and 4 is 10. 11 is 1 more than 10. If we used 10 and 6 beans were showing, 4 would be hiding. Since we used 11 beans and 6 are showing, 5 are hiding. You give the 1 to the 4 to make 5.

"Now, Kyle used his fingers as a tool. Jessica used what she knew about numbers. Let's see if we can capture what she said using only the numbers she used. She said she knew that six and four is ten. If I was going to write that using numbers, what might I write?" I asked.

"Six plus four equals ten," Jessica offered.

"Let me write that down." I recorded the equation and then asked, "How might I write the next thing she said, the part that explains, 'Eleven is one more than ten'?"

"Ten plus one equals eleven?" Jessica queried.

"You don't sound sure. How come?" I asked.

"Because the chart says eleven first. But you can't say 'Eleven equals ten plus one,'" Jessica explained.

Jessica's statement gave me the opportunity to address a common misconception about equality. Students most often see equations in which the expression (e.g., 10 + 1) is written before, rather than after, the equals sign. This concern for use of a convention can easily take precedence over what the symbols mean. In these cases, it is important to address the meaning behind the symbols. I hoped to clarify Jessica's understanding by asking some questions.

"Let me write down what you said. Do you mean that it is not OK to write this?" On the board, I wrote: *11 = 1 + 10.*

"That looks funny!" Michael said.

"Yeah, you can't do *that*!" added Sarah.

"Really? Why not?" I asked.

"'Cause the equals has to go at the end!" explained Jennifer.

"What does this symbol mean?" I pointed to the equals sign.

Jennifer responded, "It means that the first part, like eight plus three, equals the part after the equals."

"Let me see if I understand what you mean," I said. "Are you saying that the equals sign comes between the parts you are adding together—eight and three—and the answer?"

"Yeah," Jessica answered. "Eleven."

"But"—I pointed to what I had written on the board, touching each part of the equation as I mentioned it—"that is what I wrote here, except with different numbers. The equals sign is between the answer—eleven—and what we are adding together—one and ten."

"But you have to put the answer at the end!" insisted Brad.

Rarely are there times when I can just explain an idea to students by feeding them information. Usually, students need to come to their own understanding of mathematical relationships, in this case, connecting symbols to a problem-solving context. It seemed as though the students had a misconception about the use of the symbols. While they possessed a great deal of information about what the symbols represented, they believed there was only one conventional order to the use for these symbols: that the operation is written before the equals sign. I needed to clarify the misconception about order by telling students that their understanding of the symbol was accurate, that the symbol represented equivalence, regardless of the location of the 'pieces' of an equation.

"You all know a great deal about how to use these symbols, especially the equals sign. The equals sign comes between two parts of the equation. It shows that both parts of the equation are equal to each other. Eleven is equal to six plus five and six plus five is equal to eleven." There was only so much I could *tell* students about equivalence right now. Clearly, this was a concept that would need to be revisited many times in the future.

"Let's go back to Jessica's words and see if we can write the symbols to match the words she used. 'Eleven is one more than ten.'"

Several students called out, "Eleven equals one plus ten."

"And that makes sense because?" I asked.

"She said 'Eleven' first, then the one and the ten," one student explained.

"It doesn't matter . . . you can put the answer at the beginning or the end," another said.

I added to the chart: *11 = 1 + 10.*

"What about the next part: 'If we used ten and six beans were showing, four would be hiding'? How would I write that with numbers?" I pondered.

Brad attempted, "Ten equals six plus four."

"But you have that!" said Sarah.

"No she doesn't!" argued Troy.

"Do we or don't we? How can we be sure?" I asked.

"Ten equals six plus four isn't up there," said Brad.

"But six plus four equals ten is the same thing," said Sarah.

Troy countered, "But the numbers are in different order."

"But Ms. Scharton said that it doesn't matter what order the things are in, it still means the same!" Sarah tried.

"'Six plus four equals ten' and 'Ten equals six plus four' do *mean* the same, yes. If we were to write numbers to match Jessica's words, what should we write next?"

Many responded in kind, "Ten equals six plus four!"

"I told you!" agreed Troy.

I added the equation *10 = 6 + 4* to the chart, then asked, "Now what? Her words say, 'Since we used eleven beans and six are showing, five are hiding.'"

Most students called out, "Eleven equals six plus five."

I added *11 = 6 + 5* to the chart. "What number was the unknown, the number Jessica figured out when using her method?"

"Five!" said Michael. "Make a box around five."

I said, "One more idea to put into numbers: 'You give the one to the four to make five.' What do you think? How shall we record that in numbers?"

"One plus four equals five," was the unanimous response. I added *1 + 4 = 5* to the chart as well.

"Kyle used a counting-on strategy. What did Jessica use as a strategy for finding eleven's missing piece?" I questioned. "Numbers!" the students answered. Under Jessica's strategy on the chart, I wrote *Use of Numbers*.

"There are some really interesting things on this chart," I said. "We have worked on Jessica's strategy for a long time. Please look at the equations we wrote. See if you notice anything about those equations. Are any of them related? Do any go together? Talk to someone next to you and tell them what you see." After a couple of minutes in which they talked among themselves, I asked if anyone wanted to share what they, or their partner, had noticed.

"There's six plus four equals ten and ten equals six plus four!" said Jennifer.

"Yeah! And ten equals six plus four and eleven equals six plus five!" added Kyle.

"Look! There's one plus four equals five and one plus ten equals eleven, except it's written the other way," observed Troy.

"Sometimes the equals comes at the end and sometimes it's at the beginning," added Sarah.

"What a lot of observations you have made. Terrific!" I said. "Let's see if we can find a way to record this situation on the recording sheet you will be completing when you do this on your own. Let me draw another picture on the board, similar to the one that is on the paper you will get." I asked for students' input to represent eleven's missing piece—the portion of eleven hiding behind the folder—for this last combination. Collaboratively, we came up with the following:

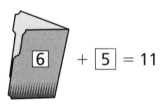

"I wonder if anyone can use Kyle's strategy to show how to solve this problem?" I said.

Sarah tried it. "Sure! You start with six and you count on to eleven, using your fingers." Sarah showed us a fist, then unfolded one finger at a time, saying a number each time, until she had five fingers opened, "Seven, eight, nine, ten, eleven. See! There's five fingers! Six and five make eleven."

"I'd like you all to try this method now," I said. "Start with six, then count on to eleven. Ready? Go!" I observed as the students practiced Kyle's method using these numbers.

"Let's try one more before I send you off on your own to do your own *Missing Piece* papers," I said, placing four beans in front of the folder. Students quickly placed their hands on their knees. Again, I asked, "Who solved the problem using Kyle's way? Who solved it using Jessica's way? Who used another way?" I wanted to get one more strategy recorded. I called on Troy.

"I kind of did it like Kyle," Troy began, "but I counted back, instead of up."

"Can you show us what you did?" I requested.

"I started with eleven and counted back, like this." Troy demonstrated on his hands, just like other students had done: "Ten, nine, eight, seven, six, five, four." Troy had seven fingers unfolded. "I got seven. Seven beans are hiding!"

"Can you remind us why you started with eleven?" I asked.

"That's how many we started with," Troy responded.

"I am going to write that down," I announced, and I added the following to the chart:

Troy

I started with 11. That is how many we started with. I counted back: 10, 9, 8, 7, 6, 5, 4. I got 7. 7 beans are hiding.

Troy used a counting strategy, but rather than counting on from the number of beans that were showing to the total number of beans, Troy started with the total number of beans and counted back to the number of beans that were showing. I wanted his method to be explicit to his classmates, so I asked some questions and had Troy confirm the students' replies.

"I wonder why he counted back to four instead of counting back to some other number," I prompted.

"There are four beans in front of the folder," one student said.

"That's how many we can see!" said another.

"He stopped at the number of beans showing," said yet another.

"I need to add some information to our chart, don't I? I wonder how he came up with 'seven' as his answer for the number of hidden beans," I questioned.

"He used his fingers," offered one student.

"When he said a number, he put up a finger!" said another.

"That's how many fingers he had up when he got to four from eleven," said a third.

"Kyle used his fingers as a tool, and Jessica used her brain and what she knows about numbers. I wonder what tool Troy used and how we can draw that tool to show what he did," I said.

"Draw a hand, like Kyle's," was one suggestion.

"You need two hands . . . he used both of them!" was another.

"Write the numbers he said, just like you did on Kyle's, except counting back numbers," said one student.

I did what the students suggested.

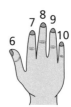

"We have used words and pictures to record Troy's method for finding eleven's missing piece," I said. "What equation could we write to record what he did?"

"He started with eleven," Sarah began.

Michael added, "But he went back, so he didn't add . . . he subtracted!"

"He subtracted on his fingers, counting back," said Kyle.

"He minused seven and got four," Michael said. "The seven needs a box around it."

The students had been focused on this activity for some time, but before we ended the group discussion I wanted them to think about how the strategies on the chart were related, realizing that we would need to take another look at these strategies during another class period. I gave them a couple of tasks while I recorded the equation that the students had helped to construct.

"I'd like you to do a couple of things before we get started at the tables, trying out this activity on our own," I said. "Please talk to the person next to you. Talk about how Troy's strategy is similar to and different from Kyle's and Jessica's. Try out Jessica's strategy and Kyle's strategy with Troy's numbers. Ready? Go!"

After several minutes, I asked them what they'd found.

"Kyle counted and Troy counted," one student said.

"Both of them used their fingers," another offered.

"Kyle counted on and Troy counted back," said a third.

"Kyle and Jessica used addition. Troy used subtraction," said yet another student.

"You could count on from four to eleven, Kyle's way," was one observation.

"You would get seven," another student added.

"Six and five is close to four and seven," said yet another.

"They all used eleven beans," observed one student.

"Eight and three, six and five, and four and seven *all* make eleven!" enthused another.

"How should we name Troy's strategy for finding the missing piece?" I asked.

"Counting back!" was the class response. I added this strategy to the class chart. The final strategy chart thus looked like this:

Missing Piece Strategies

Kyle: I started with 8. That's how many beans were showing. I counted on my fingers. I counted to the number of beans we used altogether. I said, "9, 10, 11."

$8 + \boxed{3} = 11$

COUNTING ON

Jessica: I know 6 and 4 is 10. 11 is 1 more than 10. If we used 10 and 6 beans were showing, 4 would be hiding. Since we used 11 beans and 6 are showing, 5 are hiding. You give the 1 to the 4 to make 5.

$6 + 4 = 10 \qquad 10 = 6 + 4$
$11 = 1 + 10 \qquad 11 = 6 + \boxed{5}$
$\qquad\quad 1 + 4 = 5$

USE OF NUMBERS

Troy: I started with 11. I counted back: 10, 9, 8, 7, 6, 5, 4. I got 7. 7 beans are hiding.

$11 - \boxed{7} = 4$

COUNTING BACK

I next recorded Troy's strategy as they would on their recording sheets, drawing a model of the folder on the board (see below).

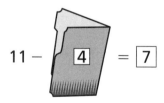

$11 - \boxed{4} = \boxed{7}$

It was now time for the students to pair up and try *The Missing Piece* on their own. We had accomplished a lot during this whole-class lesson. The students received directions for an independent activity that focused on seeing many ways in which one number could be decomposed and recombined. By listening to various methods used to determine a missing quantity,

students were coming to realize that there are many strategies that they could use for this type of problem. Lastly, recording their problem-solving strategies allowed students to see that their strategies were valued and could be represented in words, pictures, and numbers. Communicating these methods through writing and talk allowed students to acquire new methods for solving problems while finding ways to relate their own methods with those of their classmates.

Extension: *What's in the Bag?*

What's in the Bag? follows a similar sequence and shares the same objective as *The Missing Piece*. Pairs of students place a predetermined number of objects in a paper bag. One partner pulls out a handful. Students count the number of objects removed, then use different strategies to figure out the number of objects that remain in the bag. Both students record their strategies in number sentences and discuss the relationship between the number sentences, as well as the operations they used. *What's in the Bag?* provides an opportunity for students to develop addition and subtraction strategies and explain these strategies to their classmates. Recording and discussing these strategies allows students to examine the relationship between numbers and the operations of addition and subtraction.

Linking Assessment and Instruction

As you observe the students work, think about the following:

- What strategies do the students use to figure out the "hidden quantity"? Do they count back from the total or on from the amount removed? Or do they use knowledge of known number combinations?
- Do they use the same strategy repeatedly or are they able to employ a variety of strategies? Are students able to acquire or adapt the strategies of their classmates?
- How do the students symbolically represent these situations: what is hidden, what is showing, the total?
- Can they understand the relationship between addition and subtraction?
- How comfortably and effectively do students communicate their strategies, both aloud and in writing?
- Can the students see the relationships between different strategies?

Tile Riddles

CHAPTER 5

OVERVIEW

In this lesson, students choose a collection of color tiles and then write clues about their collection so that other students can determine what is in the collection. Careful wording and ordering of the clues are critical for the successful solving of the riddles. Students use algebraic thinking to narrow down a range of possibilities. They must think logically, organize information, and understand various number relationships.

MATERIALS

- color tiles, 20–40 of various colors per pair
- small brown paper bags, 1 per pair of students
- optional: transparent overhead color titles
- optional: *Tile Riddles* examples and instructions (see Blackline Masters)

TIME

- two class periods

Teaching Directions

1. Before you meet with the class, compile two tile riddle bags with a set of clues for each. For example, a bag containing four green, four yellow, and four blue tiles might have the following clues: *I have 12 tiles; I used 3 colors; There are no red tiles; There are the same number of green tiles and blue tiles;* and *I have 4 yellow tiles.* Consider the total number of tiles you will use.

2. Give students access to their own set of color tiles.

3. Present each tile riddle to the class by reading the clues one by one. As each clue is read, ask students to narrow down the range of possible tile combinations by using the tiles at their tables.

4. Have students solve the riddles, then view the contents of each bag to confirm their solutions.

5. Discuss as a class what makes a "good clue" and how clues can best be ordered.

6. Have students, working with partners, create their own tile riddles.

7. Have pairs of students test out their tile riddles on other students.

Teaching Notes

Students enjoy writing and solving riddles. While writing riddles may seem to be a simple task, it is actually quite complex: in this activity, students must consider the total number of tiles, the number of tiles of each color, and the relationships between these groups. The makeup of the actual set of tiles is only obvious to the person who wrote the clues about that set; it is difficult for young children initially to see the numerous possibilities for a given clue. The teacher's careful structuring of this activity—beginning with a total number of tiles within a range, writing clear, simple statements about the group and subgroups, and ordering the clues from general to more specific—is important when introducing *Tile Riddles* to students.

The Lesson

Day 1

Before the students came in from recess, I placed a couple of handfuls of color tiles at each table. I knew that they had used them before, so I wasn't too concerned about their need for exploration, as I would have been if they had not been familiar with these manipulatives. Still, I wanted to make sure that they were ready to hear about the purpose of the tiles. After they sat down, I stated, "I see that you have noticed the color tiles that are out on your tables. I want to thank you for leaving them be and giving me your attention while I explain to you what we're going to be doing with them."

I began the morning lesson by asking students to think about what they already knew about riddles. "I have a riddle to share with you today. But before I tell it to you, it's probably a good idea to ask you what you know about riddles. When I say the word *riddle*, what does it make you think of?"

"It's like a joke," said Mark.

Serena added, "It has rhymes in it, like 'pen' and 'hen' and 'when.' Well, sometimes it does!"

"It's kind of like a poem," answered Ernie.

"You've made some interesting observations," I said. "Yes, sometimes riddles rhyme and that makes them sound like poems. And they can be funny, like jokes. One thing about riddles that is really important for us to know is that a riddle is a puzzle that we are going to try to solve. Sometimes a riddle is in the form of a question. Let me give you one of those. What is black and white and read all over?"

"A zebra with chicken pox?" quipped Jorge. His classmates giggled.

"That's true! A zebra is normally black and white. Chicken pox would certainly make it red, also! But that isn't the answer to my riddle."

"A newspaper with some red in it?" asked Lindsey.

"That could be, couldn't it? Newspapers have black text on a white background. Sometimes other colors are in the newspaper as well," I commented.

"A paper that you read," said Fred.

"How so?" I asked.

"My brother told me that one! It's black and white, like you said. But you 'read' it, you know, with your eyes. It isn't the color kind of red; it's the reading kind of read. 'Black and white and read all over.'"

"Ohhhh!" said many students.

"You got it!" I said. "That is a really old riddle that I learned when I was your age. It was difficult for

me to understand until someone explained it to me. Keep your eyes and ears open for riddles like the newspaper riddle. There are lots of them. The newspaper riddle asks a question. Many do. The type of riddle I have to share with you has statements, or sentences. Let me show you what I mean."

I turned on the overhead. On it, I had placed a transparency with two sets of clues for two separate riddles. I had these clues covered as I said, "My riddle is about the color tiles I have hidden in this paper bag." I held up a small lunch bag that had four green, four yellow, and four blue tiles inside. "It has several clues written as sentences. I am going to read you one sentence at a time. After I do, with a partner or as a table, I want you to make a set of tiles that is true for that sentence. We will talk about the possible sets of tiles as we go. Any questions?" None of the students raised their hands, so I proceeded to show them the first clue.

1. *I have 12 tiles.*

Students quickly took tiles and began counting out twelve of them. Most students worked as a group of four; some worked as partners. Each set of tiles was different from table to table.

"Have you solved the riddle?" I asked. "When I look around the room, I see many different possible solutions for the clue that I have read. Could they all be the solution for what I have in the bag?" There was a resounding "no!" from the class.

"It seems as though you need another clue." I showed the students the next sentence on the overhead.

2. *I used 3 colors.*

"What do you know about color tiles and colors?" I asked.

"They are bright," Jorge said.

"Some aren't so bright," added Elizabeth.

"How many colors are there?" I pressed.

"Four!" several quickly responded.

"What are they?" I asked. Students named the four color tile colors: red, green, yellow, and blue. "That's important information, especially for this second clue."

Students began removing a color from their arrangements, but most did not think to add tiles back to make the number twelve. "Let's take a look at what has to be true about your group of tiles," I said. "The first clue tells you there are twelve tiles and the second clue tells you there are three colors. Both of these things have to be true. Take a look at your sets of tiles and make sure that your pile matches both of the clues."

"Oh!" many students said, as they fixed their groupings to match the clues. There were still various configurations of tiles on the tables.

"Do you know what is in my bag?" I asked. Some students clearly thought they did, while others clearly realized they did not. A few looked puzzled. "Look at a table that is near to yours. Check to see that they have twelve tiles and three colors." Students checked a neighboring pile to confirm. "Does that group have the exact group of tiles that your group has? Is there more than one solution for both clues?" Students nodded in agreement. It seemed as though they could see that more information was needed.

"Do we have a solution, or is another clue necessary?" I asked.

"Give us a clue!" some of the students said.

"We need another one!" others sang out.

I revealed the next clue.

3. There are no red tiles.

"What do you know now?" I asked as students began adjusting their tiles to reflect the three displayed clues. Some students had four tiles in each of the three colors possible, but there were other arrangements as well.

"There aren't any red ones!" said one student.

"There's three colors," said another.

"There's twelve," said a third.

"Do you know what colors of tiles are in my bag?" I asked.

Maria was confident. "If there are not red ones, there has to be only green and blue and yellow!" Her classmates nodded in agreement.

"Do you know what is in my bag for certain? Or do you need another clue?" I asked.

There was a resounding, "Another!" from many students. I uncovered the next clue.

4. There are the same number of green tiles and blue tiles.

"Oh!" several students exclaimed as they began moving and exchanging tiles.

"What do you know now?" I asked.

The students repeated the clues that had been read so far. Again, I asked, "Do you know what is in my bag?"

Most students eagerly nodded. Fred was certain. "There are four green and four yellow and four blue. I know! I used multiplication to tell me!" he said. Lots of students were smiling and nodding in agreement.

I was pleased to see that Fred and his classmates were using some familiar information to determine what tiles were in the bag. As I quickly circulated the room, I noticed that several other groups had the same set of tiles as Fred's. Jorge had a different set of tiles in front of him. I asked him if he was willing to share what he had done.

"I don't have those tiles. I have something different," said Jorge. "I have one green, one blue, and ten yellow."

"How could that be?" I pondered aloud. No hands went up. I pressed the students to use the information we already had. "What do we know about the tiles?" One by one, students read a clue from the overhead. One by one, we could see that Jorge's set of tiles matched the clues we had read. At this point, I stopped to introduce a table that might help them see there were still other possibilities besides the most "popular" one. "What colors of tiles do we know, for sure, are in my bag?"

"Green!" said several students.

"Blue!" said a few more.

"Yellow!" said some of the others.

Across the board, I wrote the three colors.

"Could there be one green tile?" I asked. Thumbs went up, heads nodded, and several students uttered "yes."

"The fourth clue says, 'There are the same number of green tiles and blue tiles.' If there is one green tile in my bag, how many blue tiles would there be?"

"One!" most students responded.

"Yeah! That's what I have!" Jorge exclaimed.

"How many yellow tiles does Jorge have?" I asked.

Overwhelmingly, students answered, "Ten!" I wrote the following on the chart:

Green	*Blue*	*Yellow*
1	1	10

"Fred and many others had four green, four blue, and four yellow, so I will put that in our chart," I said. I recorded this possibility on the chart, leaving spaces for other numbers to be filled in between Jorge's solution and Fred's solution.

Green	Blue	Yellow
1	1	10
4	4	4

"We have one green and four greens as possibilities. I wonder if there could be a number of greens in between one and four. Talk at your tables." Students began discussing with their table groups. A few students argued that the posted ways were the only two possible sets of tiles in my bag. However, at each table, there were students that could convince their tablemates that there were more than two possibilities. As conversations began to die down, I asked for more information.

"What else is possible?" I inquired.

"There could be two green," reported Serena.

"How could you prove that to us?" I asked.

Serena came up to the overhead and used the transparent overhead tiles to show us. She said, "There could be two green, and then there would be two blue." She placed two of each color on the overhead. "There have to be twelve altogether, so there have to be eight yellow ones, too." She placed eight yellow tiles on the overhead as well.

The class discussion continued to explore the other possible combinations for my bag of tiles. It was clear that some students already had memorized some of these combinations for twelve, while others had not: some students were able to quickly report the number of remaining yellow tiles, when given the numbers of blue and green tiles, while others counted on their fingers to determine the remaining quantity. However, all of the students seemed to have a way of determining the number of yellow tiles, the missing quantity. We continued exploring the possibilities until the chart looked like this:

Green	Blue	Yellow
1	1	10
2	2	8
3	3	6
4	4	4
5	5	2

"How about six greens? Could there be six greens and six blues?" Many students nodded, but a few quickly raised their hands, certain that this was impossible.

"No way!" said several students.

"That's too many!" said several more.

"Really? Why do you think so?" I pressed the students for an explanation.

Serena offered, "You can't have six and six. That's twelve!"

"Anyone else?" I asked.

Mark added, "There's only twelve. If you have six and six, that's already twelve!"

Ernie expanded on this. "You got to have yellows. If you have six green and six blue, that's already twelve. You need some yellows. The clues say!"

I decided to see what the class consensus was. I asked students to talk at their tables: Should we continue the chart or stop? After a brief conversation, we reconvened. Students thought the chart needed to stop with five green, five blue, and two yellow tiles.

I wondered if students realized how I had organized the information. "Do you see any patterns on the chart?" I asked.

"Two, four, six, eight, ten going up the chart," was one response.

"One, two, three, four, five going down," was another.

"Counting by twos!" one student said.

"Counting by ones!" said a second.

I pointed to the top of the chart and said, "What about here? Could there be zero greens and zero blues?"

"No!" many students replied.

"There have to be the same blues and greens!" added Mark.

"But zero and zero are the same!" I countered.

"There have to be three colors, Ms. Scharton! If there is zero and zero, that leaves only yellow. There have to be some greens and blues," argued Maria.

"All right. You have convinced me. Well, how many possible solutions could there be, and how do you know?" I wanted to see if students were using the information from the table to determine what could possibly be in the bag. Some students could see five possibilities right away and their hands immediately went up, while others counted the number of ways from their seats. Most students raised five fingers. I asked three or four of them to explain how they came up with five possibilities. I wanted to make sure that most students were able to use the chart to determine the number of ways and could explain how to "read" it in various ways. I uncovered the last clue on the overhead:

5. *I have 4 yellow tiles.*

Smiles and quiet conversation erupted and it was clear that the students knew the contents of my bag of tiles. I spilled them out on the overhead and cheers and high fives filled the room.

I wanted the students to hear another tile riddle so that they could have more experience with the process of eliminating possibilities and responding to the clues. It would also provide the class the opportunity to compare the clues and examine the features of "good clues," so that students could successfully use these features when writing their own riddles. One by one, I uncovered the following three clues. Each time, we discussed the possibilities, rather than use the tiles to show them. We devoted some time to discussing the second and third clue, for several reasons.

1. There are fewer than 10 tiles.

2. I used 2 colors.

3. I have no green or red tiles.

This set of clues provided an opportunity for students to examine what is a "good," "helpful" clue. We talked about whether the second and third clues were both necessary. Some students preferred the third clue and the elimination of the second one as "unnecessary": since there are only four colors of color tiles, eliminating two of these colors makes it obvious that only two others are being used. Other students thought the second clue left a wide range of possible two-color combinations to consider and the third clue helped to narrow down the possibilities to just one combination. I don't want to appear to be the ultimate "authority" in the classroom. I want students to see that I don't always have the "right" or "best" answer and realize that they are quite capable of independently solving problems. By giving them an example of clues that possibly provided redundant information, I could let them see that I was questioning what makes a good clue, and learning about clue writing along with them. I uncovered the next clue, giving students a chance to discuss the possible sets of tiles in my second bag.

4. I have twice as many blue tiles as yellow tiles.

Clue four was challenging for them. I asked a few students to explain how they figured out "twice as many." This clue gave us a way to connect our prior experience with doubles and multiplication to the context of a riddle. It also gave us another

opportunity to display a table organizing what we knew "so far":

Yellow	Blue
1	2
2	4
3	6

We discussed the possible configurations of tiles in my bag and then I revealed the final clue:

5. I have 2 yellow tiles.

When the students saw the final clue, they realized the composition of tiles was two yellow and four blue. I confirmed their success at finding the answer. At this point in the lesson, I wanted to help prepare students to write their own clues. The overhead transparency that I had used with my tile riddles listed the sets of clues for both riddles. Both riddles began with a general clue, followed by clues that became increasingly more specific. This movement from the general to the specific is an important support for children in solving riddles, but is a difficult concept to transfer to students who are just beginning to understand how riddles are crafted. However, the ability to analyze the type of information provided in the increasingly more specific clues seemed well within their grasp.

"Tomorrow you will create your own tile riddles," I explained. "You will need to write clues so that your classmates can guess what arrangement of tiles is in your bag. Before you do, let's take a look at the clues you have seen today and see if they help you in understanding how to make up your own clues." I showed both riddles on the overhead. I pointed to the first clue from the first tile riddle and asked the class to help me read it aloud; I pointed to the first clue from the second tile riddle and they did the same.

1. I have 12 tiles.   1. There are fewer than 10 tiles.

"What do you notice about these clues?" I asked.
"They tell about how many," said Mark.
"One tells twelve tiles and one says less than ten," added Serena.
Ernie said, "One tells the number. The other tells you less than a number."
"I will write down something to help us remember the type of information each clue gives." I began a chart with this statement:

Clue 1: Number of tiles

"That is something you may want to consider when you write your own clues," I offered. "You may want to begin with a clue that tells about the number of tiles you are using. Let's take a look at the second clue in both riddles." I pointed to these second clues, each time asking the class to help me read them.

2. I used 3 colors.   2. I used 2 colors.

"What do you notice about these two clues?"

Our discussion continued. We compared the second, third, fourth, and fifth clues in each set to determine the type of information each clue provided. We ended the day's lesson with a chart that would help us begin writing clues in the next lesson. Our completed chart looked like this:

Clue 1: Number of tiles
Clue 2: Number of colors
Clue 3: A color not used
Clue 4: Compare two colors of tiles
Clue 5: Tell the number of tiles of one color

Day 2

I called the students' attention to the chart that we had completed at the end of the previous session. "We did a lot of things during yesterday's math time," I said. "Let's take a moment to think about all of the things we did leading up to making this chart." Many of the students raised their hands.

"You had some bags with tiles in them," one student said.

"We had to guess what tiles were in the bags," said another.

"You put up clues. They helped us figure out the tiles," said a third.

"We had tiles at our table. We tried to make the tiles the clues were telling us about," said one student.

"You showed us the clues and we talked about them," was another response.

"We talked about how the clues were the same," a student added.

"We made the chart to help us write clues, to help us remember what to write about."

"You have done a thorough job of remembering many parts of yesterday's math time," I said. "Let's read the chart we made together and see if we can remember what it is for." I pointed to each sentence on the chart and the students discussed how the statement was meant to guide them in writing their own tile riddle clues.

I wanted students to have some support in what I knew was a rather complex task. I decided to have them work with a partner so that they could share the writing and as pairs check the accuracy of their clues.

"Today, I want you to choose a buddy with whom to work," I explained. "A pile of tiles is at each table. You will first select a group of tiles and then you will write your clues. I'd like you to use less than fifteen tiles." On the board, I wrote:

1. Choose less than 15 tiles.

"Look carefully at the tiles that you and your partner have chosen, then write the clues about your collection." I added this to the list:

2. Write clues about what you have chosen.

"Please use the chart we made yesterday to help you think about the type of clues you are writing." I wrote:

3. Think about the order of your clues. Do you have enough clues? The right amount? Too many?

I continued. "After you and your partner are done with your clues, put your collection of tiles in an empty bag and find another pair of children that have also finished writing their clues. I'd like you to test out your clues on another pair of students. Read your clues to them. Have them use another set of tiles, just like you did yesterday, to figure out what selection of tiles is in your bag." I added to the list:

4. Try out your clues with someone else.

I then dismissed the students to find a partner. I asked each pair of students to retrieve an empty brown paper bag and a sheet of paper on which to write their clues, and then find a table and get to work. I began walking around the room to watch how students were beginning to tackle the task. I wanted to ensure that they understood the directions but I also wanted to gather information that would be helpful when we came back together for a whole-class discussion. I was interested not only in the mathematics they encountered, but in the social dynamics that were at play in working with a partner and finding other pairs with which to test clues.

Serena and Ernie had some tiles on the table in front of them and were eagerly discussing what clue should be their first.

"I want to tell about the colors!" said Ernie.

Serena countered his idea. "We are supposed to write about the number!"

"How is it going?" I said, inserting myself into their spirited disagreement.

"Serena says we have to write about the number. I want to write about the colors!" said Ernie.

I was unsure if they needed my help in clarifying the directions I had given or if they wanted me to negotiate the disagreement. I tested out my confusion with a question. "Is there something you need my help with?" I asked.

"Yeah. Do we have to write about numbers first?" asked Serena.

"What do you remember about comparing the sets of clues? Why did we talk about those?" I wanted to see if they remembered that comparing the clues and realizing the similarities between the sets were only suggestions to guide their own clue writing.

"The first clues were the same . . . almost the same," said Ernie.

"What about the rest of the clues?" I asked.

"They were the same, too," said Serena.

"Almost the same," corrected Ernie.

I continued. "And why did we talk about the two sets of clues?"

"To help us write our clues," Serena inserted.

"Yes. To help you. Do you have to have to write a certain type of clue as the first clue? Where can you look if you need a reminder?" I asked.

Both students replied, in unison, "On the board."

"See number three?" asked Ernie. "It doesn't say you have to write that kind of clue. It says 'Think about the order of clues.' It doesn't say you have to write the clues like Ms. Scharton's!"

"So, now what will you do?" I asked them. It was clear now that the directions were understood. That left the issue of how to clear up the disagreement. Rather than solve the problem for them, I decided to see if they were capable of figuring out an equitable solution on their own.

"How about if we take turns? You get the first clue, I get the second clue . . . like that?" asked Serena.

"OK!" said Ernie.

I realized that this would leave someone with an odd number of clues for which to be responsible. But I thought I'd leave them to take care of that on their own. I could always step in and assist them later, if needed. I moved on.

"Hi, how's it going?" I asked Lindsey and Maria. "This is hard!" they said.

"Why do you think so?" I asked.

"We don't know what to say!" said Lindsey.

"Yeah. This is really tricky!" Maria added.

"What can you do to make it easier for yourselves?" Again, I wanted to help these students find their own solution, rather than providing one for them. Asking a question might help them realize that they were capable of taking care of their own difficulties. "Is there something you could do that would help you?"

"It's hard to write the clues! We can't see the tiles!" said Maria.

"Oh! I bet that is hard! So, what can you do so that you can see the tiles? I would have trouble writing clues if I couldn't see the tiles!" I said.

"But if we pour out the tiles, everyone will see what is in the bag!" said Lindsey.

I realized that although I had made it clear in our class discussion that looking at the tiles was a necessary first step, I had neglected to write this on the board. As I took a quick survey of what students around the room were doing, I realized that Lindsey and Maria had lots of company: most other pairs of students had put their collection of tiles in the bag, rather than leave them on the table. I quickly got the students' attention.

"Boys and girls, I need your hands off the materials and your eyes on me. I made a silly mistake. I forgot to make something very clear. When you are writing the clues, it is important to have the tiles sitting in front of you and your partner. Then it will be much easier for you to tell what is true about your collection of tiles. If you keep them in the bag, they are difficult to see. Lay the tiles on the table and talk about the clues with them in front of you."

"But people will see them!" Jorge said.

"If someone sees them, do you think they will remember each and every tile?" Fred said. "They are just as busy writing clues as you are!"

Students giggled at this remark and then dumped the contents of their bags out onto the tabletops. I continued to circulate the room. Mark and Elizabeth seemed to be having trouble. They looked somewhat dejected.

"Hi, you two. How are you doing?" I began.

"Not so good," responded Mark.

"We lost some of our tiles. I think we accidentally moved some back into the table pile. We don't remember what we had," added Elizabeth.

"What could you do?" I asked.

"We don't know. We are stuck," Mark admitted.

It was clear that these two students needed some suggestions. I wanted to help them as little as possible, because I realized that this was a perfect opportunity for them to do some real problem solving. "I think we can do something," I said. "Let's read what you have so far and see if the clues are true." One by one, Mark and Elizabeth read their clues aloud. After they read each one, I asked them if the clue was a true one for what tiles they had in front of them.

"'We have thirteen tiles,'" Elizabeth read, while Mark counted the tiles.

"Yep!" Mark confirmed.

"'We used three colors,'" they both read and then both added, "yep!" They continued. "'There are the same number of red and blue tiles.'" Elizabeth counted the red tiles and the blue tiles. There were three of each, and she said, "Yes, that's true, too." They both read, "'There are no yellow tiles.' Yep!" Then they read the last clue, "'There are three red tiles.' Uh oh . . ."

"We don't know how many green ones we should have," said Mark.

"What do you know for sure?" I asked.

"Our clues are true, except we don't know about the greens," Elizabeth said.

"And that is good news: that your clues are true. Which clue tells how many tiles you used?" I encouraged.

"Oh! The first clue! It says we used thirteen! We have three red and three blue . . . that's six!" said Mark. "And the rest are green!" Mark counted on from six to thirteen, moving the seven green tiles toward the pile of red and blue tiles they had already made. Elizabeth didn't look convinced.

"What could you do to make sure that your clues are still true?" I assisted.

Elizabeth said, "Read the clues again. See if they are true."

"Why don't you do that and see what happens," I suggested. I stood nearby as they went through this process. They read each clue and checked their collection. Sure enough, they had what they needed. "What will you do now?" I asked.

"Find someone to read our clues to!" Elizabeth said with a smile. They searched the room for another pair of students who were ready to exchange tile riddles.

As soon as the first finished pair found another finished pair, students became motivated to finish writing their clues so that they could try them out with their classmates. Students needed little help

locating classmates on whom to test their tile riddles. If a pair of students was unable to locate another pair of students, a pair that was eager to exchange riddles quickly approached them.

After most of the students had had about fifteen minutes to read their riddles to others, I asked everybody to come to the rug with their riddles and brown bags of tile collections. These riddles would be shared with the whole class, a few at a time, at subsequent class meetings. At this time, I wanted the students to be able to share the process of writing clues with their classmates. While it is important to discuss the mathematics involved in writing tile riddles, it is also important to discuss the social issues associated with working in pairs: how to fairly make decisions, what to do when you disagree with a partner, how to share the task, what works well and what difficulties were encountered.

"You were really involved in the clue writing with your partners," I began. "Most of you have had the chance to share your riddles with at least one other pair of students. Throughout the week, we will share a few riddles at a time. You will have the opportunity to read your clues to us, while we try to figure out the collection you have inside your bags. Right now, I want to give you a chance to talk about how you worked together. What worked well? What was difficult? How did you share the job of writing clues for your tile riddles? If you had any disagreements with your partner, how did you solve them?" Several students put their hands up.

"We had an argument," admitted Ernie. "But we solved it. Serena thought we had to write a clue and I said we didn't. Ms. Scharton helped us."

"We decided to take turns," Serena added. "We worked it out."

Lindsey spoke up next. "We had trouble writing clues because we couldn't see them. We poured them out on the table. It was a lot easier!"

"We did that, too!" others added.

"Writing clues was hard. I'm glad I had help!" Mark admitted. Many students nodded.

"Would you rather write your own clues, or write clues with a partner?" I asked.

Students had differing opinions. Many thought it was not easy to write tile riddles, and help from a partner was beneficial. Others thought the initial support from a classmate made them ready to try writing clues on their own.

"It's more fun with a partner!" one student said.

"I liked having help. I think I could do it on my own, though!" asserted another.

"You could check with your partner to see if you were doing it right," was another comment.

"It was hard to take turns and share the clues," said one student.

"You had an interesting mathematics period today. Not only was it challenging to write riddles. It was also challenging to work with partners. We have learned a lot about what makes a riddle, the steps to go through in writing good riddles, and how to work with other people. Right now, I'd like you to place your riddles in a pile in the center of the room. We will read a riddle or two daily and see if we can guess what tiles you and your partner wrote about."

I was anxious to review the work that pairs of students turned in. I found many interesting features in the riddles that students had written. Many students felt comfortable and successful with the structure provided from analyzing the two sets of clues on the first day of the lesson. The clues written by Jimmy and Fred were representative of many who had followed this structure. (See Figure 5–1.)

Some students provided unnecessary information, as was the case with Maria and Jorge's final clue. (See Figure 5–2.)

Ernie and Serena took a risk and attempted the use of "twice as many" when writing about the relationship between two quantities of tiles. (See Figure 5–3.)

Reading and guessing tile riddles was an engaging activity for some time. At the beginning of our math period for the next several weeks, students regularly

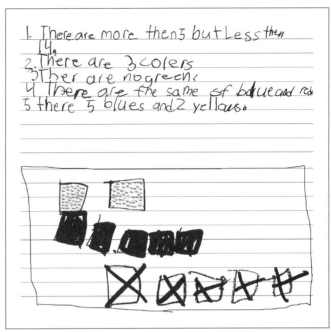

FIGURE 5–2 Maria and Jorge had a solvable riddle, yet used more information than was necessary (the number of yellow tiles).

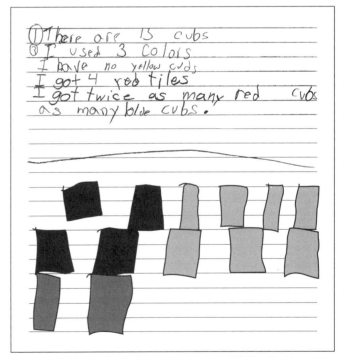

FIGURE 5–3 Ernie and Serena used multiplicative relationships when comparing two group of tiles.

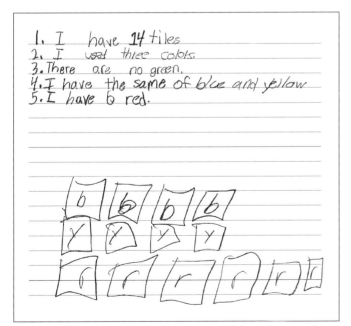

FIGURE 5–1 Jimmy and Fred's clues were representative of those of many pairs of students, following the structure compiled from a class discussion.

asked if they needed to get out some tiles for "riddle time." Students suggested that riddle writing be added to the list of options for Choice Time. When interest in *Tile Riddles* waned, we had a discussion about other objects that could be used for writing riddles. As a class, we generated a list of objects about which we could write riddles. Students initially focused on mathematics manipulatives, but soon realized that they could use other objects as well.

Linking Assessment and Instruction

As the students work, think about the following:

- Do the students understand what a "clue" is: information that leads one toward, but does not reveal, a solution?

- Are they able to build collections that match a set of clues? Do they understand vocabulary expressing comparisons and quantity, such as "more than," "twice as many," and "equal to"?
- Can students identify various attributes about objects in a collection, including quantity, color, size, and other distinguishing characteristics?
- Can students write clues that correspond to a collection?
- Can students recognize multiple solutions for a given set of clues?

Numbers and Me

CHAPTER 6

OVERVIEW

Young children tend to see numbers as symbols bound to a particular context: the mathematics classroom. Numbers and Me challenges this notion by making students aware of important numbers that have meaning in their own lives, numbers that they see and use on a regular basis, both inside and outside the classroom. In this exercise, students think about numbers that have particular significance to them and then write statements about the purpose these numbers serve in their lives. Students then share their special numbers with their classmates.

MATERIALS

- *Numbers and Me* recording sheet, 1 per student (see Blackline Masters)
- strips of paper on which to write statements
- chart paper

Numbers and Me

- Think of some numbers that are special to you.
- Record them.
- Write a sentence about each of your numbers.

My number	A sentence about my number

TIME

- one class period

Teaching Directions

1. Before you meet with the students, prepare a list of three to five numbers that have special significance to you (e.g., number of siblings or children or pets you have, your street address, years of teaching experience) and create a large sentence strip for each that explains what the number refers to (i.e., "This is the number of pets I have").

2. Post your special numbers for the students to see and read through them as a group.

3. Explain to the students that each number is meaningful to you, and that you have a set of clues that explain why each of the numbers is important to you. Randomly post each sentence strip, parallel to the list of numbers but with space in between.

4. Read the sentences aloud and have students discuss which numbers could describe each statement and which could not, until all the numbers have been "matched" to the appropriate sentence strip.

5. Have the students pick three to five numbers that have importance to them and then write a statement for each number, explaining its significance and/or the context from which it came.

6. Ask individual students to post their numbers and read, in a different order, the statements about each number. As a class, attempt to match the correct number with the statement.

Teaching Notes

Children demonstrate various levels of awareness about the importance and usefulness of numbers in the real world. Many associate numbers primarily with school, mainly in the context of arithmetic instruction. It is important to expose children to a range of contexts in which numbers reside, and allow them to consider why numbers are used within those contexts. Expanding children's awareness of where numbers are found and what purpose they serve leads to an appreciation of numbers as more than abstractions. Other issues, including magnitude of number and use of notation (e.g., decimal points and commas) arise within this lesson, providing a springboard to discussion about number conventions, as well as plausibility. Because one class period will not enable all students to share their special numbers, this is a good activity to return to when you have "filler time" of five to fifteen minutes on subsequent days, when one or two students at a time can present their special numbers and have their classmates match them to the corresponding statements.

The Lesson

In the beginning of the school year, we spend time getting to know who is in our class. *Numbers and Me* is an engaging and meaningful way for students to learn about their classmates, by learning about the numbers that are important to each of them. On this day in the fall, students were seated at their desks when I posed a challenge to get them ready for the main part of the day's lesson. I wanted them to become aware of some special numbers that were important to the class. "I wonder if any of you are 'number detectives,'" I began. "If I asked you to find the many places in which there are numbers, would you know where to look?"

"Sure!" one student said.

"No problem!" said another.

"That's easy!" said a third.

"Here is what I would like you to do. I am going to give you about five minutes to do your detective work. With your table group, I would like you to brainstorm a list of locations in which numbers are used. Make sure you write down your group's list of locations. Does that make sense?" I asked.

"Do they have to be in the classroom?" asked Denise.

I answered Denise's question with one of my own. "Is that the only location in which numbers can be found?"

"No, they are found . . . *everywhere*!" she countered.

"Then you can list places that are outside of the classroom," I confirmed.

"Do we each write down our ideas or just one list of ideas?" asked Jeff.

"'As a table group' means you only need one list," I answered.

"What if we can't spell the name of the place?" Julie asked.

"Try your best spelling," I said.

No more hands were in the air, so I asked students to begin. Conversations immediately began and there was a buzz of activity as groups of students began suggesting places where numbers could be found and the recorder at each table tried to keep up with writing down the ideas as they were generated. At some tables, this "job" rotated so that most of the group members got a chance to be the recorder.

After about five minutes, I asked for the students' attention and explained the next step. "'When I say 'Go!'" I said, "I would like your group to read through the list of ideas you have come up with. Decide as a group one location on your list that is your favorite place where numbers can be found, or a location that you think no other group has listed. When I ask for your attention, we are going to hear ideas from the different groups. Ready? Go!"

Each group of students read through their lists to decide on favorites. There was some disagreement at a few tables, but students were able to rectify the problem through voting. After a couple of minutes, the conversations died down and it appeared as though groups were ready to report to the whole class.

I called on tables, one at a time. A student from each table volunteered to read his or her group's ideas aloud.

"On the door of the classroom," one table reported.

"Our mailbox cubbies have numbers on them, *our* numbers!" said a student from table two.

"The calendar," was the choice of table three.

"The number line around the room," was group number four's location.

"The hundreds chart has *lots* of numbers!" said a student from table five.

"That was speedy reporting!" I announced. "Those numbers are numbers that are important to many of us. There are some numbers that are important to us that you cannot see as symbols. Eighteen is a number that is special to us. Why do you think I would say that?"

After a few seconds, Denise raised her hand. "It's how many of us are in the room?"

"And two is an important number," I continued. "Why do you think I would say that about us?"

"It's our grade?" suggested Tom.

"Here's another: five. Why would five be a number that is important to us?" I asked.

"There's five groups of tables!" said Joshua.

"So there are lots of numbers that are important to us," I said. "I have a list of numbers that are especially important to *me*. I am going to write this list on the board."

I had previously settled on a list of appropriate numbers to share with my students. I wanted them to appreciate that numbers serve a variety of important purposes: to quantify, label, measure, and locate. I wanted to give types of numbers that they had some familiarity and experience with, and that were of a magnitude that was accessible to them. I wrote the following numbers in a list on the board:

23

16

60

2.99

1,550

"Let's take a look at these numbers," I said. "As I point to each one, I want you to read the number aloud, in one 'class voice,' OK?" As I went down the list, students had no difficulty reading the first three. The last two, however, were difficult for them. They were inconsistent in their responses, and some looked at me with befuddled expressions.

I pointed to the fourth number, 2.99. "Let's take a look at this one," I suggested.

"What's that period for?" asked Julie.

"I think it means money," said Tom.

"How would you read this number?" I asked.

"Two hundred ninety-nine?" asked Jessica.

"No, two hundred ninety-nine doesn't have a period!" asserted Joshua.

"Two dollars and ninety-nine cents?" asked Kristen.

"Two period ninety-nine?" asked Tom. "Nah . . . that doesn't sound right."

"Let's go on. We have some ideas and those ideas might become clearer when we get some more information." I pointed to 1,550 next. "What about this number?" I asked.

"That's a big number!" Jeremy said.

"Yeah! It has four numbers!" added Kate.

"Yes, it has four digits," I clarified, pointing to each of the digits as I said, "A one, a five, another five, and a zero."

"It has a comma, too!" noticed Jeff.

We spent a few minutes discussing how to read the last number in the list. We discussed various ways to read the number. Some students said, "One thousand, five hundred fifty," while others read it as "one five five zero," or "fifteen fifty."

I went on. "I have thought of a sentence that matches each of these numbers. I have written each sentence on a sentence strip. Each sentence tells why one of the numbers is important to me. Here is the tricky part: the sentences are not in order. Your job is to guess which sentence goes with which number."

"Uh oh . . ." said Kristen.

"So we have to match them?" asked Kate.

"Yes, you have to match them. We will talk about each one, discussing which numbers could fit the sentence and which could not. Let's give it a try, OK?" I asked. "Here is the first sentence. It goes with one of my numbers, but not necessarily the first one: 'This is the number of feet that live at my house.'" As I read the sentence, I posted the strip on which it was written on the board. "Which numbers could match with that sentence? Which could not?" Hands went up in the air.

"It couldn't be one thousand, five hundred and fifty!" exclaimed Tom. "That's way too many!"

"I know it's not the fourth one. That wouldn't make sense," offered Joshua.

The students were quiet for several moments, and then I asked, "What about sixty?"

"Sixty is a lot of legs," said Julie. "I don't think it could be sixty." Several students nodded in agreement.

"What about twenty-three? Could twenty-three feet live in my house?" I asked. I was curious to see if children would rule out twenty-three as an odd number, in favor of an even number of feet.

After a short silence, Jessica spoke. "That's a lot. Let's see," she began. "You have two legs. I know you are married, so your husband has two legs. That's four. I know you have some dogs. They have four legs. That's eight. I don't know. This is hard!"

I waited to see if anyone would come to Jessica's assistance. After a few minutes, I reiterated what I had heard. "So, it sounds like it couldn't be sixty, one thousand, five hundred and fifty, or two period nine nine. It might be sixteen or twenty-three."

I posted the next strip as I read it aloud: "'This is the number of years I have been a teacher.'"

"It could be sixty! I know you have been teaching a long time!" said Kristen.

"Nuh-uh! Ms. Scharton isn't even sixty! That can't be right!" declared Joshua. The students giggled and I smiled.

"Not two ninety-nine or fifteen fifty," said Kate.

Again the class got quiet. I waited a few moments and then asked, "Nobody mentioned twenty-three. Could twenty-three be the number of years that I have been a teacher?"

"Yeah," said one student.

"Maybe," said another.

"Sure!" exclaimed a third.

I summarized what the students had suggested so far. "So, maybe I have been a teacher twenty-three years," I said, pointing to that number.

I posted and read the next strip: "'This is the number of minutes in my favorite television show.'"

"Well, most TV shows are thirty minutes," said Jeremy. "But thirty isn't up there."

"Two ninety-nine still doesn't fit," said Jeff.

"That last one doesn't fit either. It's too many again," offered Julie.

"Sixty could work!" said Denise. "I think sixty minutes is an hour. Can't TV shows be an hour?" Many of her classmates nodded in agreement.

"So, what are you thinking?" I asked. "Is sixty the only one that fits?" At first, students were very quiet, but after several seconds, most nodded their heads. "Does that help us to know, for sure, which number matches the number of feet at my house or the number of years I have been teaching?"

"No . . ." said one.

"Not really," said a second.

Several other students agreed that they couldn't be certain.

"Well, let's look at the next sentence," I said. I posted and read the words on the next strip: "'This is how much I paid for a carton of ice cream last night.'"

"It could be sixty," Tom said somewhat doubtfully.

"I don't think so," said Kristen. "I think it's two ninety-nine. Two dollars and ninety-nine cents."

"Yeah!" said several students.

"That's it!" said others.

"Yeah . . . it's the one with the period. That means money," one student explained.

"If it is a number that represents an amount of money, why is the period there?" I asked.

"It's two dollars. So the two comes before the ninety-nine," said Joshua.

"If it wasn't there, it would be two hundred ninety-nine. If it was two hundred and ninety-nine dollars, no one would have *that* much money!" said Tom with a laugh.

"The period comes after the dollars and before the cents," I explained. "If this number represents an amount of money, I would read it 'two dollars,'" I said, pointing to the 2, "and 'ninety-nine cents,'" I said, pointing to the 99. "I could write a dollar sign here and that would help," I said, adding a dollar sign to the number, which now read $2.99.

"Could it be any other numbers?" I continued. "What about twenty-three? One thousand five hundred and fifty?" Each time I read and pointed to one of these numbers, the students giggled and responded with "No way!" and "Too much!"

I then read and posted the final strip: "'This is my house address.'"

"Hmm . . . ," thought Jeff.

"It could be sixty or twenty-three. We have apartments where I live and they have those numbers!" said Denise.

"Yeah, me too!" agreed Tom.

"But she said 'house address.' I don't think houses have those numbers," said Jeremy.

"Yeah," confirmed Julie.

"What is the difference between a house and an apartment?" I asked.

"Houses are flat. Apartments have stairs," one student said.

"My grandma's house has stairs!" offered another.

"Lots of people live in apartments close together. Houses are kind of by themselves," another stated.

"Houses have yards and apartments don't. They might have a park or a yard close by though," said a fourth.

I knew that some of my students lived in houses and some lived in apartments. There was a mobile home park within the school boundaries, but none of my students lived there; if they had, they might have referred to a "space number." "Some of you live in houses and some of you live in apartments. Let's list the numbers for apartment addresses," I suggested, so that no one would be left out. Students gave me the following numbers, which I listed on a chart:

12
4
25
17
233
9B
413

"How about those of you who live in houses?" I said. "What numbers are your house address?" Again I listed on the board the numbers that students gave me:

27560	*2558*
1952	*26950*
2660	*3350*
19740	*15745*
1264	*2472*
1964	*8460*

"The last sentence I put up stated that one of the numbers was my house address," I said. "Which one of the five numbers do you think is my house address, from looking at the house addresses of your classmates?"

"The last one!" exclaimed several students.

"Fifteen fifty," said others.

"Yeah! That's it for sure!" agreed several others.

I drew a line from this posted sentence strip to the number 1,550. "Are there any other matches you can agree upon?" I asked. Students suggested that I draw a line between 60 and 'This is the number of minutes in my favorite television show' and between $2.99 and 'This is how much I paid for a carton of ice cream last night.' Two sets of statements and two numbers were left: 'The number of years I have been a teacher' and 'The number of feet that live in my house,' and 16 and 23. "What is a question you could ask to help you know which of these last numbers match with which of these sentences?"

The students were silent for several moments as they thought about this.

"We know you have a dog, maybe more than one," offered one.

"Do you have any cats?" asked another.

"How many dogs do you have?" several students asked simultaneously.

"How many cats do you have?" another student asked.

"Do you have any other pets?" queried yet another.

"Wow! A lot of questions!" I said, laughing. "Maybe this will help: I have no children, one husband, and three dogs."

Students immediately started mumbling to themselves and counting on their fingers. After a minute or two, several excited hands were waving back and forth in the air.

"When I say 'three,'" I directed, "whisper the number you think goes with 'This is the number of feet that live in my house.' One . . . two . . . *three*!" I said, and most of the students loudly whispered, "Sixteen!"

I asked for volunteers to explain what they did to decide that sixteen was the most appropriate choice.

Jessica carefully explained what she had done. "I went 'two, four,' for you and your husband. Then I imagined three dogs right here and they have four legs. So I went, 'six, eight,' for one dog, 'ten, twelve,' for another dog, and 'fourteen, sixteen,' for the last dog. It's sixteen."

Jeremy shared his idea. "I used my fingers. I did four and four for two dogs," he said, showing four fingers on each hand, "That's eight. Then another dog: that's nine, ten, eleven, twelve," he added, putting down four fingers, one at a time. "Then there's you—thirteen, fourteen—and your husband—fifteen, sixteen! The answer's sixteen!" Jeremy was very proud of himself.

"I counted by fours. Each dog is four and you and your husband together is four, too. So it's four, eight, twelve, sixteen! Sixteen feet!" said Kristen.

"Should I draw a line between sixteen and 'This is the number of feet that live in my house'?" I asked. Most students enthusiastically agreed that this was the correct match. I drew a line to connect 16 with its sentence strip.

"I notice something about my numbers," I said. "Some of these numbers stand for how many of something I have. Can you find any numbers like that?"

It took about thirty seconds, but finally Kristen's hand went up. "Sixteen?"

"Why do you think so?" I asked.

"Well, it's how many feet you *have* in your *house*," she explained.

Tom raised his hand. "You had two dollars and ninety-nine cents, but then you spent it on ice cream! So you *had* two ninety-nine."

I waited to see if there were any more ideas, then I went on. "Some of these numbers are like a label or a name. They help you to name something or find something. Can you find any that are labels or names?"

"That big number—one, five, five, zero—it's kind of like the name of your house. If you didn't have it, nobody could find where you live!" offered Joshua.

"Just like our numbers in the classroom—and on our cubbies—are like that. My number is seventeen. It's like another name for me!" added Tom.

"And your cubbie: if we want to put your papers in your cubbie, we know how to find it because it has your number on it!" said Jessica.

"Our room number is like an address, sort of like your house!" said Jeff.

"So, special numbers can be those that represent how many of something you have or they can be labels or names that help you find or locate something," I said. "Some numbers can also be a measurement: they might tell how long or how tall or how wide something is. Can you look to see if any of my numbers are a measurement?"

This was a difficult type of number for students to locate. I gave students a minute to think and then I offered them some more information. "Some of my numbers tell about lengths of time that are pretty special to me. Maybe that will help you," I said. Some hands finally went up in the air.

"I think sixty," Kate said tentatively.

"Why do you think so?" I asked.

"Well, it is how much time—minutes—your favorite TV show lasts."

"Oh yeah! And twenty-three! It is how many years—that's like time, only longer—you have been a teacher. That's a long time!" added Julie. Many of the students giggled at this remark.

I decided that the students were now prepared to hear about the independent task *Numbers and Me*. "The uses of numbers that we've been talking about might help you decide which numbers have a special meaning for you," I began. "Numbers that tell how many, numbers that name or label or locate, numbers that are measurements: we all have special numbers that we use in our own lives to help us with these things. Now it's your turn. You are going to do what I did: think of some numbers that are important to you and write a sentence that matches each number." I showed the class an overhead transparency of the *Numbers and Me* recording sheet.

"Here is the sheet you will use," I began. The directions ask you to think of some numbers that are special to you, just like I did. Write those numbers down in this column," I continued, pointing to the column labeled *My number.* "Next to each number, write a sentence to explain each of your numbers."

"Can we use your numbers?" Jeremy asked.

"Is it possible that one of your numbers is the same as one of my numbers?" I asked.

Some students nodded and others shook their heads.

"There are numbers that might be the same for more than one person in the class. I would like you to think of numbers that are particularly special to you. What are some numbers that might be special to the people in this room?" I asked. I got my pen and chart paper ready to record ideas.

"How about the number of people in my family?" one student suggested.

"My phone number!" said another.

"How many stuffed animals I have?" said a third.

"How old I am," was another response.

"My classroom and cubbie number!" a student said.

"How much I weigh?" one queried.

"How big—tall—I am?" responded another.

"The number of friends I have," one student offered.

"My address," said yet another.

I wrote these ideas on the chart. "You can use any of these ideas or any others you can think of. I wonder if there are ideas out there that you can come up with that none of your classmates will think of. Try to be 'tricky,' because we will do the same thing with your numbers that I did with mine. You will put a few on the board and then you will read a sentence about one of them and we will try to guess which number matches which sentence."

"But if we write down the number and the sentence, people will know!" stated Jessica.

"So this is one of those activities that you will try to keep 'secret,' so that others can have fun guessing, like you did with me and my numbers," I explained. "It might be a good idea to talk with some people at your table to get some ideas. You also might want to think about your home, think about where you see numbers."

"When will we get to read them?" Denise asked.

"We will read them over several days. We will read a few at the end of math time today but it will take many days for everyone to get a chance to read their own," I told them.

The students looked excited and ready to begin. I passed out the recording sheets. Most students immediately began writing. Others sat for a moment and looked pensive. Rather than intervene immediately, I decided to give students a chance to think and talk with the other people at their table. Eventually, students were all working independently: all were able to write down at least three numbers and corresponding sentences in about twenty minutes.

I asked for the students' attention. "When you hear me call out a type of number you picked, please check your paper to make sure you've written your name in the space at the bottom, put your pencil away, and join me on the rug with your paper."

"If one of your special numbers is a number that is a measurement—how long or how wide or how tall," I continued, "please come to the rug." A few students responded to this directive.

"If one of your special numbers is a label or name—helps to find or locate something—please come and take a seat," I said. More students joined the first group. "And if one of your numbers tells how many of something you own or have, please join us." The rest of the group joined their classmates on the rug.

I first acknowledged students' effort and enthusiasm. "You have been quite busy, thinking of good ideas, talking with the people at your table, and writing. I know that many of you are excited to share what you have done. I also know that you realize that only a few people will be able to share only a few of their ideas today. The rest of you will have a chance on another day. Everyone will get a turn."

"Jeff, would you like to go first?" I asked. "Pick three of your numbers and write them on the board." Jeff had recorded only three numbers on his paper. He wrote each on the board: 8, 6, and 2.

"Now, read a sentence that matches one of the numbers. Here is the tricky part of the direction: I don't want you to read them in the order you wrote the numbers. Why do you think I would give you that tricky direction?" I said.

"Because that would give it away!" he said.

"Right. And we don't want you to give it away, because we want to guess!" I said.

Jeff searched his paper and then read one of his sentences. "'I was this years old two years ago.'"

Hands went up right away. But before students guessed the actual number, I wanted them to eliminate numbers that would not match. "What numbers probably don't match that sentence and why do you think so?" I asked.

"It couldn't be two. That would mean he was four right now!" said Joshua, laughing.

"It couldn't be eight, because then he'd be ten! He's like seven or eight," added Kristen.

Students were engaged and eager, not only to guess what the number could be, but also to consider what was not possible. And by asking for students to explain their thinking, they had to do some authentic calculation to determine the number that corresponded to the statement.

"When I say *three*," I said to the class, "whisper the number that you think matches Jeff's sentence, 'I was this years old two years ago.' One . . . two . . . three!" Most of the students whispered, "Six!"

"Is that correct, Jeff?" I asked.

"Yes!"

"It's like your sentence, Ms. Scharton. You used years for how long you have been a teacher!" Jessica said. I was pleased to see that she had made a connection between my sentence and Jeff's.

"Can I read another sentence?" Jeff asked.

"Go right ahead," I answered.

"This is the number of parents I have," he read. Again, although given the numbers that Jeff had listed the choice was fairly obvious, I wanted to explore the "impossibilities" as well as the "possibilities." I asked, "Which numbers could match and which couldn't, and why do you think so?"

"Well, eight would be too many!" said Julie.

"Why do you think so?" I asked.

"He couldn't have that many parents!" she added.

"I have four parents," said Kate. "I have a mom and a dad and stepdad and a stepmom. But that's not six or eight."

"Think about what number matches Jeff's clue, 'This is the number of parents I have.' On three, whisper your idea. One . . . two . . . *three*!" All of the students whispered, "Two!" and Jeff confirmed their guess.

"Here's my last one: 'I am this many years old,'" read Jeff.

We had eliminated all other possibilities and students were excitedly whispering, "It's eight!" Still, we could discuss why the other numbers were not a match for the sentence Jeff just read.

"I hear that many of you have a good idea for what number matches Jeff's last sentence. Who would like to talk about which numbers could not match and why?"

"If he was two, he wouldn't be in school. Well, maybe preschool!" said Denise.

"I was six in first grade, so he couldn't be six!" added Tom.

"It's got to be eight!" said a few students.

"Is that correct?" I asked Jeff. Jeff smiled and nodded.

Two other students followed Jeff. One at a time, they listed three numbers on the board. Each student read one of his or her sentences. Before guessing the actual number, we discussed which numbers to eliminate and why. Students benefited from talking about and listening to their classmates explain why certain numbers were plausible matches for certain statements and why others were not. They had to regularly add or subtract when determining numbers that matched the sentence that was read. They continued to build on their experience with the matching exercise, and to make connections between the special numbers chosen by their classmates.

At the end of this first sharing session, I reviewed student work to get a sense of the kinds of numbers students chose, as well as their explanations for each. Students rarely chose numbers that were used as labels or locators. One chose the number of her favorite month (her birth month), a couple of students identified room numbers of a sibling or ones they had been in during previous years of school, and a few students identified their address as a special number. Numbers identifying measurement of time were commonly used, with age being a familiar choice. Some students wrote down ages of family members: Kate wrote, "This is how old my mom is," and Jeremy wrote, "My great-grandmother used to be this old." Some students used ages that were important markers in their own lives. Joshua's entries identified the age in which he learned how to read, "count by sixes," and "knew times," and Kristen identified what her age would be two years in the future. Quantity of items in collections was a popular choice for special numbers.

Denise wrote about "how many water animals" she has, Tom shared the number of pets in his family, and Julie identified the number of "best friends." Gabe's special numbers clearly showed his interest in visiting theme parks: he wrote about the number of times he had been to Sea World and the number of times he had been to Disneyland. While this activity focused on students' ability to develop an awareness of and an appreciation for the many uses of numbers in their world, it allowed me an opportunity to take a small glimpse into what was important to the students I was just beginning to know. This information was rich and complex, including the number of days that a student had used his new set of markers, the number of times the Dallas Cowboys had won the Super Bowl, and a student's "favorite number of old."

Linking Assessment and Instruction

As the students work, think about the following:

- Do the students realize that numbers are useful and serve a purpose?
- Are they able to locate and identify numbers that are important to them? Do they understand the purpose of numbers: to locate, label, quantify, and measure?
- Can students identify numbers that represent reasonable locations, labels, quantities, and measurements?
- What print conventions associated with numbers (decimal points, commas) are students able to recognize and/or use?

The Purse

CHAPTER 7

OVERVIEW

The Purse *by Kathy Caple is a story in which the main character spends and earns money. It provides a context for a class discussion focusing on the possible combinations of coins that make five and ten cents. Students then pursue an independent investigation of the possible ways to make twenty-five cents. Number sense involves understanding a variety of ways to compose and decompose numbers. It is important to expose students to problems in which they have an opportunity to see that numbers can be "broken apart" and "put back together" in many different ways. Not only does this lesson provide many points at which mental math can be used to address what is happening in the story, it also provides opportunities for students to consider many different combinations for given quantities of money.*

MATERIALS

- *The Purse,* by Kathy Caple (Boston: Houghton Mifflin, 1986)
- zip-top bag of 25 pennies, 2 dimes, 5 nickels, and a quarter, 1 bag per pair of students
- optional: small metal box (like those containing adhesive bandages) with some coins in it

TIME

- one class period

Teaching Directions

1. Read the story aloud to the class, to the point where the main character, Katie, has completed chores to earn twenty-five cents from her sister Marcia.

2. Review with the class coin values, and ask the students to solve a simple problem: "What possible combinations of coins equal five cents? ten cents?"

3. Present to the class the following problem: "What possible combinations of coins could Marcia have given Katie to equal twenty-five cents?"

4. Give pairs of students a bag of coins, and ask them to solve the problem, using both numbers and pictures to record their solutions.

5. Gather the class together to share how the students solved the problem.

6. Read aloud to the class the end of the story.

Teaching Notes

Number sense includes the understanding that numbers can be taken apart and combined in many different ways. The ability to flexibly decompose and recombine numbers is important for students to develop in order for them to be successful operating on larger numbers. Students who understand this characteristic of numbers are more able to invent and make sense of alternative strategies for adding and subtracting numbers.

The Lesson

"Have you ever wanted something, and you had to find creative ways of earning enough money so that you could buy it yourself?" I asked a group of second-grade students.

Many children immediately put up their hands. So that all the students could have the opportunity to share their stories, I asked them to find a "thumb buddy": When I gave the word, they were to turn to someone next to them and put their thumb on the thumb of that person, even if it was someone they didn't normally work next to or play with at recess. Anyone left "thumbless" was asked to raise his or her hand so that a quick match could be found (and feelings spared). When I said, "One, two, three, *go!*" all of the students were quickly able to find a thumb buddy, with little intervention from me.

"Now, tell your story about how you've earned money to buy things to your thumb buddy," I said. "When you are done, it will be your buddy's turn to tell their story. When you both have finished, turn back toward me and put your hands on your knees so I know that you are ready to hear a story I have to read to you." After several minutes of animated chatter, the students settled down and turned back in my direction.

I showed the class the book *The Purse* by Kathy Caple. "This is the story of a little girl who wanted to buy a purse. Listen to the story of how she spends and earns money. We will stop partway through to talk about a problem that occurs in the story. Then I will ask you to find solutions to the problem."

I read the story aloud. The book first introduces the reader to the main character, Katie, who keeps her money in a metal bandage box. Her sister Marcia teases her for keeping her money in a box rather than a purse. (At appropriate points in my reading of the story I stopped to shake a metal bandage box that I had partially filled with change. Each time they heard these special sound effects, the students giggled.) I read on to the part where Katie has purchased a purse. She has spent all of her money on this item and now has no money to put inside it. She begins doing chores for her family members in order to earn money. The first person for whom she works is her sister, Marcia. Katie offers to clean Marcia's room for twenty-five cents. At this point in the story, I stopped reading.

"Suppose you were Katie," I said. "You have just cleaned your sister's room. Let's pretend that you had agreed to clean it for five cents. Talk to your thumb buddy about some possible coins that Marcia might use to pay you."

The students turned to talk to their buddies. The conversations were animated, but brief.

"So, what do you think?" I asked after they'd turned back to me. "What are some ways that Marcia could pay Katie, if Katie agreed to clean her room for five cents? Casey?"

"There are only two ways," Casey responded quickly. "Five pennies or a nickel. That's it!"

"Casey, you named two types of coins: pennies and nickels. I wonder if someone could remind us about the value of a penny and the value of a nickel."

Jason raised his hand. "A penny is one cent," he said. "A nickel is five cents."

"I think it could be two cents and three cents. And one cent and four cents . . ." Jessica said tentatively.

"That's still the same, though," answered Casey. "If you put the two pennies with the three pennies, it's five pennies. The same with one and four: it's still five pennies." Most of the class nodded in agreement with Casey.

"Oh yeah," Jessica said. "I made a mistake."

To be certain that she was clear on this point, I asked, "Jessica, what is your thinking now? Is your way different than Casey's or the same as Casey's? How do you know for sure?"

"It's still five cents. See?" Jessica explained. She came over to my place on the rug, where a zip-top bag of coins was lying. She took out five pennies and laid them down on the rug. "Here's five cents. Two cents," and she separated out two pennies, "and three cents," and she separated out three more, "are still five cents. So is one and four." She repeated the same process with one penny and four pennies and then put the five pennies back in the bag.

"Can someone else explain it a different way?" I asked. "Tyler?"

"You can't cut a nickel, because there's only one of them," he said. "But with five pennies, you can break them up into groups. You can do that lots of ways, but it's still five pennies. You asked us what coins Marcia used. She could use pennies or a nickel. There's only two ways to make five cents: five pennies and one nickel."

Most students seemed to understand this point, but I wanted to be absolutely sure before I continued. "Talk with your buddy for another minute. See what other ways you can think of to make five cents." Students briefly conversed with their partners and then turned back to me and put their hands on their knees.

"So, what other ways did you find?" I asked. No hands went up.

"OK," I summed up, "so far we have found that there are two ways to make five cents: five pennies and one nickel. What if Katie cleaned Marcia's room for ten cents? Talk with your partner and see what possible combinations of coins Marcia could use to pay Katie." While students were talking, I wrote on the board:

Ways to make	Coins
5¢	5 pennies
	1 nickel
10¢	

Students talked with their partner for several minutes. When they had again faced front and put their hands on their knees, I said, "We found that there are two ways to make five cents. I am curious to find out if there are more than two ways to make ten cents." I pointed to the chart that I had made. "While you were talking, I got an idea. I decided to make a chart. I wrote down the amount Marcia might have paid—five cents—and the number of pennies and the number of nickels it would take to make that amount." I pointed to the columns I had constructed. Many students raised their hands to share their ideas. "What if she paid her sister ten cents? What coins might she use to make that amount?"

"Well, she could use ten pennies!" Tiffany offered.

"And two nickels!" Michael added.

"How about five pennies and a nickel?" Sarah piped in.

"You have a lot of ways! Hold everything!" I went to the chart and filled in what had been offered so far:

Ways to make	Coins
5¢	5 pennies
	1 nickel
10¢	10 pennies
	2 nickels
	5 pennies and 1 nickel

"I wonder if someone can help prove one of these ways, so that we know for sure that each way does, indeed, equal ten cents."

Tiffany spoke first. "Well, a penny is one cent. Ten pennies is one, two, three . . ." and she counted all the way to ten.

"OK. I understand how ten pennies equals ten cents. What about another way?"

Michael had an idea. "Nickels are five. Two nickels are five, ten!" Michael counted by fives, extending a finger each time he said a number.

Sarah explained her way next. "One nickel is five cents. Then the pennies make six, seven, eight, nine, ten!" Like Michael, Sarah extended a finger for each number as she counted on. Sarah had counted by ones for pennies, while Michael had counted by fives for nickels.

"But that's not all the ways! What about just a dime!" Elizabeth said.

"Your brains are working hard and fast," I commented. "I need to catch up with you! First, though, I need a reminder about the value of a dime." After several students called out, "Ten cents!" I revised the chart to look like this:

Ways to make	Coins
5¢	5 pennies
	1 nickel
10¢	10 pennies
	2 nickels
	5 pennies and 1 nickel
	1 dime

"How is this?" I asked, referring to the revised chart. The students nodded in agreement. "OK. I think I have caught up with you. Whew! That was not easy! Look at the chart. See what other ways you have talked about that I don't have recorded."

The students turned to talk with their partners. I heard some mention ways that were already up on the chart and I saw others pointing to the places where the combination had been recorded. After they had talked for about five minutes, I asked for their attention. "What ways have you found that aren't on our chart yet?" I asked.

When no one volunteered another way, I said, "I am curious about how many ways to make ten cents that we have found so far. Look at the chart, and see if you can tell, and explain your thinking to your buddy." Students quickly confirmed that there were four ways recorded. I asked Jordan to come up and show his thinking, and he quickly counted the rows that matched the quantity we were addressing.

"OK. So far we have found that there are two ways to make five cents and four ways to make ten cents. Here is the problem I would like you to solve. Pretend you are Katie. You have cleaned Marcia's room and she is going to pay you twenty-five cents from the coins in her piggy bank. I am going to ask you to work with a partner. First, I want you to make a prediction for the number of ways that you think there are to make twenty-five cents. Tell your partner your prediction, and explain how you got your prediction. Then, find all the possible combinations of coins Marcia could use to pay you. Keep track on your paper. I have bags of coins for you to use if you would like. On the board, I will list the number of coins of each type in the bag. When it is time to clean up, you will need to check your bags to make sure that the coins of each type match the list on the board. Any questions?" When no hands went up, I continued. "In just a moment, when I wink at you, I want you to choose someone with whom to work. That might be someone that you don't usually play with or someone you don't sit next to. Gently tap your partner on the shoulder and come up to get one paper that you will both work on together."

"What if we want to work alone?" Lindsey asked.

"Many times you do work on something by yourself," I responded. "Today I want you to work with someone else. I want you to be able to check your partner's ideas and make sure that each way is a possible way to make twenty-five cents."

"What if you choose someone and they tell you that they want to work with someone else?" Casey asked.

Her question gave me an opportunity to establish my expectations for the class with respect to choosing and accepting partners. "You know, Casey, I know that won't happen in this class. I know that when someone gets a tap from you, they will look at you and say, 'I am so happy you chose me to work with you!'" Casey smiled.

I proceeded to dismiss the students from the rug. I had thought that some pairs of students would attempt to solve the problem without the use of the coins. I was surprised that all students wanted that support, or at least liked having the shiny coins to handle!

Students quickly got started on the problem. I watched as coins were spilled out onto desktops and students quickly started counting the coins that were inside. While they were doing so, I drew a large picture of a zip-top bag on the board. "Inside" the bag illustration, I wrote the quantity of each coin that was inside the bag (see below).

I circulated the room to see if students were having success solving the problem and to observe how they were dividing up the task. Michael and Sarah were working together. Michael had the coins and was arranging them into groups and counting, while Sarah had a pencil in her hand and was beginning to jot down some combinations.

"It looks like you are getting a start at solving the problem," I observed. "Can you tell me a little about what you are doing?"

"Michael is finding some ways to make twenty-five cents," Sarah replied. "We think there will be five ways because there were two ways to make five cents and four ways to make ten cents. I am writing down what he does."

On the paper, Sarah had written:

2 dimes
1 nickel

"I see," I said. "Can you show me how you know that two dimes and one nickel equals twenty-five cents?"

"Two dimes is . . . ten . . . twenty," Sarah said. She got two dimes and a nickel and as she named a coin, she touched it. "And a nickel is twenty-five."

"I understand," I said. "Can you think of something else that needs to be on your paper?"

"Oops! Names!" Sarah and Michael each wrote their names on the paper.

I continued to make my way through the class. I stopped at a table where Jessica and Jason were working. On their paper, they had written:

1 corter
2 dimes and 5 pennies
2 dimes and 5 nickels

"I see you have found three ways so far," I told them. "You have been busy! Can you prove your ways to me?"

"Well," began Jason, "a quarter is twenty-five cents. That's easy . . . and one dime is ten cents and two dimes is . . . ten, twenty cents . . . and five pennies more is"—Jason moved two dimes in front of him and then five pennies, one at a time as he counted— "twenty-one, twenty-two, twenty-three, twenty-four, twenty-five!"

"Great counting," I said. "Can you show me the last way?"

Jessica took the two dimes from in front of Jason, along with a nickel from the group of coins that lay on the desk. She said, "See? Ten, twenty . . . and a nickel is twenty-one, twenty-two, twenty-three, twenty-four, twenty-five cents! Just like the last one. Except instead of pennies we used a nickel."

"I understood how you counted, Jessica. I wonder if it is the same as what you have written on the paper." Jessica looked at what she had written but did not see how it represented something different from what she had just demonstrated. Her partner, however, did.

"Oh! You wrote 'five nickels.' It should be 'one nickel,'" Jason said. "We used one nickel, not five nickels!" Jessica began erasing, but I was not sure that she understood her partner's explanation. "Before you erase, Jessica," I said, "make sure that you really need to erase. What do you think Jason just said? Can you tell me what you think?"

Jessica said, "I wrote the wrong thing. I was thinking 'five cents' . . . only one of them . . . but I wrote 'five nickels.'"

Sometimes students understand what they are doing mathematically, but the language they use to describe their understanding is unclear or undeveloped. I wanted to make sure that Jessica knew the reasoning behind what Jason had said. "You said you were thinking 'five cents' . . . 'only one of them.' What did you mean by that?" I asked.

"I know that two dimes is twenty and I still need five cents to make twenty-five cents. I only need one five cents, not five of them."

"Show me what you mean when you say 'one five cents,'" I said.

Jessica touched a nickel. "I need one five cents more," she said.

"Oh, I see. You need one more of these," I said. "You are telling me how much the coin is worth when you say 'one five cents.' Can you remind me of the name of the coin you are talking about?"

"A nickel?" Jessica responded.

"Yes, that's right," I said. "It is a nickel and it's worth five cents. But we call it a nickel. Now look at the paper you and Jason are working on. See here?" I touched the place where "2 dimes and 5 nickels" was written.

"That should be 'one nickel,' not 'five nickels'!" said Jessica. "Five nickels is too much. Five nickels and two dimes would be . . . too much! It would be more than twenty-five cents, because two dimes and one nickel is twenty-five cents . . . so two dimes and five nickels would be . . ."

"See if you can figure it out," I said as I moved on to another table. As I walked away, I heard Jason counting aloud as Jessica watched. "Two dimes is twenty. We know that right? And a nickel, that's . . . twenty-five, right? And another nickel is . . ."

As I looked around the room, it was clear that the students found this to be an engaging activity. They were talking about the possible coin combinations, using the coins to demonstrate the combinations, and finding ways to share the task of recording the combinations that they had found so far. I stopped at the table where Jeffrey and Lucas were working. On their paper, they had written the following:

2 dimes and 1 nickel
5 nickels
25 pennies
20 pennies and 1 nickel
15 pennies and 1 nickel and 5 pennies
10 pennies and 1 nickel and 10 pennies

"Hi guys!" I said. "How are you doing?"

"Great! Look how many we have!" exclaimed Lucas.

"Wow, that's a lot. That's really great, you two," I said. "Well, you know me: I am always wondering about your thinking. Could you pick some of these ways and prove them to me?"

"Sure!" said Jeffrey.

The boys quickly showed me the first four ways that had been written on their paper. The coins for the fourth way—twenty pennies and one nickel—remained on the table, and they were getting ready to show me how fifteen pennies, one nickel, and five more pennies was another way of making twenty-five cents.

"See?" Lucas separated five pennies from the pile of twenty, so that there were three sets of coins: fifteen pennies, one nickel, and five pennies. He touched the appropriate set as he named them: "Fifteen pennies, one nickel, and five pennies." Before he moved on to the last combination, I stopped him.

"What if I told you that that way looked the same to me as another way? What would you think I meant?" I questioned.

"Hmm?" mumbled Lucas.

"This one?" Jeffrey asked, pointing to the twenty pennies and one nickel on their list of combinations.

"Why do you think so?" I asked.

"Well . . . If you put these"—Jeffrey moved the five pennies over to the group of fifteen pennies—"with these, then it's, one, two, three, four . . ."

"It's twenty pennies," Lucas said. "Oh . . . then it's twenty pennies and one nickel. We already had that."

"Then this one is the same, too," said Jeffrey, as he pointed to "10 pennies and 1 nickel and 10 pennies" on the list. "If you put the ten with the ten, it's twenty pennies."

"Does that make sense?" I asked.

"Yeah. I guess you can't take out the coins," Lucas said.

I suspected that Lucas meant that you had to keep like coins together, but I wasn't sure, so I asked, "What do you mean?"

"You have to keep the pennies with the pennies and the dimes with the dimes and the nickels with the nickels. If you didn't, you'd get mixed up," Lucas explained.

The student had worked for about thirty minutes. Most pairs had about four or five different combinations written on their papers. It was important for students to find ways of determining the different possible combinations of coins that could be used to make twenty-five cents. It was also important for students to realize that a quantity—in this case, twenty-five—could be decomposed in many ways. I got the students' attention and said, "You have been working hard to find many different ways of making twenty-five cents. Raise your hand if you think you and your partner found all of the possible ways." Two hands went up. I commented, "Not many people think so. Raise your hand if you think that, as a class, we found more ways than you could think of in pairs." Most students raised their hands. "Let's come back together and see. And then we will hear the rest of the story. When I say 'Go,' we are going to start cleaning up. Check to see that the number of coins inside your coin bag is the same as what is written on the board. Place the coins back in the bag, and bring it to the rug along with your paper. I'd like you to sit in a circle with your partner so that we can all see each other. Ready? One, two, three, *go*!" When the students were seated in a circle on the rug, I spilled out one set of coins in the center of the circle so that we could use them to confirm the various combinations. I asked the students to spill out their coins between the partners.

"Let's see what we found out," I began. "Listen carefully to what you hear your classmates saying. Watch the board also. I will record the combinations that pairs of people give us. Make sure that your idea is different from one that we have already talked about. As we hear a combination, build that combination with your partner to make sure that those coins equal twenty-five cents." I was concerned that students would begin arranging the coins in patterns or not using them to make combinations rather than listening to the ideas contributed by their classmates, so I said, "Remind me what the coins will be used for while we are on the rug."

Casey said, "We are going to make what you write on the board."

"Exactly," I said. "It would be fun to make patterns and designs or other combinations, but we can do that some other time."

"Like at recess!" Lindsey said.

"That would be a great time. Let's begin. Who has a combination of coins that equals twenty-five cents?" I said.

I called on students to share different combinations. As a combination was given, I added it to the list on the board. After each combination, students built that combination with their partner to confirm the correct total. After about fifteen minutes, students had begun to get fidgety. It seemed like a good time to stop generating more combinations for the list and finish the story. The list looked like this:

2 dimes and 1 nickel
5 nickels
20 pennies and 1 nickel
2 dimes and 5 pennies
1 quarter
4 nickels and 5 pennies
1 dime and 3 nickels
1 dime and 2 nickels and 5 pennies
1 dime and 1 nickel and 10 pennies

"Let's see how Marcia decides to pay Katie and if the coins she used are the same as one of our ways," I told them. I read the rest of the book. Marcia pays Katie a quarter. Katie approaches other family members and earns money in other ways. Each time she earns some money, she puts it in her purse and gives it a shake. The purse does not make the sound of the coins in the bandage box. Katie eventually uses her money to purchase a metal box of bandages, keeping the box inside her purse and selling the bandages to her father. She places her money inside the box, and the box inside the purse. Now, when she shakes the purse, it makes the familiar "clinkity clinkity" sound.

I wanted students to see that, as a class, they were able to come up with more combinations than was possible in pairs. "Count the number of ways you and your partner were able to find. Hold up that many fingers." Students held up between three and seven fingers. "As pairs, you found up to seven ways to make twenty-five cents. As a class you found . . ." Students counted the list of combinations from where they were sitting.

"Eight, no nine!" said one of the students.

"Nine! Wow . . . nine ways!" several of the others exclaimed.

"You were able to find more ways as a class," I said. "It pays to work together."

"Does it pay more than twenty-five cents?" Lucas asked. We all laughed.

Linking Assessment and Instruction

As you observe students work, think about the following:

- How do the students count collections of coins? Do they begin with the coin of the greatest value? Or do they randomly choose coins and count?
- Are the students able to count on by ones, fives, and tens? Can they count on by fives and tens from a given quantity?
- How do they use the information from the practice problem—the number of ways to make five cents and ten cents—in this investigation? Do they use one of the listed collections from the practice problem and build on to make the greater quantity? Or do they begin the investigation in some other way?
- Do the students have a systematic way in which they approach the problem? Do they start with greatest number of pennies (twenty-five) or the greatest number of dimes (two), then build on to make twenty-five cents? Do they take one collection they have already made and substitute coins to make another combination?

CHAPTER 8

Visualizing Numbers with Ten-Frames

OVERVIEW

Visualizing Numbers with Ten-Frames *is a series of activities in which quantities are represented in a patterned arrangement based on an important landmark number: ten. A ten-frame—a grid made up of two rows of five cells each—is a tool for visualizing this quantity. These activities give students experience with visible recognition of quantity, and building, decomposing, and combining numbers that are represented in easily recognized ways. When students can easily recognize quantities, they are able to use numbers more flexibly. Flexibility with numbers allows students to compute with smaller numbers—then larger ones—in ways that are both efficient and meaningful.*

MATERIALS

- *Ten-Frames* recording sheet, 1 per student (see Backline Masters)
- *Ten-Frames Models* sheets, 1 per pair of students (see Backline Masters)
- beans, Unifix cubes, or other small counters, 20 per pair of students

TIME

- two minilessons over a one- to two-week period, followed by one class period

Teaching Directions

1. Have students observe you as you build numbers on one or more ten-frame recording sheets in various ways. Begin with a single ten-frame, leaving some cells open and some cells filled with counters.

2. Ask the students to imagine combining ten-frame quantities so that the top row, then the bottom one, is filled by visualizing the movement of the prearranged counters. Then report methods for combining.

3. Have pairs of students work with ten-frames to:
   - build numbers
   - guess numbers a partner has built
   - explore ten-frame models

Teaching Notes

Number sense is dependent upon an understanding of how numbers relate to one another. In order to develop this understanding, it is critical for students to have mathematical experiences that focus on landmark numbers and relationships between numbers. Viewing, discussing, and building patterned arrangements of quantities helps students develop number sense in many ways: students see that numbers are made up of numbers and they learn how to recognize quantities up to ten—and more than ten—without counting. The ten-frames organize quantities around an important benchmark in our number system. Students' experience with this method of organization helps them become familiar with combinations of ten and larger. As students add ten-frame quantities together, they realize how regrouping "works." Use of ten-frames and similar patterned arrangements helps students understand larger quantities and leads to greater flexibility in visualizing and computing numbers: students realize that larger quantities can be "taken apart" just like smaller ones, an important idea when developing meaningful strategies for computing with multidigit numbers.

The Lesson

Day 1

"Good afternoon!" I said as students came into the room and sat down at their desks. "I have brought something to share with you. I've put it on the overhead and I want you to look at it carefully and discuss with your classmates what you notice. Ready?" I displayed the empty ten-frame (see below) on the overhead, and after a few moments several students raised their hands.

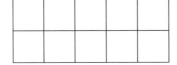

"I see lots of boxes," contributed one student.

"There's one big rectangle," another said.

"There are lots of lines," said a third.

"There are four sides," was another observation.

"I see four corners," one student said.

Because I wanted the class to consider some very particular ten-frame attributes, I acknowledged their contributions and then turned off the overhead so that they could closely attend to what I had to say. "You have many observations about what I displayed," I said. "I am going to turn the overhead back on. This time, I would like you to pay close attention to *numbers* of things. Ready?"

This time when I turned on the overhead, I saw that many students lifted an index finger to count the boxes in the display. After a few moments, several students had raised their hands.

"There are ten boxes," one commented.

"There are five on top," another observed.

"There are five boxes on the bottom, too," added another.

"There are two different types of lines: ones going up and down and ones going across," a fourth stated.

I wanted the students to be familiar with some vocabulary unique to charts and tables that would help them verbalize their observations. This seemed like an opportune time to introduce such a discussion.

"There are some words that may be helpful in talking about what you see," I said. "You noticed that there are five boxes up here." I pointed to the top row of the ten-frame. "These boxes that are arranged across—horizontally—are in a 'row.' You noticed that there are five boxes in the top row . . ."

"And five in the bottom!" answered Daniel.

"Yes! That's right," I continued. "There are five in each row. How many rows do you see?"

"Two," said many, while others held up two fingers.

"We can also look at the boxes that are on top of each other, the boxes that go up and down, vertically. We call this a 'column.' How many boxes are in a column?"

"Two," responded the class.

"Yes," I confirmed, while pointing to each box in each column, "two here, two here, two here, two here, and two here. So there are . . ."

"Five!" the students answered as one.

"Yes, there are five columns. These are rows"—I traced the five boxes in each—"and these are columns"—I traced the boxes in each of the five columns. "*Column* and *row* are important words for talking about charts and tables like this. This picture has a special name. It's called a *ten-frame*. I bet you know why the word *ten* is in the name."

"Because there's ten boxes!" several children called out.

"Exactly," I answered. "Now, I have many frames in my home. And frames hold something. My frames at home hold pictures, paintings, or photographs. This ten-frame isn't holding anything yet. I am going to turn off the overhead and add some counters—I am going to be using lima beans—to the ten-frame. I am going to turn it back on and your job is to again see what you notice." The students nodded their heads eagerly.

I turned off the overhead, placed three beans in the top row of the ten-frame, and then turned the overhead back on. The projected ten-frame looked like this:

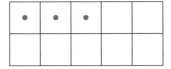

I let students observe for a minute and then I asked them to talk about what they noticed.

"I see three on the top . . . what's that word? *Row*!" said Ken.

I was not sure if Ken counted the boxes individually or if he visually recognized—subitized—three. "Did you go like this, 'One, two, three,'" I said, pointing to each box on the screen that had a bean inside, "or did you just *see* three?"

"I just saw it," said Ken.

I don't typically ask students such leading questions, but in this case I wanted them to appreciate their ability to visualize quantity. "Isn't it amazing how your brain works?" I exclaimed. "Sometimes it is easy to just *see* numbers of things. Ken did not need to count each bean. He just knew that there were three because three is easy to see. Ten-frames can help you to *see* certain numbers of things. What else do you notice?"

"There are three boxes with beans and seven with no beans," said Andrea.

"How did you know that there were seven boxes with no beans?" I asked.

"There are five on the bottom and two on the top. I went"—and she held up five outstretched fingers—"*five*, six, seven." As she counted on from five, Andrea unfurled two fingers on her other hand, one finger at a time.

"What else did you notice when you looked at this ten-frame?" I pressed.

When no one raised a hand, I decided it was time to change the arrangement. I turned off the overhead and said, "When I turn the overhead back on, I want you to again make some observations." I added two beans to the bottom row and then turned on the overhead (see below).

A number of students raised their hands.

"There are five full boxes and five empty boxes," said Julie.

"How could you tell?" I asked.

"I see three beans on the top and two on the bottom and I know three and two is five. The same with the empty boxes," she explained.

"There's two and two and one beans," said Irene. "And two and two and one empty boxes."

"The boxes with beans make an interesting shape," said Tommie.

"I am going to change the ten-frame again," I announced, turning off the overhead. I added two beans to the ten-frame. This time, I wanted students to see a "quick image" and use what they knew about the configuration of the ten-frame to make sense of the visual display. "This time," I said, "I am only going to keep the overhead on for a short while. See what you can quickly notice about the display." I turned the overhead back on for several moments (see below), then switched it off.

"I see five and two and three," Josh observed.

"There's five on top and two on the bottom," said Ruth.

"There are three empty boxes," said Ken.

"Seven are filled and three are empty," said Julie.

"Three" is a quantity that is easy to subitize but "seven" is not. I asked Julie, "How did you know that there were seven filled boxes?"

"*Five*," she said, displaying five fingers, and counting on to two more, "six, seven." Her explanation made it clear that Julie had not internalized these number combinations but she did have an effective strategy for determining the total: counting on from the larger number. Perhaps she remembered Andrea's method from earlier in the discussion.

It was time to move on to the focus of today's mathematics lesson. Before we did, I wanted to assess the students' thinking about the importance and practicality of using ten-frames.

"I have a question for you," I said. "Why might ten-frames be a good tool to use when looking at numbers of things?"

"They help you to see numbers fast," said Josh.

"You can add numbers fast, too!" added Irene.

"You don't have to count things like this: one . . . two . . . three . . . four . . . five . . ." Daniel's exaggerated pauses between numbers amused his classmates. "You can just go: *five*!"

Day 2

A few days later I wanted to expand on the work we had previously done with ten-frames. Today's lesson would also be an abbreviated one, like the last: rather than take up the entire mathematics period, it would be a minilesson preceding the bulk of "math time." As students sat down at their desks, I positioned myself at the overhead projector in front of the room. I put a double ten-frame transparency on the projector, covering up the second graphic. To support the students in extending what they had done in the introduction to ten-frames, I thought it was important to have them recount what they had previously discussed.

"I have something here that I showed you a few days ago," I said. "I wonder if you remember what it is called, what we did with it, and why it might be a useful tool to use." I turned on the overhead. Students smiled knowingly and many hands went up.

"It's got ten squares on it," commented one student.

"You can use it to count numbers fast!" said another.

"It's a ten thing," said a third.

"A ten-frame!" corrected a fourth.

I turned off the overhead projector. "Great!" I said. "You remembered many things about the ten-frame. I have something new to show you. I want you to look at it carefully and raise your hand if you have an observation about what you see." I uncovered the second ten-frame and turned on the projector so that the students could see two ten-frames on the screen (see below).

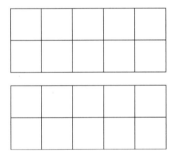

A few students began pointing to the screen, making motions with their index fingers as if they were counting each box one at a time. Other students immediately raised their hands.

"There's *two* ten-frames," said Daniel when I called on him.

"There's twenty boxes," added Ruth.

"How did you know there were twenty?" I asked.

She responded, "Ten on top and ten on the bottom. That's ten, twenty!"

"I see four fives," commented Tommie. "Five, ten, fifteen, twenty!"

"They are both empty. There's no beans in any of the boxes," another student observed.

"If all the boxes were filled, you'd have twenty beans," said Irene.

While this last statement had already been stated in a different way, I was still curious about how Irene

figured out the total number of beans needed to fill every box. "How did you know that?" I inquired.

"I counted them," she answered. "I went, 'one, two, three,' all the way to twenty." I was not sure if Irene had, indeed, counted each and every box by ones. However, she had added some information about counting to what some of her classmates had already said.

"I heard some of you count by tens. Does anyone know what I mean?" I asked.

"Yeah. Ruth did. She said, 'Ten, twenty,'" Josh informed us.

"I counted by fives!" Tommie eagerly added.

"Yes, you did," I confirmed. "Do you remember how you did that?"

"He went, 'Five, ten, fifteen, twenty!'" recalled Julie.

"Irene counted in a different way," I began.

"I counted by ones!" Irene informed us.

"I can see twos!" said Ken. "If you look at the boxes on top of each other, they go by twos. Look." Ken came up to the screen and touched each column, counting aloud. "Two, four, six, eight, ten . . . twelve . . . fourteen . . . sixteen . . . seven—I mean eighteen—twenty!"

"It's so interesting how people counted in different ways," I said. "Some of you counted by ones, some by twos, some by fives, and others by tens. No matter how people counted, they all ended up with the same number: twenty! I wonder why?" Many second graders know that a quantity remains unchanged regardless of how you count it. Others need many more experiences with counting large numbers of objects by ones, twos, fives, and tens in order to be convinced that a quantity does not change when the method of grouping changes.

I turned off the overhead projector. "Now I'm going to put some beans in some of the boxes," I explained. "I am going to turn the overhead back on and I would like you to observe what you notice. Raise your hand if you have an observation you would like to tell to the rest of us. Ready?" Students nodded. I added some beans to the ten-frame and turned on the overhead projector. The projected image now looked like this:

Several students raised their hands eagerly.

"There's five on the top row and two more. That makes . . . six, seven!" said Josh. "I can just see the three on the bottom . . . I don't need to count them."

"I see seven and three," said Andrea.

"There's ten. Seven on the top and three on the bottom," said Ruth.

"I understand how you see seven and three," I responded, "but how did you know there were ten?"

"I just know," answered Ruth. "Seven and three equals ten!" Ruth had connected her knowledge of number combinations to the displayed picture; it did not seem as though she was relying solely on a visual picture of ten.

"I know a different way!" said Daniel. "We know there's ten boxes in a ten-frame, because it's a ten-frame, right? If you move the bottom three to the open boxes in the top, that makes ten!"

"People are using different methods to find the total number of beans," I stated. "Some know number combinations: seven and three equals ten. Some are seeing numbers broken up in different ways: seven is made of five and two"—as I said this I pointed to the first and second rows of the top ten-frame—"and some people are seeing a whole quantity of beans with their eyes." I again turned off the overhead, added some beans to the bottom ten-frame, and continued. "I have changed the picture again," I said. "When I turn on the overhead, pay attention to what you see. Raise your hands to share an observation."

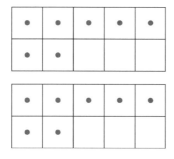

Several students raised their hands after only five or ten seconds.

"I see fourteen," said Tommie. "Seven and seven make fourteen."

"How do you know there are fourteen?" I asked.

"I just know that 'double': seven plus seven," he explained. Tommie used a strategy for doubles, as well as visualizing the quantity.

"Did anyone see something different?" I asked.

"Well, I see fourteen in a different way," said Ruth. "I can move three from the bottom to the open boxes on top."

I knew that some of the students would have trouble conceptualizing how Ruth visually "moved" a group of beans from ten-frame to ten-frame. "Ruth, could you come up and show us? I am not sure if I understand your method."

"See?" Ruth explained, pointing to the bottom ten-frame first. "I moved these three up to the top boxes. That makes ten, because it fills up this ten-frame. That leaves four on the bottom." She pointed to the remaining four beans in the bottom ten-frame. "Ten and four make fourteen." Ruth had decomposed seven: she easily visualized moving three from one set of seven to the other in order to "make a ten." Ruth also easily visualized the four that remained from the decomposed set. The action that Ruth performed demonstrated an important number-sense concept and a fundamental understanding of place value: seven and seven is equal to ten and four. Ruth had just done some critical "regrouping."

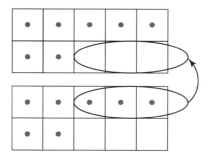

Her classmates were impressed.

"Wow!" said one.

"That's cool!" said another.

"So, we just heard about what Tommie and Ruth observed. I wonder if there is someone who observed something different," I said.

"I do!" said Andrea, walking up to the screen and pointing to the beans to which she referred. "I see five and five . . . that makes ten. That leaves two here on top and two here on the bottom. Ten and two make . . . eleven, twelve . . . and two more make thirteen, fourteen!" Andrea quickly explained how she "saw" fourteen. Yet her quick explanation yielded some important number-sense concepts. She visualized ten by "pulling out" fives from each of the seven beans displayed in each ten-frame. She recombined these pieces in a flexible and efficient way. Andrea was able to keep track of the parts of each seven that remained in the ten-frame. She used a counting-on strategy to add the first set of two, then the second. She had regrouped as well.

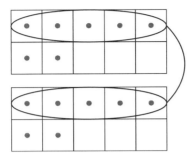

Before ending the lesson, I wanted to do two things: give students a chance to talk about their new ideas and get a sense of their ability to visualize numbers through this representation. Giving students opportunities to talk in small groups would provide them with a less threatening arena in which to share their ideas, allow them a chance to rehearse ideas they might share with the whole class, and make it easier for students to utilize careful listening strategies. Sharing with the whole class would expose students to a larger pool of ideas and give me some information that would help in my planning for our next session. I said, "You have done some thorough observations of the ten-frame bean arrangements. Before we end, I wonder what new understandings you have made about numbers and ten-frames, based on today's activities. I would like you to first share your ideas with the people at your table. Then we will share with the whole group."

After students talked for a couple of minutes, I asked for their attention and invited them to share with the whole class what they had talked about and heard.

"You can use two of them!" said one student, referring to the ten-frames.

"Yeah, and you can still move beans from one to the other . . . with your eyes!" said another.

"People can see numbers in lots of ways," one student offered.

"You can put numbers together in different ways," added another.

"Seven and seven can be made into ten and four," was another response.

This summary contained some important ideas. Students understood the ten-frame's power as a visualization tool; they saw the purpose in using two ten-frames. Students were able to see that multiple models could represent the same number; this realization was crucial to the understanding that numbers can be decomposed and recombined in a variety of ways. In the process of recombining quantities, students were acquiring fundamental place-value knowledge: two-digit numbers can be regarded as groups of tens and ones.

Day 3

This third lesson took place a couple of weeks later, but between the second and third lesson the students had continued working with ten-frames as part of their "morning routine." Three or four times a week, they observed different bean configurations on the double ten-frame overhead, discussed the quantity displayed, and explained different ways to visualize the number. Today's session would use the entire mathematics period.

Before students came into the classroom, I had placed a *Ten-Frames* sheet at each of their desks. Unifix cubes were available in the plastic shoeboxes in the middle of each group of desks, and students were familiar with the use of these snap cubes. Students came in from the morning recess and took their seats. They seemed very excited to find the ten-frames materials at their desks.

"Hey, *we* have ten-frames!" one student exclaimed.

"Neat! We can make our own numbers!" another enthused.

"Good morning!" I said as I introduced the lesson. "You've noticed that you all have your own double ten-frame and you sound like you have a pretty good idea of what we will be doing today. Yes, you are going to make your own numbers. Before we get started, why don't you take a few minutes to explore the ten-frames, using the snap cubes for counters?"

I walked around the classroom as the students familiarized themselves with the materials. Students at each table quickly opened up the shoeboxes and removed handfuls of cubes. They filled the frames in a variety of ways and "tested" their classmates on the quantities they made, discussing their different arrangements. This exploratory time was more than just "free play"; it gave the students time to experiment, so that they would be able to focus on specific directives during the actual lesson. This time also allowed me—and the students—a time to observe the variety of numbers and patterns that could be built. After about five minutes, I got the students' attention.

"You did and said some interesting things with the ten-frames. Let's take a few minutes to talk about what you did or said, or what you noticed someone else doing." Many of the students raised their hands.

"I made a pattern, going across," one student said.

"We guessed each other's numbers . . . it was fun!" said another.

"I filled up both of them. It took twenty cubes," another commented.

"We did *hard* problems . . . but we could figure them out," said a fourth.

After I acknowledged the various contributions, I introduced the activity. "Today you are going to build some numbers of your own. Before you do, I have some special directions about building numbers in the ten-frame," I explained.

I turned on the overhead; it displayed an empty double ten-frame transparency. "When you place counters in the ten-frame, you can only put one counter in each box, just like we have been doing. But you also have to begin with the box in the top left-hand corner. You cannot skip any boxes as you move across the top row, placing one counter in each box. I will give you a trick to help you remember. Fill up the ten-frame in the direction that you read: start in the upper left and move across. When you get to the end of the boxes, you make a 'return sweep,' as if you are reading! Let me show you what I mean, by building the number six."

I had chosen a number greater than five because I wanted the students to see what I meant by "return sweep." I demonstrated on the transparency (see below) as I explained. "I will start at the top of the ten-frame, just like I am 'reading' it. I am going to fill each box that I need for the number by going across the ten-frame. I reached the end and I still need to use one more box, so I am going to make a 'return sweep.' When I do, I go back to the left of the ten-frame, using the box right under the box where I started. I only need one more box to make the number six."

•	•	•	•	•
•				

While this "rule" seemed like an easy one to understand and follow, I did not want to assume that everyone understood what I had just done. I decided to have a few students explain how to build a number. As they did I followed the directions they gave, building the number on the overhead. "I think you understand this rule about the order in which to fill boxes when building numbers. I would like a few of you to choose a number for me to build. I will try to build the number by following your directions about where to place the counters. What is the largest number I can build? And why do you think so?"

"Ten . . . I mean twenty!" one student called out.

"You only have twenty boxes, so it can be twenty or smaller . . . not bigger," said another.

"It could be one or two or three or four, all the way to twenty," said a third.

"Can you build a number bigger than twenty by using all the boxes? You could put the extras on the sheet, just not in the boxes," one of the students suggested.

"You could. That's true," I replied. "For this demonstration, though, let's keep the numbers below twenty."

Julie went first. "OK . . . my number's twelve," she said. "So here's what you do: count out twelve counters." I did what she asked.

"Then you put one in each box," she continued. I waited a few seconds to see if Julie would revise her directions. She did not, so I started placing the counters randomly in boxes.

"No!" she exclaimed. "You got to start up there." She pointed to the upper-left box. I put a counter in the first box. "Then you got to go across," she continued. I placed the remaining four counters in the top row and then waited for her next direction. Some students giggled at my seeming inability to build twelve.

"OK, now you got to fill up the next row," Julie instructed, "the one underneath. That will make ten." I filled the bottom row with counters from left to right.

"OK," Julie said. "Now you have two more. Put one in the first box in the bottom ten-frame. The top . . . um . . . the top left box. OK. Then put the last one in the box next to it." I did what she instructed.

"That was hard to explain!" she exclaimed.

Below is a picture of what I built:

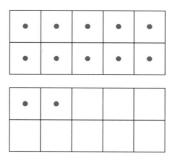

Students seemed anxious to build their own numbers. "You look like you are ready to build some numbers of your own. Here are some things you can do with a partner," I said, picking up a piece of chalk so that I could record the ten-frame options for the class. As I told the students about the different options for their ten-frame work, I wrote each down on the board. "I am going to give you three different things you can do with the ten-frames," I explained. "For the first one, one person can choose a number and the other person can build it." I wrote this down on the board next to the number 1. "The second thing you can do is choose a 'hider' and 'guesser.' The hider will write down a number and then build it; the guesser tells the number as quickly as possible, without counting by ones. The guesser has to explain what he or she did to figure out the number."

Ten-Frame Partner Work

1. Choose a number for your partner to build.

2. One person is the *hider* and the other person is the *guesser*. The hider writes down a number, then builds it. The guesser tells the number and explains how he or she figured it out.

I could see that the students were not clear about what Option 2 entailed. "Let me demonstrate for you," I offered. "Daniel, will you be my partner?"

Daniel came up to the overhead. "I am going to be the 'hider' and you are going to be the 'guesser,'" I explained. "Let me read the directions on the board: 'Hider writes down a number, then builds it.' OK, I will write down a number." On a slip of paper, I wrote down *15*. I wrote it big enough for the students to see and I showed it to them while hiding the number from Daniel. My exaggerated attempt to keep Daniel from seeing the number was met with general amusement. "Now I need to build it, following the rules," I said. I quickly placed fifteen cubes on the double ten-frame transparency (see below).

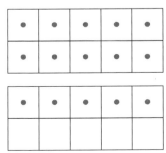

"I am going to read the directions on the board again," I said. "'The guesser tells the number and explains how he or she figured it out.'"

Daniel quickly responded, "It's fifteen!" He pointed to each row of cubes and explained, "Five, ten, fifteen! That's easy!"

"I guess I need to show Daniel what I wrote down, to see if he was right," I said, showing Daniel the slip of paper on which I had written *15*. He smiled. "Now it's Daniel's turn," I said. Students now seemed clear about Option 2.

"Those are two different things you can do for your ten-frame work with a partner," I continued. "I have one last thing to explain to you." I removed the previous transparency from the overhead and placed a new overhead—*Ten-Frames Models*—on the projector. I had already duplicated a two-page copy of these ten-frame models for each pair of students. The first page contained ten ten-frames showing the quantity ten; the second page contained ten-frames for quantities of one to nine.

"Cool!" several students exclaimed.

"They're like *pictures* of ten-frames!" said one.

"Yeah, they're already filled!" said another.

"I have a copy of these for you and your partner," I said. I removed the first page of the copy from the overhead and showed the students an overhead of the second page. "The first thing I would like you to do before using these is to cut them apart. Cut around each ten-frame, leaving a small margin, like this." I traced around one of the ten-frame models to show the students where to cut. "It should look like this," I said, showing them one of the models that I had already cut out (see below).

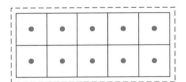

"Once you have cut each of them out, what could you and your partner do with them? Talk among yourselves at your tables and see what ideas you come up with."

These models could be used for addition and subtraction of multidigit numbers in the future. Before they would be useful, students would need some time to explore them. Today's math period seemed like an appropriate time to let the students investigate the ten-frame models and use some of their own ideas in the process of this investigation. While students talked for a couple of minutes, I added to the list of ideas on the board (see below).

Ten-Frame Partner Work

1. Choose a number for your partner to build.

2. One person is the *hider* and the other person is the *guesser*. The hider writes down a number, then builds it. The guesser tells the number and explains how he or she figured it out.

3. Explore the ten-frame models.

"What ideas did you talk about at your tables?" I asked after about five minutes.

"You can build numbers and your partner can guess the number," one student said.

"You can see how big a number you can make!" another suggested.

"You can add some numbers using the ten-frames," said a third.

"You can do the guessing thing: you can write down the number and build it. Then your partner has to figure out the number you built!" said a fourth.

"And tell you *how* they figured it out!" another clarified.

"In the directions for 'Ten-Frame Partner Work' that I wrote on the board, I have just written 'Explore the ten-frame models.' Use some of the ideas your classmates suggested or ideas you might think of. When you are done with the ten-frame models, please paperclip them together so we have complete sets to use in the future. You have three different things you can work on today with a partner. Any questions before we get started?" When none of the students spoke up, I directed the class to begin. Students began working with the double ten-frames as I distributed the *Ten-Frames Models* sheets to pairs of students.

I gave the students about twenty minutes to work independently on the choices that I had listed on the board. While they worked, I listened to their conversations and watched how they used the materials. Rather than being a time for me to instruct students or assess their thinking, this was a time for them to practice using the materials that they had only observed me using. I was curious to see how the students determined the quantities displayed in the various ten-frames; they were comfortable counting by ones, and I was anxious to see if they would use the structure of the ten-frame to count by fives and tens. We had not used the ten-frame models to examine or construct quantities greater than twenty. I was interested

in how the students would use these materials to consider numbers of greater magnitude.

Several students had begun the activity by exploring individually, building numbers in the double ten-frames. I decided not to intervene; this behavior seemed like a logical step before working with a partner.

"I built a really easy number . . . look: one!" said one student.

"Mine's trickier . . ." said his partner.

Many students were involved in the "guessing game": young children often find enjoyment in keeping something secret or "hidden."

"OK . . . what's this number?" one student asked her partner.

"Easy," the other responded. "Fifteen, sixteen . . . seventeen!"

"Yep! That's the number I wrote down, except you have to tell me how you got that number," the first student said.

"I know this first one's ten," her partner explained. "Five more is fifteen. Then I went, 'Sixteen, seventeen' for the two on the bottom."

That the ten-frame models were a novelty to the students was obvious: many children eagerly began cutting out the models and arranging them to build numbers.

"I made . . . eighty-five!" one student said.

"I can make a number bigger than *that*!" said the student's partner.

"I wonder what the biggest number is . . ." the first student responded.

"Let's see: ten, twenty, thirty, forty . . ." said the partner.

"I think all the tens make a hundred!" the first student exclaimed.

"Hey! We can put the nine with the one to make a ten . . . and the eight with the two to make a ten . . . and the seven with the three . . . and the six with the four . . . and that's ten, twenty, thirty, forty . . . There's just a five left . . . that's . . ."

"Forty-five!" said his partner. "And the forty-five with the one hundred makes . . ."

"One hundred forty-five? Whoa!" said his partner.

It was time to bring this session to a close. I was interested to hear about the students' discoveries with ten-frames. "You certainly have been busy with your ten-frame partner work," I began. "I would like to know what new understandings you have made about numbers and ten-frames, from the work you have done today."

"It was fun guessing numbers. I was really good at it!" one student exclaimed.

"I don't have to count by ones. Tens are a lot faster," said another.

"I liked making *big* numbers with those ten-frame pictures," said a third.

"Yeah! Numbers like ninety-eight and eighty-five," another added.

"We used *all* the pictures. We made a hundred and forty-five!" exclaimed one student.

"We added some numbers together. I made a number and my partner made a number. Then we pushed them all together to see what we got!" said yet another.

This whole-class discussion was illuminating to me. The information provided by the students would be useful in my construction of future ten-frames explorations. I was pleased that the exercise had proven so fruitful. Students had been inspired to build multidigit numbers, and had been successful at counting those quantities by ones, fives, and tens. The ten-frame models had pushed students to consider more efficient ways of counting; the ability to visualize and understand ten both as ten single objects and as a single group of ten was an important place-value understanding. Experience with these models gave students experience in considering number magnitude. Students were capable of comparing numbers with visual models: finding the difference between two quantities was something within their grasp, once the models were built. Once the students had been exposed to these materials, they had begun using them quite naturally to satisfy their own curiosity: performing operations independently, building a foundation of experience that we would expand on in future explorations. Most important, students saw that this important work with number-sense concepts was not only well within their means, it was something they really enjoyed doing.

Linking Assessment and Instruction

As the students work, think about the following:

- Are they able to "see" arrangements of counters on ten-frames and double ten-frames in flexible and multiple ways? Can they describe how they see these arrangements? Can students flexibly represent numbers on ten-frames and double ten-frames?

- Can students "read" multidigit numbers made with ten-frame models? Can they build multidigit numbers with ten-frame models?

- How do students talk about numbers made with ten-frames, double ten-frames, and ten-frame models? In what ways do they find these tools useful? How do they generalize their understanding of visual models to symbolic ways of representing numbers?

CHAPTER 9

Number Strings

OVERVIEW

Number Strings *provides a context in which students can use a variety of computation strategies to flexibly and efficiently recombine numbers. Students look at a "string" of single-digit numbers, consider different ways to combine the addends in this string, and then discuss these ways with their classmates. Work with number strings illustrates that numbers can be decomposed and recombined in lots of different ways. It gives students continued practice with developing strategies, such as "making tens" and using "doubles." These experiences help students to build important understandings necessary for operating with multidigit numbers.*

MATERIALS

- chart paper, several sheets
- optional: preprinted copies of a number string (e.g., 3 + 4 + 8 + 2 + 7), 1 per student

TIME

- three class periods

Teaching Directions

1. Post a string of numbers (e.g., 6 + 5 + 7).

2. Ask students to combine the numbers in the string and pay close attention to the methods they use.

3. Ask individual students to share their solutions and methods with their classmates.

4. Demonstrate how to represent solutions, using words, symbols, and/or diagrams to make the methods explicit.

5. Have students discuss representations and the similarities between methods.

Teaching Notes

These lessons focus on giving students opportunities to develop, explain, and represent their own methods for operating on numbers, rather than "acquiring" methods demonstrated by the teacher. Students are given a set of numbers and are expected to construct strategies for combining them and explain these strategies to each other. In order to do so, students must make sense of the strategies they are using. Emphasis is placed on a student understanding his or her own method, rather than on memorizing someone else's.

In this lesson, students explain their solution strategies to their classmates. Class discussions that focus on sharing strategies accomplish several important goals. Students (1) acquire methods they may not have considered on their own, (2) deepen their own understanding by explaining their methods to others, (3) learn ways of representing their ideas orally and in graphic form, and (4) supply important assessment information to the teacher. Classroom discussions provide opportunities for students see important connections between a variety of approaches and the ways to represent them.

The Lesson

Day 1

Before being introduced to number strings, my students had had numerous experiences with combinations of numbers equal to ten. They had also examined and worked with "doubles," such as 6 + 6, 7 + 7, 8 + 8, and 9 + 9. While second-grade students may be unfamiliar with the term *doubles*, they have already committed many of these number pairs to memory. A whole-class discussion about number strings might explore "near doubles," a simple two-number string that is related to a double. I began a discussion with my second-grade students by writing 6 + 7 at the top of a sheet of chart paper.

"I'd like you to take a look at what I have written," I said by way of introduction. "I am interested in knowing the answer to this problem, but I am most interested in hearing how you decide to solve it. Pay close attention to what you do in your mind as you look at this equation. Everyone will get to share their answer and method for finding the answer, but we only have time and room on the chart for me to write down the ways explained by two or three people. Please solve the problem, pay close attention to how you solved it, and put your hands on your knees when you have the answer, so I know you have finished." After fifteen to thirty seconds, all of the students had their hands on their knees.

"OK," I said, "if you feel comfortable sharing your answer and how you got your answer, please raise your hand."

Most of the students raised their hands, and I called on Michael.

"I know six plus six is like two dice, and that's twelve," Michael said. "Seven is the number after six, so the answer is the number after twelve."

"I'm not sure about the 'number after' part," I said. "Can you tell me what you mean?" I had followed Michael's reasoning, but I wanted him to explain it in a way that his classmates would understand as well.

"You have a six and a seven," Michael said. "Seven is after six. You take twelve—that's the answer to six plus six—and you say the number after twelve: thirteen."

"Let me see if I can write what you just said," I suggested. I wrote Michael's name on the chart paper and then began recording his exact words. As I wrote, I read the words aloud to him and his classmates. "'I

know six plus six is twelve. Seven is the number after six. The answer is the number after twelve. It's thirteen.' Does my writing show what you said?" I asked. Michael nodded his assent.

"Michael explained to us in words how he solved this problem," I said. "We are also going to use numbers to show his thinking. How did he start thinking about 'seven plus six'?"

"He added two sixes," Darien said.

"How would I write that using numbers?" I asked.

"Six plus six equals twelve!" many students shouted. Underneath Michael's words, I wrote this equation.

"Then what did he do?" I asked.

"He knew it was six plus seven, not six plus six," Carolyn explained. "He knew the answer was the number after twelve."

"Why did that work?" I asked.

A few hands went up. Allison wanted to share. "See, six plus six is twelve," she explained. "You wanted to know seven plus six. Seven is one more than six so the answer has to be one more than twelve. So it's thirteen. The answer's thirteen."

Hearing several students explain Michael's method gave me confidence that most of the students understood it. Moreover, explaining their classmate's ideas gave students an opportunity to clarify their own understanding of Michael's method, and gave other students additional opportunities to understand this approach.

"What should I write next?" I asked.

Michael's hand went up. "Write 'twelve plus one' under 'six plus six equals twelve.' That's what I did. I added one to twelve."

I wanted to offer the students a way of identifying Michael's method. I explained, "Michael used a 'method,' or 'strategy,' for solving seven plus six. He started with a double. But he did something to that double. He added one. Do you remember why he did that?" Most students nodded "yes." "If he had just used a double, we would have called his method, or strategy, 'doubles.' But he added one to one of the numbers. We call his strategy 'doubles plus one.'" I wrote *Doubles + 1* next to Michael's strategy. "Did anyone else use 'doubles plus one'?" Two or three students raised their hands. "Did anyone use a different way to solve the same problem? Darien?"

"I took the seven—that's the biggest number—and I counted six more on my fingers and I got thirteen," Darien said.

"Could you show us how you did that?" I asked. While this is a common strategy, not all students were using it. Darien could show them how to count on, using a familiar tool: his fingers. He was also addressing how this strategy is more efficient when starting with the greater—rather than the "first"—number.

"I put seven in my head," he touched his forehead, "and then I went, 'eight, nine, ten, eleven, twelve, thirteen!'" As Darien spoke each number, he unfolded one finger, until six fingers were extended. I asked a few students to explain what Darien did, again to assess their understanding, to make it apparent that listening to others was expected of them and valued, and to expose students to multiple descriptions of a strategy.

"Let me see if I can remember what you said," I began. "You started with seven and you put that in your head. Then you counted six more on your fingers. When you counted, you said numbers. Tell me if this is right." I wrote on the chart, *I put seven in my head* . . .

Darien continued from where I had left off. "And then I counted six on my fingers: eight, nine, ten, eleven, twelve, thirteen." As he spoke, I recorded Darien's words.

"I want to make sure that I show your thinking with your words," I said to Darien when I'd finished. "I also want to use some numbers or a picture to show what you did. I noticed you used these fingers"—I extended all of the fingers on my right hand and one on my left—"and each time you put out a finger, you said a number. I am going to draw the fingers and label each finger with the number you said." As I drew, I explained what I was doing and why. "Darien started with a number, and then he used his fingers to count on to the other number. We call that 'counting on.'" Next to Darien's strategy, I wrote *Counting on*. This is what Darien's strategy looked like on the chart:

Darien: I put seven in my head and counted six on my fingers: 8, 9, 10, 11, 12, 13.

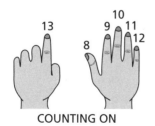

COUNTING ON

"Did anyone else use Darien's strategy?" A few students raised their hands. "We have time for one more person to share how he or she solved seven plus six. Does anyone else have a way that hasn't been shared yet?" Several students raised their hands. I called on Desiree.

"I took six and I broke it up into three and three," Desiree said. "I put the seven with one of the threes and I got ten. I got the other three and put it with the ten. I got thirteen." I recorded Desiree's words on the chart.

"I am going to use a picture and a drawing to show what Desiree did," I said. "She said she broke up six into three and three. I will write a six, and split it into three and three. Then she said, 'I put the seven with the three.' Help me think of an equation that matches what Desiree did," I said to the class.

"Seven plus three!" said several students.

Others offered, "Seven plus three equals ten!"

I wrote the equation that students suggested, then prompted the group with a new question, not only to keep them involved in helping me create a representation of Desiree's method, but to make sure they understood the steps she went through.

"And then she added another number. What should I do?" I asked.

"You need to add a three," one student said.

"You have to write a new equation: ten plus three equals thirteen," said another.

I made the additions to the class chart. Desiree decomposed six into doubles in order for her to recombine more familiar number combinations: those that make ten. I explained this to her classmates. "Desire broke six into . . ." I prompted.

"Three and three!" said several students.

"Two threes," said several others.

"What made her think that was a smart thing to do?" I asked.

"She wanted to use one of them with the seven," one student responded.

"She wanted to make ten," said another.

"Ten is a 'friendly' number. Desiree *always* makes tens! She knew the seven needs three to make ten. She got the three from the six," said yet another.

"So," I summed up, "Desiree was looking for a way to make ten. That would be a good name for Desiree's strategy: 'make a ten.'" I wrote this on the class chart. We concluded the discussion by reviewing all of the methods students had used to solve the number string 6 + 7.

6 + 7

Michael: I know six plus six is twelve. Seven is the number after six. The answer is the number after twelve. It's thirteen.

$$6 + 6 = 12$$
$$12 + 1 = 13$$

DOUBLES + 1

Darien: I put seven in my head and counted six on my fingers: 8, 9, 10, 11, 12, 13.

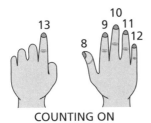

COUNTING ON

Desiree: I broke up six into three and three. I put the seven with one of the threes and I got ten. I got the other three and put it with the ten. I got thirteen.

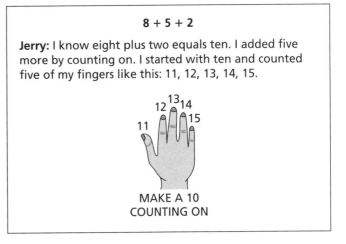

MAKE A 10

Day 2

A couple of days later, I wrote $8 + 5 + 2$ on the top of a piece of chart paper. Again I began by telling students that I was interested not only in the sum but, even more important, in how they figured out the sum. I asked them to solve the problem and put their hands on their knees to signal that they had found the solution. After about thirty seconds, I asked who would be willing to share their strategy. I called on Jerry.

"I know eight and two makes ten," Jerry said. "And then I added five more."

Jerry did not start with the numbers in the string and add them in the order written. He used a "make a ten" strategy, but it seemed as though he had used another strategy as well. "How did you add the five more?" I asked.

"I started with the ten and I counted five of my fingers, like this: eleven, twelve, thirteen, fourteen, fifteen," he answered.

"Let me write what you said. You tell me if this is right," I said. When I was finished, Jerry indicated

that what I had written was correct. I asked the students what strategy Jerry had used, and they responded by saying either "make a ten" or "counting on." I wrote both next to Jerry's method on the class chart, which now looked like this:

8 + 5 + 2

Jerry: I know eight plus two equals ten. I added five more by counting on. I started with ten and counted five of my fingers like this: 11, 12, 13, 14, 15.

MAKE A 10
COUNTING ON

When I asked the students, "Who used Jerry's way?" a few shared that they had also made a ten and then added the five by counting on.

Gil was eager to explain his way. "I know five and two make seven." Gil proved this by first putting up five fingers and then putting up two more. "I know that eight plus eight is sixteen, because I know my doubles. But I am adding seven plus eight, so I take away one. I got fifteen." I wrote down the words as Gil said them. When I finished writing, he quickly added, "I used doubles, but I didn't add one. I took away one. I think my way should be called 'doubles minus one.'" I wrote on the chart:

$$5 + 2 = 7$$

$$8 + 8 = 16$$

$$16 - 1 = 15$$

$$DOUBLES - 1$$

Alexandra explained her method next. "I know five and two make seven. I took the seven and then I counted on to eight. I got fifteen. My strategy was 'counting on.'" I recorded Alexandra's way with words, numbers, and a picture. I also recorded the strategy that she used and asked the other students if they had used a similar way. We concluded our second discussion of number strings by reviewing all of the ways that the students had used.

8 + 5 + 2

Jerry: I know eight plus two equals ten. I added five more by counting on. I started with ten and counted five of my fingers like this: 11, 12, 13, 14, 15.

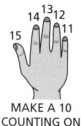

MAKE A 10
COUNTING ON

Gil: I know five and two make seven. I know that eight plus eight is sixteen, because I know my doubles. But I am adding seven plus eight, so I take away one. I got fifteen.

$$5 + 2 = 7$$
$$8 + 8 = 16$$
$$16 - 1 = 15$$
DOUBLES − 1

Alexandra: I know five and two make seven. I took the seven and then I counted on eight. I got fifteen.

$$5 + 2 = 7$$
$$7 + 8 = 15$$

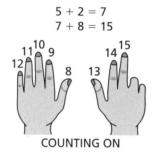

COUNTING ON

Day 3

After several discussions using strings with three or four digits, I was eager to give the students a longer string of numbers, one that might look challenging but could easily be solved using the methods they had already tried. The purpose of today's activity was not to teach, but to assess. I wanted to see what students could independently do to solve a number string: I wanted to look at the strategies they used and the ways in which they represented these strategies on paper. I wrote the following string of numbers on the board: *3 + 4 + 8 + 2 + 7.*

"Good morning!" I began, "I am glad to see that you have noticed the number string I have written on the board—I know it's a long one, but I think you're ready for it. You have been working on strategies for a while and you have used these strategies to solve

many number strings. We have talked about and charted your strategies and discussed how they are alike and different. We have looked at the different ways that you can represent your strategies using words and numbers and pictures. Today, we are not going to discuss the different ways to solve this problem. I would like you to think about all of the ideas you have been using over the last several days. Think about all the ideas your classmates have shared as well. Look carefully at the number string and think about the best way you know to add these numbers together. What methods have you heard your classmates use?"

"Counting on!" several students sang out.

"Making tens . . . I like making tens!" one of the children called out.

"Doubles . . . they are easy!" another affirmed.

"Doubles plus one and doubles minus one . . . they are trickier, but they are easy, too!" another student offered.

I was pleased to hear the students commenting that the use of different strategies made this problem accessible; their attitude was very positive. This was a problem they knew they could do. Rather than be dissuaded by the length of the number string, the students sounded eager to try out their strategies on a longer string of numbers.

"You have remembered many strategies we have used on other number strings. Look at this string and think about the strategies that would work best. Solve this number string. You might use words, you might use numbers, you might use pictures—you might use all three—to tell me what you did to figure out the answer. Check your papers over carefully. If you finish before it is time, you can turn your paper over and make up your own number string to solve." I handed out papers to students. As they received their paper, they quickly got up to go to their desks and begin working.

Students appeared capable and confident. There was little reluctance either to get started on solving the string or to record the methods used. Because my purpose was to assess students' use of strategies up to this point, my comments were more about acknowledging what they were doing rather than asking questions or commenting to prompt new understandings. After about ten or fifteen minutes, I called for the students' attention. I wanted to get a sense of how they were feeling about the task. After hearing their comments, I would give them a few minutes to finish up their work and then I would collect their papers for review.

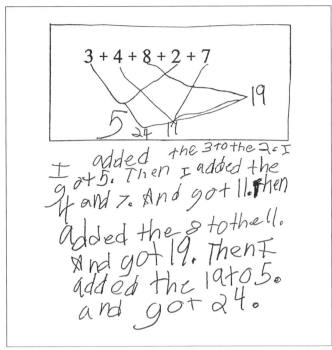

FIGURE 9–1 Perry clearly showed the process he went through, but his addition strategies are unclear.

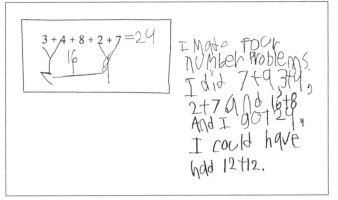

FIGURE 9–2 Matt also combined number pairs and was less effective in communicating strategies.

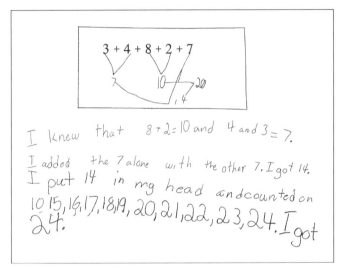

FIGURE 9–3 Liz looked for tens and made use of doubles.

"It looks like you really know what to do. You got started right away and there were no questions about what to do; everyone seemed to have a way to solve this long number string. How did it feel to work on this number string today?"

"It was easy!" said several of the students.

"Yeah, it looked hard but we have already used strategies, we know lots of them!" one stated.

"I finished really quickly!" another commented.

"I drew pictures, words, *and* numbers!" one student said.

"Can we do another one?" another asked.

"I want to finish this one so I can do my own on the back!" yet another exclaimed.

"It looks like most of you are just about finished solving the number string and explaining how you solved it," I said. "Take a couple more minutes to finish up your work and read what you have done and then I will collect your papers."

The students' work, which I later reviewed, revealed both understandings and confusions; it also gave me a good base on which to build future such exercises with these students. Perry's work was particularly interesting to me. (See Figure 9–1.) Perry clearly stated the process he went through: which numbers he added and the order in which he added them. I was curious about why he chose particular numbers to combine and whether he had internalized these number combinations or whether he used some

other kind of strategy. His explanation made it difficult for me to tell.

Matt's work was somewhat similar to Perry's. (See Figure 9–2.) I was not sure about the strategies he used to combine the number pairs he had chosen. He included some information about a related number pair, 12 + 12, that would result in the sum for this number string. Could he find the numbers within this string that could make this familiar double?

Liz's work made use of some familiar strategies; some were implied and some were clearly explained. (See Figure 9–3.) She had looked for tens and made use of doubles; Liz stated how she counted starting with fourteen and counted on ten. Again, I had questions. When she was left with two numbers to combine (10 and 14), did she deliberately choose the greater one from which to count on, or was this a random choice? Was she recording a strategy that had been demonstrated (counting on) or did she already know how to count on by tens from any number?

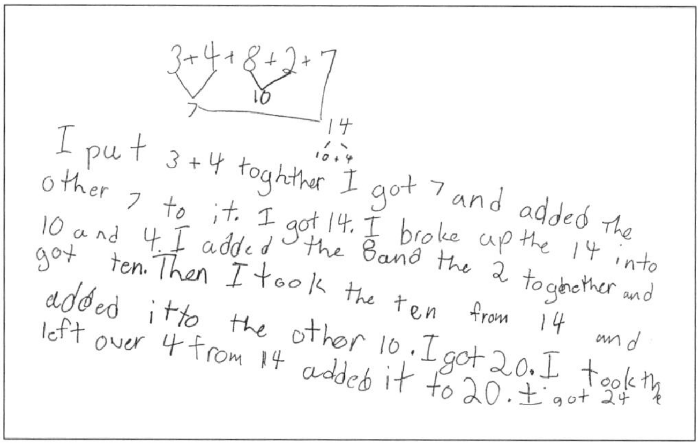

FIGURE 9–4 Shelley's paper demonstrates some place-value understandings that she made use of in efficient and flexible ways.

Shelley combined the first two pairs of numbers in the string in order. I wondered if combining these numbers first was due to the order in the string or some other reason. Shelley combined tens, as well as doubles. She also made use of tens in some flexible ways: rather than continually combining pairs of numbers like many of her peers, Shelley decomposed a sum—14—into 4 and 10. This decomposition allowed her to "pull out" another ten and combine it with the other ten. This decomposition let me know that Shelley had some place-value understandings that she made use of in some efficient and flexible ways. She was able to see that 14 could be made from a familiar double—7 + 7—and from tens and ones. This kind of understanding would be beneficial for Shelley when efficiently and flexibly operating on multidigit numbers. Sharing this understanding with her classmates would help them to develop this place-value knowledge as well. (See Figure 9–4.)

Linking Assessment and Instruction

As the students work, think about the following:

- Which students need materials to represent all the numbers in a string? Which are using counting-on strategies? Which are making use of number combinations?
- Which students are using strategies flexibly? Which students are using the same ones repeatedly?
- Are students acquiring strategies they have heard their classmates use?
- Are students able to explain their methods for adding strings of numbers, either aloud or in writing or both?
- Do students consider all the numbers in the string before combining them, or do they combine numbers in the order in which they appear?

Working with Story Problems

CHAPTER 10

OVERVIEW

In each of the lessons in this series, students are given a word problem. They discuss the features of the problem and contemplate possible ways of solving it. Students independently solve the problem, using methods they know and understand, then come back together to discuss the various methods used. The emphasis of each lesson is on making sense of the problem and considering various strategies for solving it. Students communicate how they solved the problem verbally and in writing. Throughout this process, they deepen their understanding of their own methods and broaden those of their classmates.

MATERIALS

- mathematics manipulatives and tools (base ten materials, snap cubes, beans, 1–100 charts)
- chart paper
- preprinted story problem, 1 per student (see Blackline Masters)

TIME

- three class periods

Teaching Directions

1. Present a story problem to the class, and then discuss with students the structure of the problem and possible methods for solving it.

2. Have students work independently to solve the problem in a way of their choosing.

3. Gather students to share a range of solution methods, talk about similarities and differences between methods, and discuss ways of representing their methods aloud and in writing.

Teaching Notes

It can be challenging for teachers to gauge students' level of understanding of computation procedures. Students may demonstrate an ability to follow the steps in any given procedure without truly making sense of how and why a particular one "works." When students are given opportunities to create and use alternative computation strategies, the focus shifts from repeated use of a misunderstood procedure to creating and using methods that make sense to them.

The methods students create and use to solve a problem depend upon many things, one of them being the structure of the problem itself. In order for students to develop different strategies for solving problems, it is important for them to be exposed to various types of problems. There are a wide range of problem "features": the presence/absence of action, nature of the unknown, and number magnitude are a few of these features. Varying these features is an important consideration when helping students develop a range of strategies for solving problems.

The Lesson

Day 1

Today I visited Mrs. Mason's second-grade class. Before going into the classroom, I considered the type of problem I wanted to give this group of second graders. Because it was my first time giving them a story problem, I wanted the experience to be accessible and successful. I chose a "joining" (addition) problem using a familiar context. I also gave them a choice of numbers to use. When giving them directions, I would use smaller numbers. I didn't want students to get "bogged down" in the wording of the story problem, the choice of number pairs, and the magnitude of the numbers in the pairs. By using a simpler type of problem—joining—and numbers that made a sum of twenty or less, I was attempting to keep the focus on thinking and problem solving. My choice of number pairs in both the demonstration problem and the actual one was deliberate: I chose pairs that allowed them to simply add tens to a quantity, one that resulted in a sum that was a multiple of ten, and one that forced them to "regroup." I would ask them to discuss what the problem was about, give them time to independently solve the problem, and then ask for volunteers to share a range of methods.

After the students came to the front of the room and sat down, I began by telling them about the problem. "Good morning, boys and girls. I am really excited about our lesson today. I love mathematics: giving students mathematics problems to solve and hearing about the ways that they go about solving them is really interesting to me. I wrote a problem about your teacher and I was hoping to give it to you and see what you do to solve it. Would that be OK?" Seven- and eight-year-olds can be extremely receptive and this group was no exception: most eagerly nodded their heads in response to my question.

"Did you know your teacher loves writing about as much as I love mathematics? Because she likes writing so much, she collects pencils. She has lots and lots of pencils and this story problem is about her pencils. I am going to write the story on the board, and then I would like your help reading it. I am going to do something a little odd: I am going to put some lines or 'blanks' in the problem. When you get to a blank, just say 'mmm' and then I will show you what those lines—the blanks—are for." I wrote the following on the board and then asked the

students to read it aloud to me as I touched each word on the board:

Mrs. Mason had _____ pencils.

She collected _____ more pencils.

How many pencils did Mrs. Mason have then?

(10, 4)   (12, 8)   (7, 8)

To make sure the students understood the problem, I said, "If you remember something about this story problem, could you raise your hand to tell us? I will call on some of you to remind us what this story is about."

Samuel went first. "It's about our teacher. She has a lot of pencils!" he said.

"She had some and she got some more," added Sylvia.

"We need to find out how many pencils she has," said Michelle.

The remaining hands went down, signaling that the students were out of ideas to add to the discussion. I waited a few moments to see if other students would venture to share some new ideas, but no other hands went up.

"These blanks in the story show places that need numbers. You get to choose what pair of numbers you want to use in the story. The number choices are below the story. You can use ten and four, twelve and eight, or seven and eight. The first number in the pair goes on the first blank in the story and the second number in the pair goes in the second blank. Can anyone explain what they think I mean?" It was time to let a student inform me about how clearly I gave my directions. A student's retelling of my directions might take a form more easily understood by the group.

Abbie spoke first. "You got to use the numbers under the story." She came up to the board. As she pointed to the places in the story to which she was referring, she wrote the numbers on the board. "Say you wanted to use the first numbers. Ten would go on the first line and four would go on the second line." She sat back down on the rug.

"What if I wanted to use this set of numbers?" I asked, pointing to the pair 12 and 8. "Then what would I do?"

Pedro came up to the board. "Twelve goes here," he said, pointing to the first blank, "and eight goes here," he said, pointing to the second.

I decided to ask the students to share tentative strategies. By so doing, we would reveal some of the students' repertoire of problem-solving strategies, allow access to those students unsure of how to begin, and provide students with opportunities to begin solving the problem. I said, "I wonder how you are going to go about figuring out how many pencils Mrs. Mason has. What do you think you will do?"

Josie had an idea. "I am going to get some cubes and pretend they are pencils. I am going to get seven cubes and then I am going to get eight cubes. Then I'm going to count them all to find the answer."

Josie realized that she could use materials other than pencils to solve the problem. I wanted to be certain that she knew why she was combining the two quantities to "find the answer." If I asked her to give an explanation, perhaps it would help her classmates understand her method as well. I reiterated her method. "You told us that you were going to take seven cubes and eight cubes. And you told us that you would pretend that the cubes were pencils. You told us how you would count them all to find the answer. I wonder why counting them all would tell you the answer?"

"Well, Mrs. Mason has some pencils and then she got some more. We have to add to figure out how many she has. I'm going to add the cubes together," Josie told us.

"I am going to draw a picture," Ramon said.

"Really? How might you start?" I asked. From what Ramon said, I could not tell if he would need to draw both quantities in the story or just one. His explanation would inform his classmates and me about whether he needed to use all the numbers in the story and "count all" or use one of the numbers in the story and "count on."

"I am going to draw seven pencils and then I am going to draw eight pencils. I am going to count them and that will tell me the answer," he said.

"You have heard some possible ways to solve the problem. I am going to ask you to try a way that you know and understand. You might want to try a way you just heard about, or another way. After you finish solving the problem, please tell me—in writing— what you did to find the answer to the problem. You will be doing your writing on this paper and I am going to give you different numbers to use than these." I stopped to erase the previous number pairs and replace them with the following:

(38, 30)   (47, 23)   (57, 25)

"You will use these numbers in the same way as we did with the first problem: the first number in the pair is used in the first blank in the story and the second number in the pair goes in the second. Any questions?" I asked, as I showed them the sheet on which the problem was printed.

"What do we do when we're done?" questioned Pedro.

"I will ask you to come back together in a group after you have had some time to work on the problem. If you finish before I call you, see if there is another way that you can solve the same problem. If you understand Ramon's or Josie's way, you could try one of their ways, or another way. You can also change the numbers in the problem, and see if you can solve the same problem with different numbers," I suggested.

"What will we do when we come back together?" asked Michelle.

"We will talk about some of the ways in which different people solved the problem," I answered. "While you are working, I will be walking around to see what different ways people are using. I may ask you if you could explain the method you used to the rest of the class."

"What if we don't want to?" Samuel asked shyly.

Samuel's question gave me the opportunity to explain to the students the value of having them share their independent thinking with their classmates. "Teaching us about your thinking might be a new experience for you. Being a teacher is scary sometimes! Telling us about your ideas is like giving us a 'big gift': we might learn a way from you that we would have never thought of by ourselves! If you teach us a new way, then we would have two ways to solve the problem, instead of just one. Now, we won't have time to hear about everyone's method of solving the problem. And I won't make you if you don't want to."

I handed out copies of the story problem to the students. They went to their seats and got out pencils. In the center of each group of four desks was a plastic shoebox containing snap cubes and base ten materials. Some students pulled out base ten blocks or snap cubes from the plastic shoeboxes. Others began drawing pictures on their papers. Some students started talking to other students who were sitting at their table groups. I walked around the room to get a sense of what students were doing. I stopped at Jamie's desk. He was hard at work, drawing pencils. On each he had drawn a point and a jagged edge to show where the pencil was sharpened. So far, he had drawn four. It would take him a very long time to draw all of the pencils that were indicated in the problem.

"Hi, Jamie. How's it going?" I asked.

"Good. I'm drawing the pencils! Do you like them?" he said proudly.

"I think you are a careful illustrator," I said, acknowledging his efforts. "Tell me a little about what you are doing."

"I am going to draw the pencils Mrs. Mason had, then the new pencils. I am going to count them all to find out how many she has."

"You explained your method really well. I can understand just what you are going to do," I told him. "I forgot to tell everyone some important information earlier. I forgot to say that, if you are going to draw a picture, you don't need to make fancy drawings. Do you know what I mean by fancy drawings?" I asked.

"Yeah, like mine. Mine are really fancy!" he said.

"Why might I say 'You don't need fancy drawings'?" I asked Jamie.

"Maybe I don't have time?" he responded.

"Yes, I am a little worried that you might not have time to make fancy drawings. Can you think of a way to make a really simple drawing of a pencil?"

"Like this!" said Jamie as he made a tally mark on his paper.

"Wow, you made a very quick drawing of a pencil! That is exactly what I meant when I said 'simple.'"

I stopped next by Josie's desk. She had some of the base ten cubes lying on her desk and she looked confused.

"I don't know what to do," she confessed.

"I bet you do know," I told her. "Let's see. Tell me what you know about the problem."

"Mrs. Mason likes pencils?" she asked.

"Yes, she does!" I confirmed. "What else do you know about the problem?"

"She had some and then she got some more," Josie added.

"Yes, that's true also," I acknowledged. Determining the point of confusion is like detective work. Perhaps the size of the new number pairs was overwhelming to Josie. By encouraging her to articulate what she did know, I was attempting to locate the place at which she needed my support. Josie seemed to understand the problem, and from her contributions in the prior discussion, she seemed to have a strategy for solving it as well; I wanted to be certain. "So, what will you do?" I asked.

"I am going to get seven cubes and eight cubes and count them," she told me. Josie was referring to the number pair from the class discussion, rather than the ones on her sheet.

"Show me the problem that you are working on," I asked. She pointed to the words on her paper. "Seven and eight are number choices we practiced with," I gently reminded her. "You have different number

choices on your paper. Can you find the choices you get to choose from?" She pointed to the pairs of numbers on her paper and read them aloud. "We could have used seven and eight for this problem. But I changed the numbers. Sneaky, huh? You have new number choices. Which numbers will you choose?"

Josie thought for a moment and then pointed to her paper. "Forty-seven and twenty-three."

"All right. And what will you do?" I asked.

"I am going to get forty-seven cubes and twenty-three cubes and count them," she answered.

"And by doing that, what will you find out?" I wanted to make sure she was connecting her method to the problem she had been asked to solve.

"How many pencils Mrs. Mason has," she said.

"OK. Do you mind if I watch you?" I asked, as she began taking cubes from the shoebox. She removed them one at a time until she had about twenty. I interrupted her. "Josie, I notice you are carefully taking out one cube at a time. Can you think of another way to make forty-seven, without having to use the single cubes?"

Josie smiled and nodded. "I can use these!" she exclaimed, and took some ten rods out of the shoebox. She separated out four and then counted aloud softly, "Ten, twenty, thirty, forty," and then took some of the single cubes that were already lying on her desk to continue, "forty-one, forty-two," all the way to forty-seven. She looked at me for confirmation.

"Tell me what you are thinking," I said. I didn't want to assume she had a full understanding of her problem-solving process.

"These are the pencils Mrs. Mason had," she said, as she touched the materials on the table. "Now I am going to get some more . . . twenty-three. Then I am going to count them."

I was almost ready to let her work on her own. I asked one last question, to ensure that she knew why her method "worked." "What will you know when you count them?" I asked.

"The answer," she said. "How many pencils Mrs. Mason has."

"Would you be willing to tell the class how you solved the problem?" I asked. Josie nodded. "When we come back together, bring the materials you used, OK? That will help others to see how you built the numbers."

Josie now had a method for solving the problem. She had worked through her initial confusion of how the practice problem related to the problem on her paper. Maybe she lacked confidence in her ability to use other, larger, number pairs. Josie's articulation of her thought processes seemed to alleviate both her confusion and lack of confidence. Working with her for a short time also gave me an opportunity to gently nudge her to consider grouping by tens, rather than counting single units. This skill—counting things in groups—is a critical step in her developing understanding of place value as well as her efficiency in computing with larger numbers.

I moved on to Tommie, who was writing on the back side of his paper.

"Hi, Tommie. How are you doing?" I asked.

"Fine. I'm working on the second problem!" Tommie turned his paper over to show me what he had written on the front:

40 plus 20 is 60. I added 7 and 3 and it = 10. Then I got 70.

Tommie had comfortably separated the numbers into tens and ones and then recombined them. His method was more sophisticated than Josie's or Jamie's, yet he could still benefit from some feedback on providing a clear explanation of his method. "You have been working hard!" I commented. "Could you read it to me?"

When Tommie had finished, I commented, "There is one little part I am not sure about. Could you tell me where you got the numbers you used?"

"I got the forty from the forty-seven and the twenty from the twenty-three," Tommie explained.

"OK. That makes sense. And the seven and the three?" I asked.

"I made the forty-seven into forty and seven and the twenty-three into twenty and three. I got the seven and three from the forty-seven and the twenty-three," he added.

"I understand how you got sixty and ten. I think I know, but I am not sure, how you got seventy. Can you tell me?" I asked.

"Oh! I get it! I didn't say, 'Sixty plus ten is seventy,'" he said.

"No, you didn't. That's where I thought seventy came from. It would help me remember that if you wrote that on your paper. Could you do that?"

Tommie nodded and made the addition to his paper. (See Figure 10–1.) He agreed to share his method with the entire class.

To prepare students for the impending whole-class discussion, I got their attention and let them know that they had just a couple of minutes to finish recording. I stopped by Jamie's desk, and invited him also to share his method with his classmates. He readily agreed.

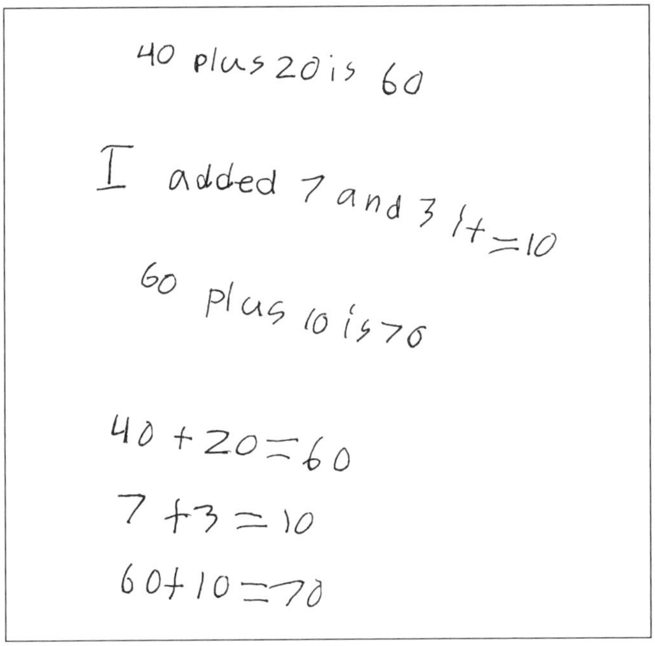

40 plus 20 is 60

I added 7 and 3 It = 10

60 Plus 10 is 70

40 + 20 = 60
7 + 3 = 10
60 + 10 = 70

FIGURE 10–1 Tommie revised his work to include missing steps.

When the students were gathered on the rug with their papers, I began our session by setting expectations for listening. I informed them that some of their classmates would be "teaching" and that they might learn a way of solving the problem that they might never have considered on their own. I asked them how they could tell if someone was listening to them and they aptly named a variety of behaviors, which we were able to condense to the following: *They are looking at you. Their bodies are still.*

I invited Josie to go first. She had brought the base ten materials with her to the rug, and demonstrated with these as she explained her method for solving the problem.

"I used forty-seven and twenty-three," Josie began, referring to the number pairs that she had picked. "I got four tens and seven ones and two tens and three ones. I put the tens together and then I put the ones together. I went ten, twenty, thirty, forty, fifty, sixty, then sixty-one, sixty-two, sixty-three, sixty-four, sixty-five, sixty-six, sixty-seven, sixty-eight, sixty-nine, seventy."

"So you counted by tens, then ones," I said.

"Yeah," answered Josie. "I counted these by tens and these by ones," she explained, touching first the base ten materials and then the single cubes.

"Did anyone else use the blocks?" I asked. A few students responded by raising their hands.

Josie had modeled both quantities in the problem using manipulatives. I asked Jamie to go next, since he

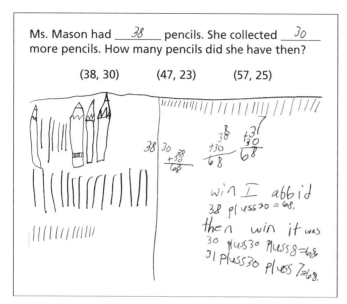

Ms. Mason had ___38___ pencils. She collected ___30___ more pencils. How many pencils did she have then?

(38, 30)   (47, 23)   (57, 25)

win I abbid
38 pluss 20 = 68,
then win it was
30 pluss 30 pluss 8 = 68,
31 pluss 30 pluss 7 = 68.

FIGURE 10–2   Jamie represented both quantities in the problem with pictures.

had also represented both quantities, but he had used pictures. This would be a good opportunity for students to see the connections between the two methods.

Jamie showed his paper to the class as he explained what he had done. (See Figure 10–2.) "I made thirty-eight pencils and thirty pencils and I counted them. I got sixty-eight."

"Thank you, Jamie," I said. "I wonder if anyone else drew a picture and counted to find the answer." Several students raised their hands.

To clarify Jamie's method of counting by ones, I asked, "Can you show us how you counted? You don't need to count them all . . . just a few."

"Like this," Jamie said. "One, two, three, four, five, six, seven, eight, nine, ten, eleven, twelve . . . is that OK?"

"That's perfect," I confirmed. "Thank you for showing us how you counted by ones."

I wanted to make it clear to the students that, while Josie and Jamie had chosen different numbers, their problem-solving methods were similar: each had represented both numbers in the problem and counted to find the total. Josie had counted using groups of tens, while Jamie had counted by ones. The tools each had used also differed: Jamie had drawn a picture while Josie had used base ten materials. I wanted them to appreciate that both methods had yielded valid solutions to the problem.

"You have seen two methods for solving the problem," I said. "Jamie and Josie chose different numbers. How were their methods for solving the problem the same?" The students did not

immediately respond. I waited in silence to give them time to think about the question.

Michelle spoke first. "Josie made the numbers. So did Jamie."

"Tell us more about that," I said.

"Josie made the numbers with the blocks. Jamie made the numbers with pencils and tally marks," Michelle explained.

"They counted," Samuel added.

"What do you mean?" I inquired.

"They had to count to get the answer," he said.

"Did anyone notice how Josie and Jamie counted?" I asked. "Were their counting methods the same or different?"

"I think they are different, because Josie counted by tens and ones, but Jamie just counted by ones," Pedro suggested.

"So, Josie's and Jamie's ways of solving the problem were similar in some ways and different in others. Are they different in any other ways?"

Sylvia spoke up. "Josie used blocks and Jamie used pictures."

"Josie showed us with the base ten stuff and Jamie showed us his pictures," Sonia added.

I asked Tommie to talk about his way of solving the problem. Tommie moved to the front of the group and held up his paper. "I used forty-seven and twenty-three," he said, and then read from his paper. "Forty plus twenty is sixty. I added seven and three. It equals ten. Sixty plus ten is seventy."

"Did anyone else use numbers, like Tommie did?" I asked. A couple of students raised their hands. Tommie's method was more sophisticated than the other two methods presented. While Josie and Jamie had represented each number in the problem with materials—Josie with base ten materials and Jamie with tally marks—Tommie's method used abstractions—numbers—to represent these quantities. Rather than counting, Tommie decomposed the numbers in the problem into "friendly" chunks: tens and ones. He recombined these chunks in ways that made sense to him. He recognized some important understandings about place value: that the 4 in 47 represented forty, and the 7 represented seven. If he had not understood the value of each digit, this method would not have "worked."

I guided a discussion of the connections between the three methods. "You have heard three different ways that students used to solve the problem," I began. "Jamie and Josie and Tommie. Think about Tommie's way. How is his way different from and similar to what Josie and Jamie did?" Several hands went up.

"Tommie used numbers and so did Jamie and Josie," one student said.

"But Tommie just used numbers. Jamie used tally marks and Josie used blocks," another offered.

"Tommie used tens. Josie used tens, too. She went, 'Ten, twenty, thirty,' like that. Tommie went, 'Forty and twenty.' Those are tens numbers," said yet another.

Students continued to share their perceptions of how the demonstrated methods were alike and different. We ended our discussion by recounting the importance of listening to another person's method for solving problems and considering the use of these three students' methods when encountering story problems in the future.

Day 2

On Day 2 of the lesson, I wanted to provide some challenges for the students while continuing to encourage them to think about ways of representing story problems on paper. The previous lesson's problem was a "joining problem": the language used "directed" the students to add two quantities. I wanted to try a new problem that had some challenging features: no obvious "joining" action and a challenging number size.

I greeted the class and asked, "What do you remember about our last lesson?"

"You gave us a problem!" one student exclaimed.

"We tried one problem and then we got a harder one to do," another offered.

"We got to do it any way we wanted to," said another.

"We talked about how the ways were the same and not the same," another commented.

From these and other animated responses, I knew that the students had found our last session challenging, yet positive. Students recalled some important features from the first session: solving problems in ways that made sense to them and explaining these methods to others. Students made connections between the methods that were discussed and realized that peers could teach each other new problem-solving approaches.

"I am impressed by what you remember about our last lesson and what you know about solving problems," I said. "We are going to do something similar today: we will talk about a problem, take time to solve it in a way that you understand, then come back together to talk about some of the methods you used. I'm hoping that we'll learn some new ways of solving problems today, and of recording those ways

on paper. I am going to write the problem on the board. Please read it to yourself as I write it down." I wrote the following on the board:

_____ *children were playing soccer.*

_____ *were boys and the rest were girls.*

How many girls were playing soccer?

(7, 3)   (20, 10)   (23, 12)

I asked the students to read aloud with me as I touched each word. After we finished reading the story problem, I asked the students to explain what they knew about the problem.

"There are children playing soccer," one student said.

"Boys and girls are playing, just like the kids at our school!" said another.

I waited for other contributions, but the students had grown quiet. I had anticipated that this type of problem would be more challenging to the students and their silence confirmed my suspicions. While the first problem implied addition, this problem was not as straightforward. Here there were two "givens": a "whole" (children playing soccer) and "a part of the whole" (the number of boys playing soccer). I quickly considered what support I could give the students to make the problem and its solution more accessible, while retaining the challenge.

"Let's take a moment to recall what these numbers are for," I suggested, pointing to the number pairs below the word problem. Perhaps inserting numbers into the problem would diminish some of the confusion. "OK, I am going to pick the first numbers," I said. "Remind me what I do."

"Write 'seven' on the first blank and 'three' on the second blank," Jamie said.

I did this and then turned back to the class. "Let's read it again and see what it says now," I suggested. I touched the words and the students read them aloud with me. "I wonder if anyone has some more information about the problem and can tell us what it is about," I said.

"There are seven children playing," one of the students said.

"Three boys are playing," another offered.

"Oh! I get it!" yet another exclaimed. "We have to find out how many girls there are!"

While we seemed to be approaching some understanding of the problem, there were still a limited number of students willing to share what they understood.

"There are some tricky things about story problems," I suggested. "There is some information given in the story problem and then some information that you have to figure out. There are some things you know, and some things you don't know. What are some things we know in the problem? What are some things we don't know?"

"We know there are children playing soccer," one student said.

"Seven children are playing," another clarified.

"We know how many boys. There are three boys," said another.

"So there are four girls!" another responded excitedly. This comment was met with opposition by several students.

"Huh? It doesn't say that!" one said.

"We don't know that!" declared another.

"Let me ask my question again," I said. "What do we know and what do we have to figure out?"

"We don't know how many girls. That's why it says, 'How many girls were playing soccer?'" one said.

"But I know! I know there's four," another said.

"The story doesn't tell you that. You figured it out!" said the first student.

It wasn't clear to me what portion of the class understood the problem. More students were engaged in the discussion of its features at this point, but I could hear in some of the students' voices both frustration and confusion. I decided to move the discussion in the direction of tentative strategies. I restated what had been discussed and asked students to think about what they might do to solve the story problem.

"Let's talk about what we do know," I began. "There is a group of boys and girls playing soccer. Do we know how large that group is?"

"Yeah! There's seven!" the students chorused.

"OK, so there is a group of seven soccer players. This group is made up of boys . . ."

"And girls!" the students sang out.

"So we have seven soccer players and some are boys and some are girls. I know there are seven players. I also know . . ."

"Three are boys!"

I wasn't sure that the entire class was with me at this point. But since I would have an opportunity to assess their understanding when they'd begun independent work on the problem, I continued.

"Seven soccer players, three of them are boys, and we don't know how many . . ."

"Girls! We don't know how many girls!" several of the students called out.

"Hmm," I said. "I wonder what you will do to figure out the answer. Is anyone willing to tell us how you might begin?"

Sylvia had an idea. "I am going to draw the children, seven of them. I am going to circle the boys. I am going to count the rest."

Samuel spoke up next. "I am going to use my fingers," he said. "I am going to start with the boys: three." Samuel held up three fingers. "I am going to keep putting up fingers until I get to seven . . . the number of kids." Samuel extended one finger at a time as he counted aloud: "Four, five, six, seven. There's four girls, because I put up four more fingers."

Pedro wanted to contribute. "I am going to use cubes: seven," he said. "I am going to take out the boys . . . three. What's left are the girls."

Although I knew that it would be a challenge for them, I decided that it was time to see what the children would do on their own with this problem. I erased the number pairs and wrote in new ones: 45 and 20, 50 and 26, and 63 and 28. I chose these number pairs deliberately. I was curious to see if students that chose the first pair of numbers would use their understanding of how to add or subtract tens to or from any number, if those choosing the second pair would connect these numbers with their knowledge of money or doubles, and if those choosing the last pair of numbers would find the need to "regroup" or "rename" a ten problematic.

"Some of your classmates have shared the ways they might solve this problem," I said. "Take a moment to think about those ways. If one of them makes sense to you, use it. If it doesn't, think of another way. Remember: It is important to use a way that you understand. I am going to hand out the problem and I'd like you to record how you solved it. You will have some time to work on your own, and then I will be inviting some of you to share with your classmates how you solved the problem. Who remembers what to do if you finish solving the problem before the rest of the class has finished?"

"You can solve the same problem in a different way," one of the students responded.

"You can use different numbers and solve the problem again," another said.

"You look ready to begin," I commented. I began distributing papers. As they took a sheet, students got up and went to their seats.

Many students began taking base ten materials or snap cubes out of the shoeboxes in the center of each group of four desks. Some retrieved 1–100 charts. A few students looked confused, but most of these second graders looked engaged, reading the problem, writing on their papers, or manipulating the materials they had gotten out to use. I began circulating the classroom to assess students' understanding, to ask questions, to clarify information, and to determine approaches that would be appropriate for students to share during our whole-class discussion.

Most students seemed to have found a way of solving the problem. A few, however, seemed only to be going through the motions: choosing numbers, selecting an operation, and performing it, whether or not the operation made sense in this particular context. Andrea was one such student. On her paper, she had drawn two groups of tally marks, one with forty-five and the other with twenty tally marks. She had carefully labeled one group *chidren all togeter* and the other *boy's*. She had obviously counted the groups by fives, marking each group *5, 10, 15*, and so on. She had circled the total number of tally marks in each and had written equations at the bottom of her paper. One of the equations was circled. Unfortunately, while all of the equations were correct, none of them represented a way to solve this particular problem:

$$
\begin{array}{ccc}
45 & 65 & 45 \\
+20 & -20 & -25 \\
\hline
\text{(65)} & 45 & 20 \\
\end{array}
$$

"Hi, Andrea. How are you doing?" I began.

"OK," she said, looking somewhat doubtful.

"Can you tell me a little bit about what you are doing?" I asked.

"Here are the children playing soccer," she explained, pointing to the larger group of tally marks on her paper, "and here are the boys."

"I see that. You labeled those groups as well," I told her. "What did you find out?"

"The answer is sixty-five," she told me. "That's why I circled it."

Andrea had told me a little about what she had written on her paper, but she had not told me what she understood about the problem. "You have really worked hard on this paper," I began. "You took some time to make these marks. You used helpful labels to show what the tally marks are for and you also showed how you can count by fives. You even included equations at the bottom of your paper. Could you remind me about what is happening in this story problem?"

Andrea read the problem aloud to me, inserting the numbers she had chosen rather than telling me what the problem was about. She was more comfortable reading what was written on her paper than explaining to me her understanding of the problem's solution. I tried a different approach: using smaller numbers. If the numbers were less cumbersome, perhaps we could put the focus on the challenging features of the problem.

"You read that very carefully, Andrea. Can we try something? What if I changed the numbers here? What if I said that, instead of forty-five children playing soccer, there were only three? And what if I said that, instcad of twenty boys, there was only one? What if the problem was this one: 'Three children were playing soccer. One was a boy and the rest were girls. How many girls were playing soccer?' What would you do?"

Andrea made two sets of cubes, one with three and the other with one. She sat for a moment, looking at what she had constructed. I waited for several moments before I spoke. "Tell me about those cubes," I prodded.

"These are the children," she said, pointing to the three cubes, "and this is the boy," she said, pointing to the single cube. "Two are girls." She put the single cube back into the shoebox. "These are the kids and *this* is the boy," she explained again, this time pulling one cube out of the group of three. These are the two girls," she said, touching the remaining two cubes.

"Tell me about that cube you put back in the shoebox," I said.

"I didn't need that. The boy is already here," she said, touching the single cube.

"What if I changed the numbers on you again? What if I said there were ten children playing soccer and three of them were boys and the rest were girls. Could you use the same strategy to figure out the answer?" I asked.

Andrea took some more cubes out of the shoebox. She counted aloud until she had ten cubes and then put the rest of the cubes back into the shoebox. "Here are the children playing soccer," she confirmed, touching the group of ten cubes, "and these are the boys." She pushed aside three cubes, then counted those remaining. "Seven are girls," she concluded. "Here they are."

"I wonder if you used the same method here with the cubes as you did on your paper with tally marks," I said. Andrea looked up at me skeptically. "Which way did you best understand, the tally mark way or the cube way?" I asked.

"The cubes," she said.

"Could you try that way, if you understand it best? There's one problem: the numbers aren't three and one or ten and three. The numbers are forty-five and twenty. What would you do if there were forty-five children playing soccer and twenty were boys and the rest were girls? What would you do?"

Andrea explained how she would take forty-five cubes and then count out twenty of them to represent the boys and then count the rest to see how many girls were playing soccer. After satisfying myself that that method made sense to her, I left her to work on her own. It was clear to me that Andrea's understanding of this type of problem was still fragile. More experience with problems of this sort, as well as hearing approaches used by her classmates, would help her to gain confidence in approaching problems with a similar structure in the future.

When I walked by David's desk, I saw that he was using a 1–100 chart. I had seen him use this tool before, and I know that it is common for students to get comfortable with a particular method and use it frequently; the 1–100 chart is a familiar tool for students to use for "counting on." While it is important that students show confidence in how and why a method and tool "works," it is important for the teacher to determine how and when to gently push a student to consider a more efficient method or more sophisticated use of a tool. If this had been the first time I had noticed David using the 1–100 chart for counting on, I would not have felt the need to intervene. My experience in observing David led me to think that this was an opportune time to help him extend his thinking.

"Good morning, David. I see you are using the hundred chart. Can you show me what you are doing?"

"Well, I started with twenty-eight. That's the number of boys. I counted the numbers to sixty-three. That's the number of children playing. I got thirty-five numbers. That's how many girls there are." David demonstrated what he had done, starting with 28 and counting the number of boxes until he "landed" on 63. David had counted by ones, something he had repeatedly done in the past. Today I would ask him to consider counting in a "new" way, although I knew that this would be new only in the context of solving a story problem. During other lessons, I noticed that David had used the 1–100 chart to count by tens, a much more efficient strategy than counting by ones.

"Wow! You explained that well. You know what I know about you? You are an expert with a hundred chart!" David beamed. I continued. "I heard you count aloud, very carefully," I said. "I heard you say, 'One, two, three,' all the way to thirty-five. Do you know what we call that type of counting?"

"By ones!" he said matter-of-factly.

"Yes! I wonder if you know a faster way to count on the hundred chart."

"I could try counting by tens!" he said. David touched 28. As he moved to 38, 48, 58, and 68, he said, "Ten, twenty, thirty, forty. Uh oh! I went too far!" David had realized that he had gone past 63. Rather than provide him with support, I bided my time to see what he would do to compensate. He thought for a few seconds, then located 28 and counted by tens again, this time stopping at 58 and counting by ones to 63. "Ten, twenty, thirty, thirty-one, thirty-two, thirty-three, thirty-four, thirty-five. Thirty-five! It's still thirty-five!"

"You sound surprised! Tell me what you are thinking," I said.

"That was fast!" he said. "I like that way better!"

"So now you have two ways. You know how to count by ones," I began.

"And tens!" he said proudly.

Most students had finished solving the problem after about fifteen minutes. I had selected a few students who had agreed to present different approaches or different representations of their approaches to the whole class. After giving the students a "two-minute warning," I asked them to put away their materials, leave their papers at their desks unless they had been asked to share, and come to the rug for a class discussion.

Students assembled themselves on the rug at the front of the room. Three students had brought their papers with them and one of them had brought some materials as well. I began our discussion by reviewing with the class our purpose in listening to classmates share their problem-solving approaches, and reminding the students what is expected of good listeners.

I had given some careful consideration to the order of the three student presentations. Two of the methods were similar: they involved showing the whole quantity, marking off or "separating out" the part, and counting what remained. Both used models that seemed to clearly represent the problem and would be accessible to the whole class. I decided to have these two students begin and have the third student, Samuel, go last. I had posted two pieces of chart paper on the board in the front of the room, so that I could record for the class each student's strategy.

I would ask questions to make sure the process was reflected through words, an illustration, and an equation. Having a model of different methods used to solve this problem would be helpful in the future. When solving new problems, we could revisit the tools, strategies, and representations to see if previous methods might be applicable to new situations.

Sylvia went first. She stood up in front of the room and looked around to see if she had her classmates' attention. When she was satisfied that the class was ready, she read her paper aloud and showed it to her classmates. Her paper was organized and neat.

When students use tally marks, cubes, fingers, or other tools for solving a problem, I want to ensure that they understand how the tool represents the problem. Asking students to help "re-create" Sylvia's method would engage them in retelling, allowing me to check for understanding and providing me with an opportunity to model representation.

"Can someone explain what Sylvia did? I want to write down her way of solving this problem. We might want to use it in the future, when we are solving new problems," I explained. "What was the first thing she did?"

I wrote Sylvia's name on the chart and turned back to the group. As the students collaborated in a retelling of what their classmate had done, I asked questions to supply missing information or clarify what was said.

"She drew tally marks," Pedro said.

"How many tally marks?" I asked.

"Forty-five," he responded.

I wrote on the chart, *I drew 45 tally marks.* "What did she do next?" I asked.

"She circled some tally marks," Ramon offered.

"What did those marks represent?" I asked.

"They were the number of boys," Michelle stated. "She circled the number of boys and there were twenty."

I added to the chart, *I circled the number of boys, 20.* "What did Sylvia do next?"

"She counted the rest of the tally marks by fives," Sonia said. "Those were the number of girls." I added this information to the chart.

"What did Sylvia find out?" I inquired.

"Twenty-five girls were playing soccer," Sylvia offered. I wrote these words on the chart.

"What did Sylvia do to show her method for figuring out how many girls were playing soccer?" I asked.

Josie spoke up. "She made groups of tally marks. She made all the kids—forty-five—and then circled the boys. She counted the rest. Those were the girls."

I began drawing on the chart. As I drew, I asked questions to make sure that the students were seeing the connection between what was being drawn and what was stated in the problem. After I had drawn all forty-five tally marks, I made an imaginary circle around them, asking, "Remind me: what did these marks have to do with the story?"

"The children," one student said.

"The boys and girls altogether," said another.

"The soccer players," said a third.

I labeled the group of forty-five tally marks *children playing soccer.* "OK," I continued. "Now I am going to circle these, twenty of them. Remind me why I need to do that."

"Those are the boys," several students affirmed.

"You have to show which ones are the boy soccer players," one said.

I circled the group and wrote *boys* inside the circle. "And what do I need to do now?" I asked.

"Count the rest," some of the students chimed.

"The rest are the girls," another said.

"That's what Sylvia found out: there were twenty-five girls," another explained.

I labeled the group of remaining tally marks: *girls.*

"Is there a way that I can write an equation to show what Sylvia did?" I asked.

"She started with forty-five tally marks, so you could write 'forty-five,'" Tommie suggested.

"She took away—subtracted—twenty," added Jamie. "So you'd write 'minus twenty.' And the answer was twenty-five, the number of girls."

As I wrote, I reiterated what Jamie and Tommie had said. Whenever I paused, various students sang out the missing information.

"She started with forty-five tally marks," I began, "the number . . ."

"Of children playing soccer!" several children finished.

"She subtracted the number of boys," I continued, "and she showed that by . . ."

"Circling tally marks!" was the response.

"She counted the rest of the tally marks . . ." I said.

"To find the answer for how many girls were playing soccer!" the students answered.

"Why do you suppose I put a box around 'twenty-five'?" I asked.

"That's the answer," one student asserted.

"That's what we were trying to find out," said another. "That's how many girls were playing soccer!"

The chart looked like this:

Sylvia: I drew 45 tally marks. I circled the number of boys, 20. The rest I counted by fives and those were the number of girls. 25 girls were playing soccer.

Children playing soccer

$$45 - 20 = \boxed{25}$$

Sylvia had used a method in which she modeled all the numbers in the problem. She showed the whole—the number of children playing soccer—and the part—the number of boys playing soccer. She used tally marks, grouped by fives, to represent her method. The method of our second student presenter was a similar one.

"Now we are going to hear how Alba solved the problem," I said. "Listen for ways that show how Alba's method is similar to and different from Sylvia's way."

Alba came to the front of the group with her paper and some base ten materials. She showed her paper to the class and explained what she had done with the materials. (See Figure 10–3.)

"I got six of these," she said, showing the six tens, "and three of these. That's sixty-three, the number of children playing soccer. I took away two of these tens, but I couldn't take away eight, because I can't break them off. So I just pretended." Alba laid two tens to

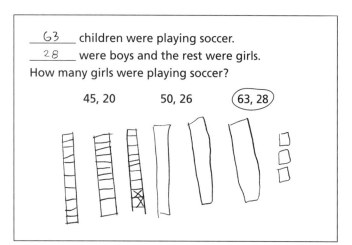

FIGURE 10–3   Alba modeled the problem using base ten materials.

the side and showed the eight on the third ten. She went on. "So there's two here," she explained, showing the two ones remaining on the ten she "pretended" to break up into two pieces: one with eight ones and one with two ones. "And so there's three tens and these three ones. That's thirty-five. There's thirty-five girls playing soccer."

Alba had modeled the problem with the materials; Sylvia had modeled it with tally marks. She had shown—and drawn—the whole and marked the part that represented the boys. The remaining materials represented the girls and she showed how she counted them to find the answer. I asked students to retell what Alba had done, again asking questions to fill in missing or unclear parts of the explanation. We collaborated on an equation to match her method. I wrote and drew the following on the chart:

Alba: I got 6 tens and 3 ones for the 63 children playing soccer. I took out the 28: the number of boys. I counted the rest and got 35. There were 35 girls playing soccer.

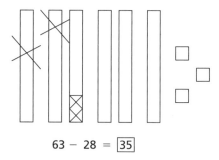

$$63 - 28 = \boxed{35}$$

Before the last student presentation, we discussed how Sylvia's method and Alba's method were similar and different. Students noticed how each had shown the number of students playing soccer, one with tally marks and one with base ten materials. Students explained how each had removed the number of boys and counted what remained to find the number of girls playing soccer. Students recognized different counting methods. Sylvia counted by ones as she made the tally marks in groups of five. She counted the remaining tally marks by fives. Alba used tens and ones to represent the players in the problem and she counted by tens and ones throughout the problem.

Samuel was the last student to represent how he had solved the problem. Whereas Sylvia and Alba modeled all of the numbers in the problem—the whole as well as the parts—Samuel used a more sophisticated method: counting on.

"I started with twenty-eight and I counted to sixty-three," Samuel explained.

Rather than making the whole and separating out the part and counting what remained—"counting three times"—Samuel knew that he could begin with a part and "count on" to the whole in order to find the other "missing part." However, Samuel's explanation was sparse. Asking him some questions would give him the opportunity to make his thinking more explicit to his classmates.

"Could you remind us why you started with twenty-eight?" I began.

"That's the number of boys there were," he replied. "I counted to the number of children there were."

"How did you keep track of your counting?" I asked.

"I used tally marks . . . right here," Samuel explained, pointing to his paper.

"How about we make a larger drawing of what you did?" I suggested. "We can count out loud while I draw the marks. Now, remind us what number we are starting with and why, and what number we are counting to and why," I requested. Samuel explained to us that we would be starting with the number of boys, and counting to the total number of children playing soccer, and that that would tell us how many girls there were.

I drew tallies as students counted aloud from twenty-eight to sixty-three. Student volunteers helped to provide an explanation for what Samuel had done so that I could record these words on the chart. It looked like this:

Samuel: I started with the number of boys playing soccer, 28. I counted by ones to the number of children playing soccer. I kept track with tally marks. The tally marks show the number of girls that played soccer. There were 35 girls playing soccer.

TᕼᏗ TᕼᏗ TᕼᏗ TᕼᏗ TᕼᏗ TᕼᏗ TᕼᏗ

Sylvia and Josie had used a "separating out," subtraction strategy. Samuel had used a strategy of "counting on," or addition. His equation would reflect this difference.

"If we were to think about an equation that would match what Samuel did, what would we do? How did he begin?" I asked.

"He started with twenty-eight," Ramon said.

Michelle added, "He counted up . . . he added."

I wrote on the board: *28 +*

The class grew silent. I waited a few moments, and a few students raised their hands tentatively.

"I think he added thirty-five," Alba suggested. "Those were the tally marks he drew."

"Yeah. He had the number of boys—twenty-eight—and he added the number of girls—thirty-five.

The answer was the number of children playing," offered Jamie.

"Does anyone else have some ideas about how to show Samuel's way using an equation?" I requested.

"He started with twenty-eight, so we have to start with twenty-eight!" Pedro insisted.

"See, that's the boys. Boys plus girls equals the kids!" added Ramon.

"Oh!" exclaimed Sonia. "So, twenty-eight plus thirty-five equals sixty-three! That's the boys—twenty-eight—plus the thirty-five for the girls—gives you the answer: sixty-three!"

"Wait!" David said. "I thought the answer was thirty-five."

Such confusion among students can be intimidating to teachers, but often children's need for clarification provides a rich opportunity to push them toward understanding. When students look at an equation, they typically regard the number that follows the equals sign as "the answer." I wanted the students to understand that in this example, an equation was a symbolic, "shorthand" way of presenting the story, another representation.

"Let's see what we have discussed so far. Samuel began with a number," I started.

"Twenty-eight!" was the unanimous response.

I pointed to the 28 I had already written on the board. "Now, did Samuel add or subtract? What do you think? And why do you think so?"

"I think he added, because he counted on," said David.

"He went, 'twenty-nine, thirty, thirty-one,'" offered Michelle. "That's counting up, and when you count up, you are adding."

"He added boys plus girls," added Jamie.

"So, he started with the number of boys—twenty-eight—and he added," I said, pointing to the plus sign on the board. "I wonder what would come next in the equation. What do you think and why do you think so?"

"He counted up, thirty-five," said Tommie.

"He added the number of girls and there were thirty-five, the number of tally marks we drew," explained Alba.

Samuel confirmed what his classmates had said. "Yeah, I plussed—added—thirty-five."

I wrote *35* on the board. "Hmm . . . now what?" I asked.

"Well, that equals sixty-three," said Josie. "That's the number of kids."

"Yeah, boys and girls together makes sixty-three. The problem told us that!" added Sonia.

I wrote = *63* on the board. "OK. I wonder where the box goes. The box goes around the number that we were trying to figure out . . . the missing number."

"It goes around the thirty-five; that's the number we had to find out," said Michelle.

"Yeah! 'Girls' was missing," said Ramon.

Most students were nodding their heads, so I drew a box around the 35.

$$28 + \boxed{35} = 63$$

"Who can explain what this equation has to do with Samuel's way of solving the problem?" I asked.

"He started with twenty-eight and he added thirty-five and he got sixty-three," one of the students said.

"He added the boys to the girls and he got sixty-three," another responded.

"He didn't know the number of girls at first. So he started with the number of boys and he counted to sixty-three. That was thirty-five. That's the number of girls," said another.

Another gave a definitive summation. "We were trying to find out the number of girls . . . that's what was missing. That's why thirty-five has the box around it. We didn't know that and we had to figure that out."

We ended our discussion by finding the similarities and differences between Samuel's method and the two previous methods. We reviewed why we were taking the time to learn about a variety of approaches to solving a problem, and I posted the chart as a resource for students to use.

Day 3

"Joining" and "separating" problems have *action*. In working with them, students are guided by this stated action; they receive support for solving the problem from the way in which the problem is worded. In part–whole situations, action is not inherent in the problem; without an obvious "joining" or "separating" context, students find it challenging to determine what to "do" with the numbers. For this reason, I decided on Day 3 to present a problem that again contained action, while also offering students a challenge in that the features of this problem would be different from the previous two. I worded the problem this way:

_____ *children were on the playground.*

Some children went inside their classrooms.

_____ *were still on the playground.*

How many children went inside their classrooms?

I provided a familiar context for the children: the playground. In Lesson 1 they had encountered a joining problem containing action: students knew the beginning quantity and the quantity that was joined to the beginning quantity, and they needed to determine the resulting quantity. Lesson 2 involved a part–whole problem, which, by nature, had no action: students knew the quantity in the "whole" and the quantity in a "part" of the whole and they needed to find the quantity in the missing part. This time, I chose a problem that involved a "separating" action. The problem began with an initial quantity, an unknown quantity was separated out, and a quantity remained. Students would choose numbers to represent the number of students playing on the playground at the beginning and at the end of the story; their task was to determine the number—the "change"—that occurred in the middle of the problem.

I gathered the students on the rug and directed their attention to the piece of chart paper on which I had written the new problem. While they watched, I wrote the word *Problem* across the top of the chart.

"It looks like we have another story problem to solve," I began. "This problem looks something like the others we worked on previously, doesn't it? It has blanks in it just like the others, and I will once again ask you to solve it using a method that you understand. We will end our math period like we did before: coming back together as a class and listening to how some of you solved the problem."

We then read the problem aloud, and discussed what is happening in the problem and tentative methods for solving it. I wrote some practice number pairs on the board, and we used them to think about tentative strategies:

(10, 7)   (15, 8)   (22, 8)

"I'd like you to choose a number pair and solve the problem," I explained. "Pay attention to how you solved the problem. When you are done, please place your hands on your knees so I know you are finished." When most of the students had their hands on their knees, I asked for volunteers to share how they'd solved the problem.

"I know!" said Samuel. "It's seven. See? I used fifteen and eight. Fifteen kids were playing and I minused until I got to eight, like this: fourteen, thirteen, twelve, eleven, ten, nine, eight." Samuel counted backward on his fingers, putting up one finger at a time, until he "got to" the number of children left on the playground. He showed us the seven fingers and said, "It's seven. That's the number of children that went in."

"So you started with . . ." I began.

"Fifteen!" many students responded.

"Yes, the number of students on the playground," I continued, "and you 'minused'—subtracted—the number of students . . ."

"The number of students still on the playground!" one of the students said.

"Yeah! To get to the number of students that went in!" another added.

"He subtracted seven," said a third.

"He counted back . . . that's subtracting," another clarified.

"Did anyone solve the problem in a different way or use different numbers?" I asked.

"I used twenty-two and eight," said Josie. "I started with eight and went up to twenty-two."

"Tell us what eight and twenty-two mean in the story," I said. I wanted to make sure that the students continued to refer back to and connect with the story, and were not just "doing something with the numbers."

"Eight is the number of kids that were on the playground in the end. Twenty-two is the number outside—on the playground—in the beginning, before some kids went in," she explained.

"OK," I said. "You said you 'went up.' Show us what you did," I said.

"I started with eight in my head and then I counted up to the number of children that were on the playground before some went in," Josie said. She put up a finger at a time, as she counted aloud, "Nine, ten, eleven, twelve, thirteen, fourteen, fifteen, sixteen, seventeen, eighteen, nineteen, twenty, twenty-one, twenty-two." Josie had used all ten fingers, then used four more. I was curious to see how she would explain. "That's fourteen. See? Ten," and she showed us ten fingers, "and four," and she showed us four more fingers, "that's fourteen! Fourteen students went in."

"So, Samuel started with . . ." I began.

"Fifteen!" the children chorused.

"The number of children on the playground," I added. "And he . . ."

"Took away the kids that were still on the playground," one student said.

"He minused eight," said another.

"He subtracted . . . to get to eight," said a third.

"He counted back," another contributed.

"And Josie did something different," I said.

"She started with the children that were on the playground at the end," one student affirmed.

"She counted on!" and "She added!" other students sang out.

"She went to twenty-two. It took fourteen to get to twenty-two," another student offered.

"So," I summed up, "one person started with the number of children on the playground at the beginning of the story and subtracted to get to the number of children on the playground at the end of the story. The other person started with the number of children on the playground at the end of the story and added to get to the number of children on the playground at the beginning of the story. Are both ways OK?"

"Yes!" was the general consensus.

"Either way, you still find the number that went inside," one student explained.

"It doesn't matter. You can count up or count back!" said another.

"I wonder if there is even another way that would work," I said.

Tommie raised his hand. "I used ten and seven," he said. "Ten children were outside playing, and then some went inside. Seven children were still outside. It's three."

"Tell us about 'three,'" I asked.

"Three is the answer," Tommie asserted. "That's how many children went inside. I know seven and three is ten, so if there's ten outside, then some went inside and there's seven still outside; three had to go in, because seven plus three is ten." Tommie had used some known number combinations; yet another way to solve the problem.

I erased the practice number pairs as I explained the new number pairs to students. "You have heard some different ways of finding the answer to the story problem using these pairs. Now you will be using different pairs: fifty and twenty-four, eighty-nine and forty-six, or ninety-three and fifty-eight. You can use one of the ways you heard your classmates explain, or another way. What is important is that you . . ." At this prompt, various students completed my sentence:

"Understand what you're doing."

"Use a way that makes sense."

"Can explain what you did."

"When you get a paper," I continued, "go ahead and get started at your seat. I will be walking around to check on what you're doing. We will come back together as a whole group in about twenty minutes so that we can hear about some of the ways you solved the problem. If you finish before it is time to come back together . . ." I passed out papers with the problem printed on the top.

"You can try different numbers," one student responded.

"You can solve the same problem in another way," chimed in another.

As previously, the number pairs that students were given for the independent activity were obviously more challenging than the practice numbers. Again I had chosen the numbers deliberately for the math possibilities they presented. Since the students had been discussing the use of doubles and had experience with combining the number 25 in the context of coins, I chose 50 and 24 to see if they would apply their previous experience with these numbers to this new context. I chose 93 and 58 to force students into a regrouping situation and I chose 89 and 46 to avoid imposing regrouping.

As the students got to work, I noticed that they were using various manipulatives to assist them in solving the new story problem. Some students got out the 1–100 charts that are kept at their desks. Other students were using the base ten materials and the snap cubes. A large pile of single cubes in front of one student caught my attention.

"Hi, Sylvia," I said.

"Hi, Ms. Scharton. I am using these numbers." Sylvia pointed to 89 and 46.

"Terrific! You already chose your numbers. Can you tell me a little about what you are doing?" I asked.

"I am counting out cubes . . . eighty-nine cubes, for the kids on the playground," she explained.

"OK. Then what will you do?" I asked.

"I am going take away forty-six," she responded.

"OK. Can you tell me why?" I asked.

"Well, the eighty-nine are the kids on the playground. Forty-six is the number of kids on the playground at the end. I will take forty-six away and that will be the kids that went in!" she said confidently.

"That makes sense," I said. "Eighty-four is a big number, though. Is there another way to count these cubes instead of counting by ones?"

She thought for a moment and then said, "I could put them into tens!"

"You could. Is there another type of material that is already in tens?" I asked.

"Oh!" she answered, reaching for the base ten materials.

"Show me how you could use those," I said.

Sylvia counted out eight tens and nine loose cubes. Using these materials, she then counted by tens up to eighty, then by ones to eighty-nine. She next separated out forty-six, first by taking four tens, then

counting out six individual cubes. She counted what was left, beginning with the four tens and then counting the three loose ones. "It's forty-three!" she exclaimed.

"That was fast!" I said. "That took much less time than it would have if you had used the single cubes, don't you think?" Sylvia nodded. "Do me a favor," I continued. "I'd like to remember what it was that you did. Could you draw a picture to remind me?"

I watched as Sylvia drew a picture of eight tens and nine ones; she then looked up at me for guidance.

"How could you show that you took those forty-six away?" I asked.

Sylvia immediately began crossing out the tens and ones she had subtracted. She looked up at me once again.

"What will you do next?" I asked.

"I could write the numbers!" she answered.

"Yes, you could. What number did you start with?" As Sylvia began writing her equation, I left to check on some of the other students.

When walking around the room, I look both for students who are obviously "stuck" and students like Sylvia who are perhaps ready to consider a more advanced method. I know that students often listen in when I am working with one of their classmates, so I try to make my way to each of the groups of desks, in order that all of the students can benefit from these teaching moments.

Michelle had five tens lying on the desk in front of her, and she looked stumped. "Hi, Michelle. How's it going?" I asked.

"OK," she said unconvincingly.

"I see you are using the base ten blocks," I commented.

"Yeah, but I can't do it!" she said. "I have fifty and I want to take away twenty-four, but I can't, because I can't break up the tens." Michelle had chosen 50 and 24 as her number pair. Although I wanted to remind her what I know she already knew about the numbers 25 and 50, I thought it was more important to support her in using her chosen strategy, by guiding her toward the understanding that she really could do this problem with the materials she had in front of her.

"So, you are starting with the number of children in the playground," I said.

"Yeah," she responded.

"And you are trying to subtract . . ."

"I want to take out the number that would leave twenty-four . . . the number on the playground on the end. That will tell me the number that went in," she explained.

"And you can't break the base ten materials, true . . . so what could you do instead?" I asked.

Michelle did what students often do in a regrouping situation: she separated out two tens and then covered up four ones on one of the tens with her index finger. This left two tens and the six "exposed" ones on another ten. She said, "It's twenty-six!"

"Wow, that was fast!" I said. "Tell me what you did."

Michelle explained that she "took away" two tens. She was unable to "take away" the four ones, so she covered them with her finger instead. She looked at what was left and quickly counted. While many teachers use base ten materials to demonstrate a standard subtraction algorithm—"trading" a ten for ten ones, then subtracting the necessary amount—Michelle constructed her own way of dealing with regrouping. The method she used made much more sense to her than one I could have shown her.

"I understand what you did," I told her. "I wonder how you could draw that."

As Michelle began drawing a picture to represent her strategy, I moved on to another table. (See Figure 10–4.)

As I stopped beside Ramon, I saw that he had his 1–100 chart in front of him and was finishing up with his writing. "Hey," I began, "how's it going, Ramon?"

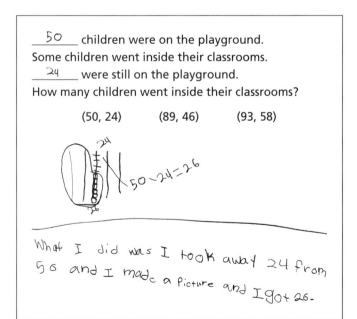

FIGURE 10–4 Michelle constructed a way to deal with the regrouping issue.

"Good. I used the hundred chart and these numbers," he answered, pointing to 93 and 58.

"Great," I said. "Can you show me what you did?"

"I started with fifty-eight," Ramon explained, touching the 58 on his chart.

"Because . . ." I prodded.

"Because that's the number of children left on the playground," he quickly replied.

"OK. What did you do next?" I asked.

"I went to ninety-three," he went on.

"Because . . ." I said again.

"Because that's the number of children on the playground first," he answered.

"And what will you find out?" I asked.

"I will count up to ninety-three and that will tell me how many kids went inside," he explained. Rather than count by ones from fifty-eight to ninety-three, Ramon counted by tens, then ones. "I went to sixty-eight, then seventy-eight, eighty-eight, then ninety-eight. Then I went back to ninety-three."

In the past, Ramon had used the 1–100 chart in a way that is time-consuming but comfortable for many children: counting by ones. This time, he was using it more efficiently: counting by tens. While he had "gone too far" and ended up on 98, he seemed confident about what he needed to do to arrive at his final destination.

"So, what did you find out?" I asked.

"It's thirty-five!" he replied.

"And how did you get your answer?" I asked.

"Well, sixty-eight, seventy-eight, eighty-eight, ninety-eight: that's forty. But I have to go back to ninety-three, so it's thirty-nine, thirty-eight, thirty-seven, thirty-six, thirty-five!" Ramon counted back from forty as he touched the 97, 96, 95, 94, and the 93 on his 1–100 chart. When he finished he looked up at me with a broad smile.

After students had been working for about twenty minutes, I got their attention, gave them the "two-minute warning," and continued to circulate the room. I then asked the students to put away their materials and join me on the rug for a class discussion.

Once again we reviewed the reasons for coming together and the types of behaviors that were most helpful when listening to their classmates share. During the independent work period, I had chosen four students to present their problem-solving methods to the class. I had decided the order in which they would share, starting with the method that would be most accessible to the students.

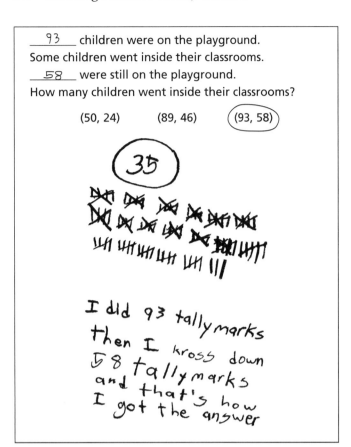

_____93_____ children were on the playground.
Some children went inside their classrooms.
_____58_____ were still on the playground.
How many children went inside their classrooms?

(50, 24)   (89, 46)   (93, 58)

FIGURE 10–5   Pedro used tally marks to model how he subtracted.

Pedro began. "I used ninety-three and fifty-eight," he explained. "I made tally marks. I drew ninety-three marks and subtracted fifty-eight. I crossed them out and I counted what was left. I got thirty-five." Pedro showed his paper to his classmates. (See Figure 10–5.)

"Could you show us how you knew that you crossed out fifty-eight?" I asked. Pedro had crossed out groups of five. I was curious to see if he'd counted by fives when crossing out the groups.

Pedro demonstrated what he had done. He touched each group of tallies and counted by fives up to fifty-five, then by ones to fifty-eight. "I counted the ones that aren't crossed out," he explained. Then Pedro counted aloud again, starting with the groups of five and then the ones: "Five, ten, fifteen, twenty, twenty-five, thirty. Then there's these three—thirty-one, thirty-two, thirty-three—and these two—thirty-four, thirty-five. There's thirty-five tally marks left."

"So, Pedro started with what number?" I asked.

"Ninety-three!" was the unanimous response.

"The kids on the playground!" one student added.

"Yeah, at the beginning!" clarified another.

"And what did he do next?" I asked.

"Crossed out the kids that were on the playground at the end!" was one response.

"Subtracted!" another student said.

"What did he find out?" I asked.

"The kids that went in!" several students sang out.

"Thirty-five kids went in the classroom!" one student noted.

Since Pedro did not record an equation for his strategy, I asked the students to consider a number sentence that would show what he had done.

"He started with ninety-three and he crossed out fifty-eight," one of the students said. "So I think it would be 'ninety-three minus fifty-eight.'"

"Ninety-three minus fifty-eight equals thirty-five," another student added.

"You should put a box around 'thirty-five,' because that's the number we were trying to figure out," suggested someone else.

I wrote the following on the board:

Pedro

$$93 - 58 = \boxed{35}$$

"Did anyone else use tally marks?" I asked. A few students raised their hands. "Pedro used tally marks to solve the problem. He subtracted groups of five and counted what was left. Sylvia used a different tool. She used base ten materials. Let's watch and see what she did."

Sylvia had brought her base ten materials to the rug. She demonstrated how she began with 89, subtracted 46, and counted what was left. She showed the group her work. (See Figure 10–6.)

"Let's see if we can explain what Sylvia did," I said.

"She used the tens and ones," one student offered.

"She started like Pedro: with the number of kids on the playground," another explained.

"Yeah! And she subtracted like he did!" said a third.

"He subtracted by crossing out. She subtracted by taking them away!" one student observed.

"He took away groups of five. She took away groups of ten," said another.

"Did anyone else use the base ten materials?" I asked, wanting to acknowledge the strategies of as many students as possible. "Did anyone else start with the number of children on the playground in the

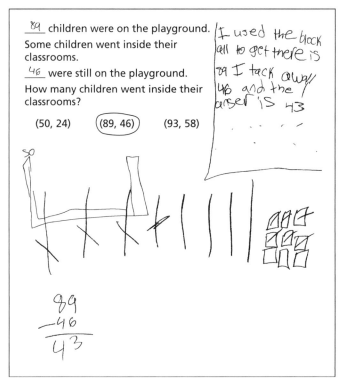

89 children were on the playground.
Some children went inside their classrooms.
46 were still on the playground.
How many children went inside their classrooms?

(50, 24) (89, 46) (93, 58)

I used the block all to get there is 89 I tack away 46 and the arser is 43

FIGURE 10–6 Sylvia solved the problem using base ten materials.

beginning and subtract the number of children that were on the playground at the end of the story?" After each question, a few students raised their hands.

Next, Michelle explained her method for the number pair 50 and 24 using base ten materials, which she also had brought to the rug. She demonstrated how she had started with the five tens, separated out two tens, and then covered up the four ones on one of the three remaining tens (see below).

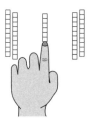

"So there's two tens and six showing," Michelle said. "That's twenty-six."

"Let's think about what Michelle did and the tools she used," I said. "How is this similar to and different from what has already been done?"

"Everyone started with the bigger number—the number of kids on the playground," one student said.

"One person used tally marks," another observed.

"Two people used the base ten materials," said another.

"Everyone minused, took away, the number of children that were on the playground at the end," said a fourth.

"Everyone counted what was left," another stated.

"Pedro counted by fives. Sylvia and Michelle counted by tens and ones!" someone else clarified.

"Everybody subtracted," another student observed.

"Well, let's see if everyone subtracted," I said. "Let's listen to Ramon."

"I used the hundred chart," Ramon began. "I started on fifty-eight, the number of kids still on the playground after kids went inside, and I counted to the number of kids on the playground first." Ramon pointed to the numbers on the large class 1–100 chart that was permanently posted in front of the group. "I went like this," he said. "Sixty-eight, seventy-eight, eighty-eight, ninety-eight. That's forty. But ninety-eight is bigger than ninety-three, so I had to go backwards to get to ninety-three: thirty-nine, thirty-eight, thirty-seven, thirty-six, thirty-five. Thirty-five children went inside."

"I wonder if we can retell what Ramon did," I said.

"He used a different tool: the hundred chart," was one comment.

"He went up, he added," one student remarked.

"Everyone else subtracted, but Ramon added," another said.

"He started with the kids left after some went in, and he added to get to the number of kids outside on the playground at the beginning," said yet another.

"He used tens to count on," one student observed.

I was not sure if everyone in the class understood where Ramon got the answer thirty-five, so I asked, "Can you figure out what Ramon's answer is and how he got it?"

"He went by tens down to ninety-eight, then he went back," one student said.

"He went back, because ninety-eight was bigger than ninety-three and he had to get back to ninety-three," another said.

The students grew silent after these two comments. I waited for a few moments after posing my questions again. "What answer did he get? And how did he get that answer?"

"He got thirty-five," several students said.

And again there was silence. "OK," I said. "Where did the thirty-five come from? Maybe you can show us again, Ramon?"

Ramon pointed at the 58 on the hundred chart, then the four boxes below it, saying, "Sixty-eight, seventy-eight, eighty-eight, ninety-eight . . . that's forty to get to ninety-eight. But I have to get to ninety-three, not ninety-eight. If I have forty, then backwards makes it thirty-nine, thirty-eight, thirty-seven, thirty-six, thirty-five." As Ramon said the numbers he touched the 97, 96, 95, 94, and finally the 93.

"Oh! Forty was too many. Fifty-eight plus forty is ninety-eight!" one student exclaimed.

"Yeah!" said another. "But fifty-eight plus . . ."

"Plus thirty-five is ninety-three!" said the first.

"Huh?" said the second.

I tried another tack. "Is there a way that we can check to see if fifty-eight plus thirty-five really is ninety-three?" I asked. "Can someone come up and use the same tool to check?"

Tommie gave it a try. "You start at fifty-eight and count thirty-five more." Tommie put his hand on the 58, then moved his finger from number to number as he and his classmates counted on together by ones up to thirty-five. They landed on the 93.

"Thanks, Tommie," I said. "Is there a different way—a faster way—to count on to thirty-five?" I asked.

"By tens! I can!" exclaimed Sonia. Sonia came up to the chart and put her finger on the 58. "Ten, twenty, thirty," she counted aloud, moving her finger from 68, to 78, to 88 on the chart. "Thirty-one, thirty-two, thirty-three, thirty-four, thirty-five," she continued, touching 89, 90, 91, 92, and 93. "See!" Sonia exclaimed. "Ninety-three!"

I was able to see that not everyone in the class understood what Ramon had done to solve the problem, but I also suspected that students who were confused by his strategy were, thanks to this discussion, now willing to use a different tool—the 1–100 chart—or perhaps try counting in a more efficient way—by tens.

Students regularly attempt to make sense of the information provided by a teacher. Mandated procedures for addition and subtraction may often confuse children. Students' repeated use of procedures that are not fully understood by them can only lead to frustration and misconceptions. Students should be encouraged to use tools and processes that are accessible to them; it is up to the teacher to continually assess their methods to determine when they are ready for a challenge. In these story problem lessons, all of the students were encouraged—expected—to solve the problems in a way that made sense to them. Rather than simply replicating a method modeled by the teacher, students were expected to create or adapt, use, and explain methods that they understood. This process results in a more thorough understanding of computation methods.

Linking Assessment and Instruction

As the students work, think about the following:

- Are students able to retell story problems in their own words? Are they able to explain what is "given" in the problem and what is "missing"?
- What methods do students use to solve problems? Which students . . .

  - need to model all numbers in the problem? Do they use manipulatives or pictures?
  - use counting strategies? Do they count on or back? Do they count by ones or tens? Do they use fingers? Manipulatives? A 1–100 chart?
  - use understanding of number combinations?

- Are students able to explain the strategies they use, aloud or in writing? In what ways do students represent the methods they use?
- Do the students repeatedly use the same strategy? Or, once they are comfortable with a strategy, are they able to use others? Are students progressing from modeling to counting to number strategies?
- Are students able to understand and use other students' strategies?
- Can students see how separate strategies for solving a problem are similar and/or different? Can students see the relationship between operations? Given a problem such as:

  Toby had 9 cookies.

  5 were chocolate chip and the rest were oatmeal.

  How many cookies were oatmeal?

are students able to understand why some students would solve this problem by counting on from five (addition) and others would solve this by counting back from nine (subtraction)?

Travels on the Number Line

CHAPTER 11

OVERVIEW

Travels on the Number Line *is a series of lessons in which the teacher gives students sets of problems, students solve the problems, and the teacher represents their methods on a number line; eventually students explore representing their own strategies using number lines. When constructing problems for students to solve, careful number choices on the part of the teacher may help students acquire particular computation strategies, including making use of "friendly" or "landmark" numbers, using knowledge of tens and/or hundreds, and considering alternative approaches.*

MATERIALS

- chart paper
- preprinted story problems, 1 set per student (see Blackline Masters)

TIME

- two class periods

Teaching Directions

1. Consider types of strategies students would benefit from using (e.g., making use of tens/hundreds or "landmark" numbers).

2. Write number and/or word problems using numbers and operations that would promote use of the strategy.

3. Have students mentally solve these problems and explain their methods to their classmates.

4. Chart student methods.

5. Repeat the process several times.

6. Invite the students to represent their computational strategies using number lines.

Teaching Notes

Number lines are a tool for modeling addition and subtraction strategies, comparing numbers, and examining the relationship between numbers. Certain number choices promote particular strategies. Students learn to efficiently solve problems with two "decade numbers" (e.g., 20 + 10) using knowledge of tens rather than ones. Teachers can build on student knowledge by carefully ordering problems that focus on these relationships (e.g., 20 + 11, 21 + 10, 20 + 12). With teacher support, students begin to see how numbers relate to each other; noticing these relationships leads students to understand how strategies are related as well. Other problem sets can be constructed to focus on other features and strategies (e.g., use of doubles: $25 + 25 \rightarrow 25 + 26$; use of landmark numbers: $20 + 20 \rightarrow 19 + 21$) to help students build a repertoire of strategies that are efficient, as well as meaningful.

The Lesson

Day 1

Students in this second-grade classroom had been confidently solving a variety of word problems with multidigit numbers. Their classroom teacher was responsive to letting them solve problems using methods they understood and had established a classroom climate in which a variety of approaches was valued. Students were motivated to solve problems, record their methods on paper, and share these methods in whole-class discussions. Many students had been using tools (1–100 charts, tally marks, and fingers) that supported their use of ones. My colleague, who had asked me to teach some lessons in her room, was eager to expose her students to problems and numbers that would encourage them to consider more efficient strategies for solving problems. I spent some time thinking about the types of numbers and word problems that would help students develop flexibility with number relationships and fluency with computation strategies.

I greeted students as they came in from morning recess and quietly sat down on the rug in front of the room. I had taped a piece of chart paper on the board, and I invited the students to help me read the words that were written there:

There were _____ children on the playground.

_____ more came to join them.

How many children were on the playground then?

"I wonder if you can help me to retell that story problem, so that we know what it is all about," I asked. Several hands went up. It was obvious that these students were accustomed to solving word problems and had experience with class discussions.

"There are some kids on the playground," one of the students offered.

"Some more children came out to play," another said.

"We don't know how many, because there is a blank," said a third.

"We don't know how many kids were there in the beginning or how many more came," another student said.

"We need to figure out how many children were on the playground in the end," one student suggested.

"Wow!" I said. "Have you seen this problem before?" The students smiled and I went on. "You really listened well and seem to know just what this problem is all about. You know some children were on the playground and some more students came. You know that we are trying to figure out how many children were on the playground. You also know

there are 'blanks' in the story. We need to put some numbers in the story. Let's see . . ." Beneath the problem, I wrote these numbers on the chart: *10, 10*.

I explained how we would use the numbers I wrote. "There are two blanks in the problem, so I wrote down two numbers we could use. The first number goes in the first blank and the second number goes in the second blank. Let's read the problem again. As we read this time, when we get to the first blank, we are going to say . . ."

"Ten!" called out most of the students.

"You are right! And when we get to the second blank, we are going to say . . ." I prompted.

"Ten!" they called out again.

"Hey! It's the same number!" said one student.

"You are right again. Yes, it is the same number. That will not always be the case, though. Are you ready to try?" The students smiled and nodded. They read the words along with me again, this time inserting a number when they came to a blank. "Now we have more information about the story problem. We know how many children were on the playground," I said.

"Ten," several students repeated.

I nodded and continued. "And we know how many more came out to join them."

"Ten!" they said.

"That's easy!" Juan stated.

"Think about the answer," I said. "Touch your knees when you have figured it out." Most students immediately put their hands on their knees, informing me that they had mentally combined ten and ten; only one or two students counted on their fingers, one at a time. I waited about ten seconds and then asked, "Can someone tell us what he or she did to solve the problem?"

"It's twenty. I know ten and ten is twenty," explained Danny.

"It sounds like you started with ten. Ten was the number of students . . ."

"That were on the playground first," Danny said.

"And you added another ten because . . ."

Again, Danny finished my sentence. "Those were the ones who came and played with the first group."

Often, students operate on numbers and lose track of the problem context. Keeping the context in mind can help students thoughtfully consider whether their choice of operations makes sense and if the answer is a reasonable one.

I reiterated what Danny had done as I recorded his thinking on the chart in this way:

"Danny started with ten, the number of students on the playground," I said, pointing to the 10 I had written on the chart to illustrate what number Danny had started with. "He added ten, the number of students that came out to the playground," I said, pointing to the +10 I had written next. "His answer is twenty, the number of children playing on the playground," I said, pointing to the 20 I had written last. I had joined Danny's first and last numbers with an arched line to indicate the process.

When introducing new concepts—in this case, a way of representing addition—it is often difficult to assess how students are making sense of new information. Giving students a chance to explain their understanding would not only help me to quickly assess some of the students, but it would also give their classmates a chance to hear a method repeated in some slightly different ways.

"Can someone explain what Danny said and how I made a picture to show how he solved the problem?" I asked.

Ray volunteered. He came up to the chart and pointed to the various elements as he explained them. "This is the number he started with," Ray said, pointing to the first 10. "And he added ten, so that's why it says 'plus ten' here. Ten plus ten is twenty and here's the answer," he said, touching the 20.

Sophia came up next. She also pointed to the numbers and lines as she talked about what her classmate had done. "These were the kids on the playground," she explained, pointing to the 10. "And these are the kids that came," she said, pointing to +10. "These are the twenty there are altogether," Sophia told us, pointing to the 20.

"Why do you suppose this line is here?" I asked, tracing the arc between 10 and 20.

"You went from ten kids to twenty kids," Sophia said.

"That shows that you added," one of her classmates added.

"It's like an equation but in a picture: ten plus ten equals twenty," another student said.

"We call this a 'number line,'" I explained. "When you hear the term *number line*, what do you think of?"

"We have one of those on our desks!" one of the students said.

"We have one around the board, too!" said another student, pointing to a strip of adding machine tape that had been hung above the board and had large numbers written on it. "It tells how many days we have been in school."

"Yeah. We sometimes use it for adding or take away," explained another.

"But my number line starts with zero and has a line. You don't have a line! And yours starts with ten! That's weird," one student stated.

"Now you know that there are different kinds of number lines," I said. "They don't have to start with zero, like the number line on your desk. And they don't have to start with one, like the one above your board. But we can use them for adding, just like you have already used yours.

"I am going to do something tricky," I continued. "I am going to change the numbers. What if the numbers were twenty and ten," I said as I wrote these new numbers on the chart. Where previously in such lessons I had presented the various number pairs all at once, in this case I decided to introduce the pairs one at a time. This would keep the focus on only one pair of numbers, and it would also serve to demonstrate a logical connection between various sets of numbers. Again I read the problem to the children, pausing to allow them to provide the new numbers. "'There were . . .'" I began, touching the words on the chart.

"Twenty!" most of the students called out.

"'. . . children on the playground.'" I touched the second blank and looked at the students questioningly.

"Ten!" they called out.

"'. . . more children came. How many children were on the playground?' Touch your knees when you have an answer," I said, giving the students about fifteen seconds to solve the problem. "Who would like to explain what you did to figure out the answer?" Again, several hands went up in the air. This time I called on Laura.

"It's twenty and ten and that's thirty. I just know!" She smiled.

"You really know something about using tens!" I confirmed. I explained the representation of Laura's thinking as I recorded it.

$$\overset{\overset{\displaystyle +10}{\frown}}{20,\ 10 \qquad 20 \qquad\qquad 30}$$

"Laura started with the number of children," I said. I looked at Laura, encouraging her to share in the explanation of what I had drawn.

"The ones on the playground at first," she said. "Twenty."

I pointed to 20 and then went on. "And she added ten because," I began, touching the +10 and looking at Laura.

"That's how many kids came out on the playground next," she explained. "So there were thirty kids on the playground!" I pointed to the 30 on the chart.

"Now, I made this 'jump of ten' the same size as the one before. Why do you think I did that?" I asked.

"Because you added ten both times."

"If you added ten, the jump has to be the same as the other ten."

"If you made it bigger, that would mean you added more."

"Yeah, I wonder what plus a hundred would look like!"

I wanted to continue to give students a chance to think about this method of representing an addition situation. This time, I decided to have students share with a partner, rather than have several students explain to the whole group. "Turn to someone next to you. Explain this picture of Laura's thinking to your partner. Then switch jobs so that the listener can explain Laura's thinking also. One person listens and one person talks, then . . ."

"The other person listens and the other person talks!"

I gave students a couple of minutes to discuss and then I asked that they give me their attention. "OK, I am going to change the numbers again," I said, writing *20* and *11* on the chart. Since the students seemed to be comfortable with adding ten, I wanted to give them a number that was near ten to see if they would continue to make use of this same strategy, with slight adjustments. "Here is what I would like you to do. Both Danny and Laura used tens. I would like you to look at these numbers. One of them isn't a 'tens' number. What do you think I mean?"

"One doesn't end in zero."

"Before, if you counted by tens, you would get 'tens' numbers: ten, twenty, thirty. Twenty you can get by counting by tens, but eleven you can't get. If I said that one of these numbers was a 'near ten' number, what do you think I mean?" I continued.

"You mean it's really close to ten," one student said.

"Yeah. It's not ten but it's almost a ten!" said another.

"Like nine. It's near ten, but not ten," said a third.

"'Near' means, like, 'one away.' Nine is one away from ten. So is eleven!" explained one student.

"I want you to try to do something," I said. "See if you can use what you know about tens from watching Danny and Laura. See if you can solve the problem by using tens. This problem would now

be . . ." As I touched the words on the chart, the students read the original problem aloud, inserting "twenty" in the first blank and "eleven" in the second. I gave the students about thirty seconds; after this amount of time, most had their hands on their knees.

"Who would like to explain what you did?" I asked.

Jonathon explained first. "I started with twenty and added ten, because ten is really close to eleven. That made thirty, like Laura got. But I need to add one, because it's eleven and not ten. So that makes thirty-one." I recorded what Jonathon said like this:

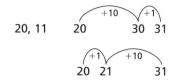

I wanted to make sure that the students understood what I had drawn. I asked for volunteers to explain my picture of what Jonathon did.

"He started with twenty and added ten," one student said. "He got to thirty. Then he added one more. That makes thirty-one."

"Twenty plus ten is thirty and one more is thirty-one," said another.

"He's adding eleven, because eleven more children went to the playground," said yet another. "He is trying to use ten, like you said. So he added ten and then one more and that's the eleven. Twenty and eleven equal thirty-one."

"What if I had drawn this?" I asked, adding another drawing below the one representing Jonathon's way (see below).

$$20, 11 \qquad 20 \overset{+10}{\frown} 30\ 31 \overset{+1}{\frown}$$
$$20\ 21 \overset{+1}{\frown} 31 \overset{+10}{\frown}$$

"It's the same thing, but opposite," said one student.

"Yeah . . . it's backwards," said another.

"Instead of adding ten first, you added one, then the ten," noticed a third.

"You can add ten, then one, or one, then ten. It doesn't matter," said a fourth.

"You still get the same answer," explained another student.

"You are still getting thirty-one and you are still adding eleven!" said yet another.

Many students appeared to have some understanding of the commutative property of addition: they could see that the order of the addends did not affect the sum. They also seemed to think flexibly about numbers: they realized that eleven was comprised of ten and one and one and ten. Dealing with "decade" numbers—"counting by tens" numbers—is typically easier than dealing with "nondecade" numbers. I wanted to push the students' thinking, while still encouraging them to make use of tens. I wrote *28* and *10* on the chart and said, "I would like you to use the same strategy, using tens, when solving the problem with these numbers." I noticed more students counting on fingers when asked to combine these numbers. After about thirty seconds, most students had their hands on their knees. I asked for volunteers to explain.

Lydia went first. "I started with twenty-eight and I counted on my fingers: twenty-nine, thirty, thirty-one, thirty-two, thirty-three, thirty-four, thirty-five, thirty-six, thirty-seven, thirty-eight," she said, extending a finger with each number she named.

I needed to acknowledge her efforts but I wanted to help students to consider using tens. I drew Lydia's method on the board (see below), rather than on the class chart. I did not want to "commit" this strategy to our chart, since it made use of ones:

"Lydia started with the number of students on the playground: twenty-eight," I said. "Then she added the number of students that came to join them. Why do you think I drew her method this way?"

"She counted on her fingers," said one student.

"She added one, then one, then one . . ." said another.

"She used her fingers and added one each time," said a third.

"This way worked, though," I said. "Lydia added ten. She added ten by counting on ones. I wonder if there is a way to add tens?"

Jose had an idea. "Just add ten," he said. "It's thirty-eight!"

"What do you mean?" I asked.

"You don't have to start with a 'counting by tens' number. You can add tens to any number. You could add tens to twenty-eight: thirty-eight, forty-eight, fifty-eight, sixty-eight . . . like that!" he explained.

"Hmm," I said. "Can you do that with any number? Can you start with any number and add tens?" Some students looked confident; others looked a little confused, but intrigued by the question.

Elaine attempted a guess. "I think so . . ." she said.

"Let's choose a number and try," I encouraged her.

"OK . . . thirty-six," she said.

"So, we'll start with thirty-six and count by tens . . . ready?" I asked.

Elaine began and the rest of the class joined in. As I added tens, I put up a finger each time, to model a way to keep track of the number of tens I had added.

"Thirty-six, forty-six, fifty-six, sixty-six, seventy-six, eighty-six, ninety-six . . ." Fewer voices joined in the counting as we got closer to one hundred.

"Let's stop there," I said. I showed them my six outstretched fingers. "What does this show you?" I asked them.

"That's how many tens you added," one student said.

"Yeah, we counted on six tens," said another.

"That's . . . ten, twenty, thirty, forty, fifty, sixty! We added sixty!" commented one student.

"Thirty-six and sixty is ninety-six!" said yet another.

"Can we count by tens from another number?" I asked.

"How about forty-two?" Elaine asked.

"Let's try. Ready?" I began and other students joined in: "Fifty-two, sixty-two, seventy-two, eighty-two, ninety-two . . ."

"Fifty!" said several students.

"We counted on five tens . . . that's fifty!" said one.

"So, we can count by tens from any number," I said. "Now, let's go back to what Jose did. He said you could add ten to twenty-eight and get thirty-eight. What do you think I should draw on our chart?"

Jose spoke up. "Put a twenty-eight, then that line, and a thirty-eight at the end. Put the 'plus ten,' too."

I recorded what he said:

I continued to give the students different numbers to use for the same word problem. Each time, we reread the problem, inserting the new numbers. I gave the students time to mentally find the answer after encouraging them to "use tens." I called on one or more students to explain the ways in which they found the answer to the problem, each time charting the methods students used. After charting a new method, student volunteers explained the representation to the whole class or pairs of students discussed what I had drawn. The final chart looked like this:

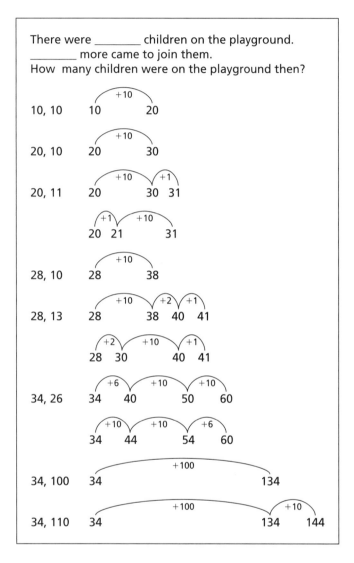

I was curious to see what students would independently do when given some time to work with different numbers on their own. I explained, "You seem to be really comfortable with the strategy of using tens with number lines as your 'tool.' I am going to ask you to use what you have learned during our time together this morning. I am going to ask you to use the same 'playground problem.' I am going to give you two number choices: forty-eight and twenty-six or one hundred thirty-eight and one hundred thirty-four." I wrote these number pairs on the board. "Use the numbers that are 'right' for you. I would like you

to represent your thinking using a number line and explain your number line with words. If you finish before mathematics time is over, you can pick another pair of numbers or you can use the same pair of numbers and solve the problem in a different way. You will have about fifteen minutes to work and then we will come back together and talk about what we learned today." I handed out papers on which the problem was written, and students quickly took their seats and began working on the problem. I was interested to see what students could do on their own. Students eagerly began working and seemed to have confidence in what they were doing. After ten minutes of independent work time, I gave the students a five-minute warning to finish up. A few minutes later, we gathered together on the rug in front of the room.

"I noticed that you worked on your own quite well," I began. "Most of you seemed to know just what to do to get started. Some of you chose forty-eight and twenty-six; others chose one hundred and thirty-eight and one hundred thirty-four. What are some of the things you learned today?"

"I learned a new way to solve problems using a different kind of number line," one of the students offered.

"I learned that number lines don't have to start with zero or one. They can start with any numbers," said another.

"It is easy to count by tens from any number, not just ten, twenty, thirty . . . like that," said a third.

"Yeah . . . counting by ones is easy, but counting by tens is pretty easy too!" added another.

"You can count by hundreds, too!" said one of the children.

It was clear that today's session tapped several aspects of number-sense understanding. Students felt comfortable using a strategy involving combining groups of tens—and hundreds—rather than just ones. They enjoyed experimenting with a new tool to keep track of mental computation and their attitude about using this new strategy and tool was positive. I was eager to examine student work and get a closer look at how individuals made sense of the problem.

Ray had used the number pair 48 and 26. He began with 48 and added two to get to the next decade number, fifty. He then added eight and two and eight before adding the final six. Rather than adding two tens and six ones to 48, Ray decomposed 28 into addends that made ten. (See Figure 11–1.)

There were ___48___ children on the playground.
___26___ more came to join them.
How many children were on the playground then?

A) 48, 26   B) 138, 134

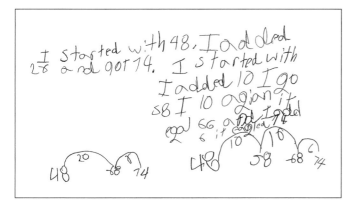

I started with 48 and added 2 then. got 50 then I added 8 and I got 58 I added 2 and got 60 then I add 8 and I got 68 then I added 6 and got 74.

FIGURE 11–1   Ray was able to show his solution with a number line, which he explained in writing.

I Started with 48, I added 26 and got 74. I started with I added 10 I go 58 I 10 again it equal 66, and 6 it equal 74 I added 48 58 68 74

FIGURE 11–2   Juan's number line showed his strategy.

There were ___48___ children on the playground.
___26___ more came to join them.
How many children were on the playground then?

A) 48, 26   B) 138, 134

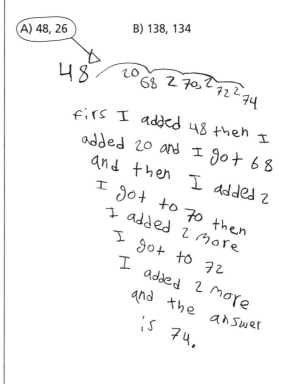

firs I added 48 then I added 20 and I got 68 and then I added 2 I got to 70 then I added 2 more I got to 72 I added 2 more and the answer is 74.

FIGURE 11–3   Aaron's paper showed his facility with adding and decomposing numbers.

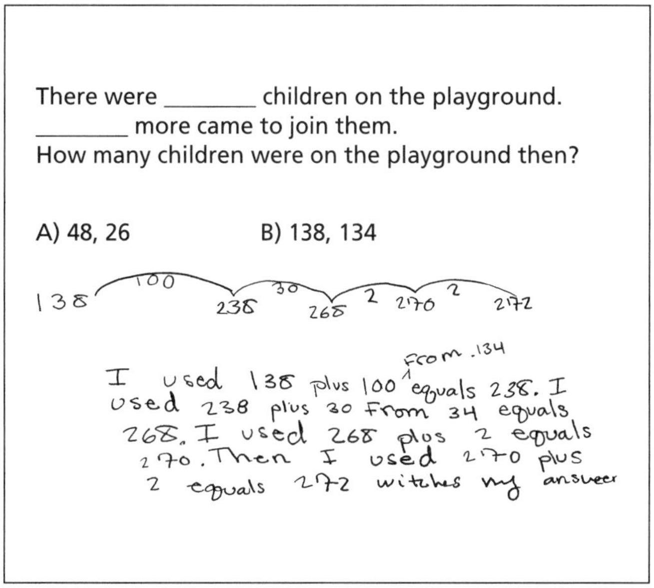

Juan also used this number pair but added in ways that were similar to what we had done as a group: he "pulled out" tens from 26, added them to 48, and then added on the additional six. (See Figure 11–2.)

Aaron added twenty first. He then decomposed the remaining six into three sets of two, adding them one at time. (See Figure 11–3.)

Several students used the other number choice: 138 and 134. Elaine added 100, then 30; she broke up the remaining 4 into two sets of 2. (See Figure 11–4.)

Jonathon used the same number pair, but added 20, then 100, then 10, then 4. (See Figure 11–5.) He seems to know what he wants the sum to be!

There were _____ children on the playground.
_____ more came to join them.
How many children were on the playground then?

A) 48, 26   B) 138, 134

I used 138 plus 100 from .134 equals 238. I used 238 plus 30 from 34 equals 268. I used 268 plus 2 equals 270. Then I used 270 plus 2 equals 272 witches my answer

FIGURE 11–4   Elaine added 100, then 30; she "broke up" the remaining 4 into two sets of 2.

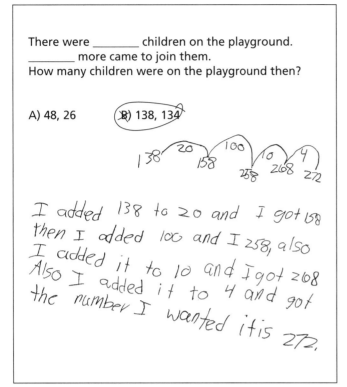

There were _____ children on the playground.
_____ more came to join them.
How many children were on the playground then?

A) 48, 26   B) 138, 134

I added 138 to 20 and I got 158 then I added 100 and I 258, also I added it to 10 and I got 268 Also I added it to 4 and got the number I wanted it is 272.

FIGURE 11–5 Jonathon used the same number pair as Elaine but added 20, then 100, then 10, then 4.

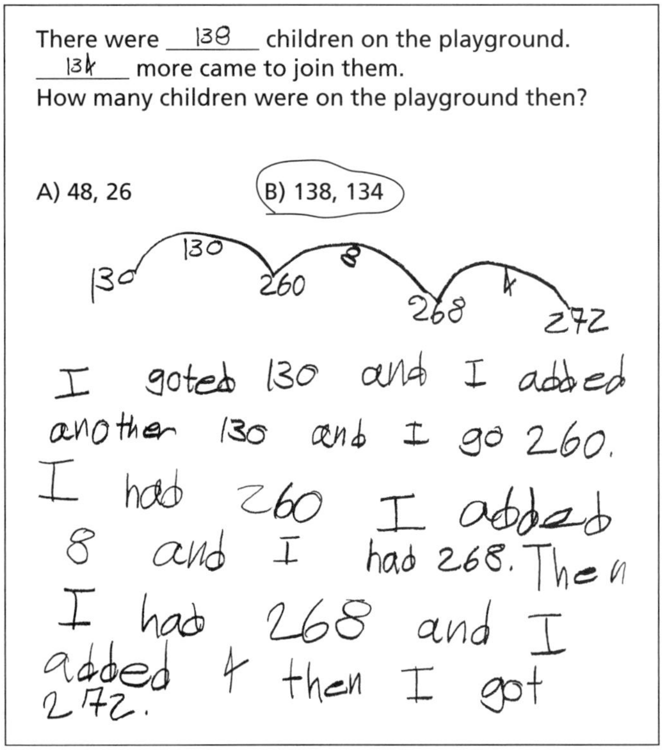

There were __138__ children on the playground.
__134__ more came to join them.
How many children were on the playground then?

A) 48, 26   B) 138, 134

I goted 130 and I added another 130 and I go 260. I had 260 I added 8 and I had 268. Then I had 268 and I added 4 then I got 272.

FIGURE 11–6 Ernesto found yet another way to map the problem.

Ernesto also used 138 and 134. Rather than beginning with 138, Ernesto began with part of that number: 130. He added another 130, then added back the original 8 from the first addend and proceeded to add the remaining 4. (See Figure 11–6.)

Day 2

My first lesson with these second-grade students focused on helping them develop a strategy of using tens and hundreds and model the use of a tool that we could use to represent this strategy. This second lesson occurred about a week later and would build on what we had done. I wanted to provide further practice with the number line, use a story problem that made use of a different operation, and introduce a new but related strategy. I also wanted to give students a chance to model their methods with their classmates. I had given a lot of thought to the story problem I would present to the students, as well as the number pairs I would introduce, one at a time.

As students came in from recess, they noticed the chart paper I had posted on the board. They sat down on the rug in front of the room. I greeted the students and asked, "What do you remember from our last lesson?" Their answers would help me assess their

understanding of what we'd previously discussed, and help set the stage for today's experiences.

"We had a story problem about the playground," one student said. "Some students were on the playground and more students came. We had to figure out how many students were on the playground altogether."

"We had to add," said another.

"We used a number line," said a third. "It was weird because it didn't start at zero or one!"

"You kept tricking us!" said one student. "You kept giving us different numbers!"

"You wanted us to use tens. Some people used hundreds!" said yet another.

"We had to solve problems on our own and we got to choose some numbers to use," another student commented.

"Many of you have already noticed the word problem we will be using today," I said. "You remembered that we used a tool—the number line—and a strategy for adding numbers—groups of tens and hundreds. You used to use ones a lot and I wondered if you would be able to use bigger chunks, like tens and hundreds. And you did! Today, we are also going to use the number line to show ways of working with the numbers in the word problem. We will talk about the strategy as we go."

I gestured to the chart. "Could you help me read the word problem I have written?" I asked. Students read along with me as I pointed to the words of the new problem on the chart:

There were _____ children in the cafeteria.

_____ children left to go to recess.

How many children were left in the cafeteria?

"Let's talk about what is happening in this problem before we solve it," I suggested.

"It must be lunch time or an assembly," one of the students suggested.

"Some kids are in the cafeteria. We don't know how many because you haven't told us yet!" said another.

"Yeah, and some left. We don't know how many," was another comment.

"We are trying to figure out how many are still in the cafeteria," one student said.

"We need some numbers!" several called out.

"This is kind of like the other problem . . . but opposite!" one student noticed.

This last comment was intriguing. It sounded as though this student was making an important connection between the problems, as well as the operations involved. I prodded, "Tell me a little more about 'like the other problem, but opposite,'" I said. Several students raised their hands.

"In that other problem, some students were on the playground and some more students came. This time, some students were in the cafeteria and some *left*," said one.

"On the playground, the students got bigger . . . there were more students in the end," another explained. "In the cafeteria, the students get smaller . . . there aren't as many after some of them went away."

"The other problem was an adding problem. I think this one is a take-away problem," said yet another.

The students were making some important comparisons between the problem from the first lesson and this problem. They commented on how the number of students increased in the first problem and decreased in the second one. They were considering how one problem used addition and the other used subtraction. And they alluded to a feature of subtraction that makes it a complex operation. Addition involves combining separate, distinct addends. In this

subtraction problem, a quantity (the subtrahend) is removed from an initial quantity (the minuend); what is removed, as well as what remains, is part of that quantity.

"You have some important understandings about this problem and about addition and subtraction. You are thinking about some ways in which this problem is similar to and different from the one we worked with last time. Let's try solving this problem with some numbers." I wrote the following numbers on the chart: *23, 3.*

"Let's read the problem with these numbers," I continued. "Do you remember that the first number . . ." When I paused, several students completed my sentence.

"Goes on the first line and the second number goes on the second line."

"Yeah, we know!" said some others.

I pointed to the words on the chart and we read the story problem aloud. When we got to the first blank, students inserted "twenty-three," and when we got to the second blank, students inserted "three." Several students raised their hands immediately, so I reminded the class what they were to do to let me know they were done mentally solving the problem. I whispered, "When you have figured out the answer, touch your knees to let me know." It took only ten or fifteen seconds before almost all students were touching their knees. I asked for volunteers to share how they'd solved the problem.

Ray went first. "Well, you got twenty-three, right? You just take off the three and it's twenty!" he said.

His explanation was brief but contained some important information. "So, you started with . . ."

"Twenty-three," he quickly responded.

"Because . . ." I prompted.

"Those are the kids in the cafeteria," he answered.

"OK. And you said you 'took off the three.' You did that because . . ."

"Those are the kids that left and went to go play," he explained.

"And when you 'took off,' are you adding? Subtracting?" I asked.

"Take away . . . subtracting. Because those kids left . . . they went away," he said.

"And when you subtracted three, that left you with twenty. And twenty is the number of . . ." I prompted.

"Twenty kids are still in the cafeteria," he said.

"OK, let me see if I can show this on the chart," I said. "Ray started with twenty-three, the number of students in the cafeteria. He subtracted the students that left: three." These students kept track of the number of days they had been in school on a number line they had constructed from adding machine tape and posted above the board we were facing. I pointed to it as I explained some features of the number line: numbers increased to the right and decreased to the left. "Now, we know something about number lines: if you move this way—to the right—the numbers get bigger and you are adding. But if you move this way—to the left—the numbers . . ." I paused.

"They get smaller," one student called out.

"You are doing 'take away,'" said another.

"You are subtracting," another added.

"Ray said he is subtracting three. So I have to move . . ." Again I paused.

Many students pointed to the left to indicate how to move backward on the number line.

"To the left," one student said.

"After we subtract three, we end up with . . ." I paused yet again.

"Twenty!" said several students.

"The number of kids still in the cafeteria," another said.

"The number of children after some went to recess," said yet another. I drew the following:

I wanted to make sure that the students understood the way I had represented what Ray had said. I asked, "Can someone explain my picture to the rest of the class?"

Elaine volunteered. "You started at twenty-three. You subtracted three and you ended up with twenty."

"Anyone else?" Hearing from different classmates would give students a chance to hear information that had been processed in a different way.

Aaron said, "Twenty-three is the number of kids in the cafeteria. Minus three is the kids going outside. You have less kids in the cafeteria, so you got to go that way . . . to the left. Twenty kids are left in the cafeteria."

Sophia went next. "You start with that many: twenty-three," she said, pointing to the chart. "You got to go to the left because you are taking some kids away . . . three. Twenty-three minus three is twenty!"

I decided to try some new, but similar numbers. First I wanted students to attend to some number features they may not have considered. "I think Ray paid attention to ways in which the numbers twenty-three and three are 'related' to each other," I said. "See if

you can pay attention to how these numbers are 'related.'" I wrote the next number pair on the chart: *43, 23*.

"Let's read the problem using these new numbers," I said. I pointed to the words of the problem and students read along with me, inserting the new numbers in the blanks. When most students touched their knees to indicate they had found a solution, I asked a few to explain what they had done.

Juan volunteered. "Well, I tried to do what Ray did, right? There is a three in both numbers. So I took away the three and that makes forty. Then I took away the twenty and that makes twenty."

"You started with . . ." I began.

"Forty-three. There were that many in the cafeteria. And I took away the three, because there is a three in twenty-three and a three in forty-three," Juan explained.

I wanted to record what he had done so far. "I am going to start with forty-three and subtract three, but can you remind me what direction I need to go if I am subtracting?" I asked.

Students pointed to the left but I wanted to make sure they knew why. "You are pointing that way," I said, pointing in the direction they had indicated. "Can you remind me why?"

"You got to go that way because you are subtracting," one of the students explained.

"You are taking away," said another.

"The numbers are getting smaller," said a third.

"If some kids left, there aren't as many. You have less," someone else commented.

I drew the following on the chart:

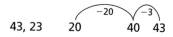

Juan continued. "There is twenty left to take away. So you have to make a *big* line that way," he said, pointing to the left, "and write 'minus twenty,' and then write 'twenty,' because you end up on twenty."

I added the following to the chart:

$$43, 23 \qquad 20 \overset{-20}{\frown} 40 \overset{-3}{\frown} 43$$

"I wonder if someone can help explain what Juan and I have created?" I asked.

"There was a three in both numbers, so he took away the three in twenty-three, then the twenty in twenty-three," Mary said.

Diego continued. "He broke up the twenty-three into two pieces: twenty and three. He took away one piece and the other piece. I did it kind of like that but a little different. I took away three and then ten and then ten."

"Let me see if I can draw what you just said," I stated, then added to the chart:

$$20 \overset{-10}{\frown} 30 \overset{-10}{\frown} 40 \overset{-3}{\frown} 43$$

"Can someone explain what Diego and I have done?" I asked.

Fernando raised his hand. "He took away three, just like Juan. Except, instead of taking away twenty, he took away ten and then ten . . . that's the same as twenty. He used tens, instead of twenty."

"I had to think hard about the length of my lines. What do you think I mean?" I asked. Students viewed the chart and then many raised their hands.

"The 'minus three' lines are the same . . . well, almost!" said Ernesto.

"Minus twenty is the same . . . and the minus ten and minus ten together are the same as the minus twenty line, see?" Laura came up to the chart. She pointed to the "−20" line, then the two "−10" lines, to demonstrate the relationships she was trying to explain.

"The 'minus three' line is the shortest and the minus twenty line is the longest and the minus ten line is in between," said Mark.

At least some of the students seemed to be aware of my attempts to demonstrate number magnitude through the length of a line. I wrote another number pair on the chart: *43, 24.*

"Before you solve this problem, I would like you to think about the ways in which your classmates have solved the other problems. They looked at the relationships between the numbers, how they were alike and different. They subtracted pieces at a time. Think about their ideas when solving the same problem with new numbers." I gave the students a minute or two to solve the problem.

Lydia raised her hand to explain her solution. "Twenty-four is close to twenty-three . . . it's just one away. I took three from twenty-four, just like we did before. Forty-three minus three is forty. Then I took away one more; that's thirty-nine. Then I took away a ten and another ten. That made nineteen."

I enlisted Lydia's help in drawing what she had just explained, asking questions to ensure I was accurately representing her ideas. "You said 'forty-three minus three is forty.' I know that I will be making my number line go from right to left, if I am subtracting. I will start on forty-three and subtract three. You said you subtracted one more, so I will write 'minus 1.' And you

said 'that's thirty-nine,' so I know that forty minus one is thirty-nine; I will write 'thirty-nine.' You said you 'took away a ten and another ten,' so I will write 'minus ten' and another 'minus ten.' I need some help though. Thirty-nine minus ten? What will I write?"

"Twenty-nine," said Lydia. "Remember how we counted up by tens and down by tens? Thirty-nine, twenty-nine, nineteen . . . you can tell by looking at the hundred chart, too. If you start at thirty-nine and take away ten, you are on twenty-nine . . . take away another ten and you are on nineteen!"

"So, thirty-nine minus ten is twenty-nine, so I will write that," I said. "And twenty-nine minus ten is nineteen. So I will write that. How does this look?" I asked (see below).

$$43, 24 \quad 19 \overset{-10}{\frown} 29 \overset{-10}{\frown} 39 \overset{-1}{\frown} 40 \overset{-3}{\frown} 43$$

"Perfect!" said Lydia.

"Let's take a moment and make sure we understand what you did," I said. Getting many students talking was important at this juncture. Not only had the students been sitting a while, but explaining their thinking to another person would help deepen their understanding after this lengthy discussion. "Turn to the person next to you," I began. "Tell them what you understand about this picture I drew and Lydia's idea. Then, switch jobs so that your partner can do some explaining as well." I gave the students a minute or two to talk. While they were talking, I added another number pair to the class chart: *65, 5.*

When I got students' attention back, they noticed the change and immediately put their hands on their knees. To keep them involved in the process and give them a chance to construct their own representation, I asked for student volunteers to come forward and record their thinking. Mark was the first. (See Figure 11–7.)

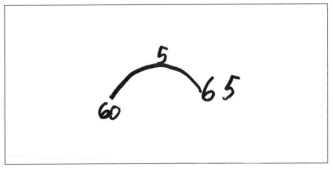

FIGURE 11–7 Mark constructed a number line to show 65 − 5.

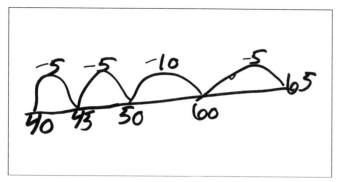

FIGURE 11–8   Mary's number line shows how she subtracted in "pieces."

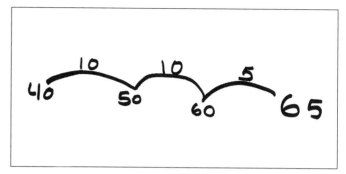

FIGURE 11–10   Danny used another way.

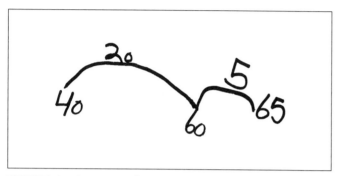

FIGURE 11–9   Fernando's subtraction operation looked like this.

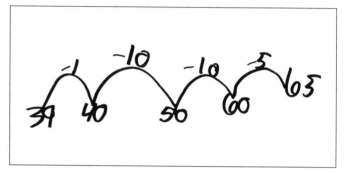

FIGURE 11–11   Sophia built another line using different numbers.

He explained, "It's easy! Sixty-five kids are in the cafeteria and five go out to recess. There's a five in sixty-five so you take away five and you get the sixty!"

"OK . . . that was easy. Let's try this number pair," I said, writing *65, 25* on the chart. Several students raised their hands. I called on Mary to come up to the chart.

Mary drew a number line and then explained what she had drawn. "I took pieces out of the twenty-five," she said. "I subtracted the five in twenty-five, since sixty five had a five in it. That made sixty. Then I subtracted ten and that made fifty. Then I subtracted five to get to forty-five and five more. That made forty." (See Figure 11–8.)

Fernando solved the problem differently. He drew while he explained. (See Figure 11–9.) "It was sixty-five minus twenty-five, right? I just took away the five, then took away the twenty. That made forty," he explained.

"I did it kind of like Mary's and kind of like Fernando's," Danny said. He explained, "It's kind of like them both because I took away the five first, see?" Danny pointed to the numeral 5. "Instead of taking away the twenty all at once, I took away a ten and another ten," he went on, pointing to the 10s as he explained. (See Figure 11–10.)

"Let's try one last number pair for today," I said, writing *65, 26* on the chart. "What information about sixty-five and twenty-five can you use to solve the same problem with these numbers?" I gave students a minute, then asked for volunteers to come up to the chart, illustrate their method, and explain what they drew.

Sophia explained, "Well, sixty-five minus twenty-six is almost like sixty-five minus twenty-five, just like that other problem, see? So, I took away the five that was in the twenty-six. That made sixty. I took away ten and that made fifty, then another ten. That made forty. I still had one to take away, because twenty-six is one more than twenty-five, right? So forty minus one is thirty-nine!" (See Figure 11–11.)

Next, Jose shared his way. "My way is kind of like Sophia's way. I started by taking five away first. But instead of taking away ten and ten, I took away twenty all at once. Then I took away the one." (See Figure 11–12.)

The students' "work time" had been spent in a lengthy whole-class discussion sitting on the rug in front of the room. Their ability to attend to further discussion was clearly decreasing but it seemed important to summarize what they had accomplished during today's session. I affirmed their efforts before asking for their final input.

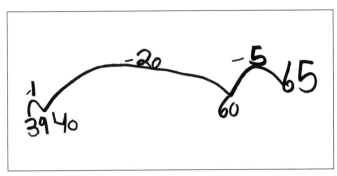

FIGURE 11–12 Jose used these numbers to build a different number line.

"You have done some hard thinking about strategies for subtraction using the number line as a tool. Before we end our mathematics time, I want to give you a chance to give me some information about what new information you learned today."

"We can add *and* subtract on a number line," one student stated.

"I can take away parts of numbers at a time," said another.

"It helps to think about the number before you take away part," said a third. "Like sixty-five minus twenty-five . . . it helps to take away the five first, because there's a five in both numbers."

"It's faster to take away a big part of the number, instead of just counting back," one student offered.

"People solved the same problem in different ways," said another.

"Subtracting is like adding . . . one goes up and one goes back on the number line," was another comment.

Students were adding to their repertoire of computation strategies and tools. They were able to use a number line to move beyond adding or subtracting by ones and to represent both addition and subtraction of tens. They were able to grow in their development of significant number concepts. Students were developing an understanding that the operations were related in some important ways, that there are a variety of ways of solving computation problems, and that some strategies are more efficient than others. Most importantly, they were able to communicate these understandings in writing and aloud, to their teacher as well as one another.

Linking Assessment and Instruction

As the students work, think about the following:

- In what ways do the students decompose or recombine numbers? Can they understand multi-digit numbers as groups of tens and ones? Do they decompose a number in multiple ways, depending on the addition or subtraction situation?
- Do students attend to "features" of numbers when deciding how to decompose them? Do they make use of "friendly" or "landmark" numbers? Are they able to explain why it is efficient and/or meaningful to use landmark numbers in certain situations?
- Can students make sense of a number line as a tool to use when adding or subtracting? How do they communicate their ability to do so?

CHAPTER 12

The Place-Value Game

OVERVIEW

In The Place-Value Game, *students are given three numbers in succession, and must record those numbers in one of three spaces on their papers, in an attempt to write the highest possible two-digit number. Each time the die is rolled, students must make a decision about whether they will write that number in the ones, tens, or "discard" place; having committed a number to one of the place-value spaces or the discard space, they are unable to move it to another space. Understanding place value is fundamental to understanding arithmetic operations.* The Place-Value Game *is an engaging way to prompt a class discussion on how the position of the digits affects the magnitude of the number.*

MATERIALS

- die
- 100 snap cubes, or 10 tens rods (longs) and 10 ones cubes (units), or 10 dimes and 10 pennies, 1 set per pair/small group of students (More than one pair/group may have the same type of materials.)

TIME

- one class period

Teaching Directions

1. Explain to the students that the object of the game is to record the highest two-digit number.

2. Ask the students to draw three lines on a blank sheet of paper: one for each digit in a two-digit number and one "discard" blank.

3. Roll a die three times. After each roll is announced, have students record the number in one of the spaces on their papers. Explain that once the number is recorded, its position cannot be changed.

4. Discuss with students the possible numbers that could be recorded from the three rolls of the die.

Teaching Notes

In order for students to understand arithmetic operations, it is important for them to realize how number magnitude relates to the position and value of each digit. Typically, teachers tell students the value of each place in a multidigit number. Students are expected to then memorize the value associated with the position of the digits. However, in order for students to understand place value, it is important that they have multiple experiences in considering the value associated with digits, as well as opportunities to compare numbers that have the same numerals in different positions. These types of experiences help students to understand that, although 63 and 36 contain the same numerals, these numbers differ greatly in magnitude.

The Lesson

The students came in from recess and sat down in a circle on the rug. In the center of the rug were three of the shoeboxes that usually sat in the center of each group of four tables. Inside were materials that the students regularly used, including sets of money, Unifix cubes, and base ten materials.

"There is something I bet you know a great deal about. I am not sure you have heard the mathematical term, but I am certain you have some knowledge about what it means," I began. The students looked at my quizzically. I went on, "What comes to your mind when I say 'place value'?" Most of the students looked uncertain, but a few raised their hands.

"Something has value," one student offered.

"There's a place for something," said another.

"There is value in the place," said a third.

I waited for about a minute for other students to volunteer, but none did. "I really appreciate your attempts to tell me about the meaning of these words, even though your expressions show that you don't seem very sure of yourselves. You were willing to take a risk and that isn't easy to do." I knew that experience with place-value concepts would give these students a foundation on which to build their understanding of this concept as well as ways to express it.

"I have a game to share with you today. I think it will help you learn more about what 'place value' means. It is called *The Place-Value Game*. Here is how you play." I drew three lines on the board:

_____   _____

_____

"I am going to roll a die three times," I said. "On each roll, I must decide on which line to write the numeral that matches what comes up on the die. I can write it on this line"—and I pointed to the one on the left—"this line"—and I pointed to the middle line—"or on this line, the 'discard' line," I said, pointing to the line to the far right, which I had drawn about an inch lower than the other two. "The object of the game is for me to come up with the highest number possible. Now, it might be a good time for me to think about what can possibly come up when I roll one die."

"You could get a six!"

"That's right! I could," I said, showing the class the side of the die that had six dots.

"You could get a five, too!"

"Yes, that's true, isn't it? I could get a five," I confirmed, again showing them the side of the die with the corresponding number of dots.

"You could get a one, a two, a three, a four, a five or a six."

"It is important for me to remember that when I roll the die. Well, let's see what happens," I said.

I rolled the die and got a 5. I asked the students for some help in deciding where to write the 5. "What do you think I should do?" I asked.

"It's almost the biggest number. I think you should put it on *that* line," David suggested, pointing to the line that represented the tens place. "That would make it a number in the fifties, right?"

"Why do you think so?" I asked him. It seemed as though David had some beginning understandings of place value that he could use to answer his own question.

"Yeah . . . that would be a fifties number," he replied. "If you put it in that middle place, it would be five ones." David's early understanding of place value had helped him to develop a strategy for what to do with a die roll that was a relatively high one.

Sonia built on what David had said. "But what if you get a six?" she said. "The tens would already be used! I think you should put it on the middle line." Sonia used "middle line" to label the place that David had correctly designated as the "ones."

"I don't think she's going to get a six. I think the five is probably the highest number she's going to roll," added Uriel. I was curious about Uriel's experience with dice and probability concepts. Sonia seemed to think that a 6 was probable while Uriel seemed to think it was not, or perhaps Sonia was more of a risk-taker.

"Hmm . . . this is not an easy decision," I said. "I could get a six; that is possible. I wonder if it is 'likely' though. Well, I think I will follow the advice some of you gave: I am going to put it on the left line, in the tens place." This is what my game board looked like:

__5__   _____

_____

"What is the highest number I could create and how would it be possible?" I asked.

"You could make 'fifty-six' if you rolled a six. But I don't think you will!" offered Kristin.

"You could make 'fifty-five' or 'fifty-four' or 'fifty-three' or 'fifty-two' or 'fifty-one,'" added Aaron, "but 'fifty-six' is the highest number you could make."

"Well, let's continue, and see what happens," I said as I jiggled the die in my hand. I spilled it out onto the table by my side and told the students what I rolled. "I got a two. What do you think I should do?"

Aaron was the first to give his opinion. "Throw it out! You gotta get a higher roll than that!"

"But what if she doesn't?" asked Sonia. "She only has one more roll!"

"So, if I write a 'two' on the middle line, the number will be . . ."

"Fifty-two!" chimed the class.

"And then what happens?" I asked.

"You are done!" said Kristin.

"Nuh-uh! She still has another roll!" said David. "And she'll have to write that number down on that line," he continued, pointing to the discard line.

"She'll be, like, wasting a roll," said one student.

"Huh?" questioned Kristin.

David continued. "Well, if it's a 'one,' it won't be wasted, because she would be throwing out the one and that number wouldn't help anyway. But if she rolled, like, a five or a six, she'd be throwing out good numbers . . . numbers that she could have used." David clearly had some experience with dice. He was looking ahead in the game and able to consider some ramifications of hasty, early moves.

"Oh yeah . . ." admitted Kristin. "This is hard!"

"Does anyone else have some ideas that could help me decide?" I asked.

"I think you should throw it out . . . write it on that line," offered Aaron, pointing to the discard line. "You want to write the highest number, right? If you put a two in the middle, then your number is fifty-two. But you might be able to make fifty-three or fifty-four or fifty-five or fifty-six. I think you should go for it!"

"OK. I think I will 'go for it,'" I said as I wrote a *2* on the discard line. There was some gentle applause. I rolled the die and told the students what I got: a 4.

"See! I told you! Yeah!" cheered Aaron.

As I wrote the last number on the middle blank line, I reminded the students of the goal of the game. "The object of the game is to make the highest number. What number did I make?" I asked. Hands went up (see below).

$$\underline{\hspace{1em}5\hspace{1em}}\qquad\underline{\hspace{1em}4\hspace{1em}}$$
$$\underline{\hspace{1em}2\hspace{1em}}$$

"You made fifty-four," said Sonia.

"I did . . . with your help! But what if I didn't put the numbers in these places? What if had decided to put the numbers in other places? What other possible numbers could I have made?" I wanted to see if students were able to see the possible combinations that could be made with the three numbers I had rolled. Some students began writing the combinations down on the paper that was in front of them, while others could quickly "see" the possibilities from looking at the digits on the board.

"You could have made fifty-two," said one.

"And twenty-five!" said another.

"Ooh! Forty-five! You could have made forty-five!" exclaimed another.

"And forty-two!" offered one student.

"What about twenty-four?" queried another.

As students named the different numbers that could be made from rolling a 5, 2, and 4, I listed them on the board. "There are lots of numbers I could have written down on the blank lines," I said in summation, "but I wrote down this one," I pointed to what I had written on the board. "Is it the highest number I could have written? How could I prove it to myself and to you? Quietly think about that, without raising your hands." I gave students a couple of minutes and then asked them to share their ideas.

"What do you think? How could I convince someone that I did make the highest number possible with a five, a two, and a four?" I asked.

"You could make them with materials . . . like the cubes!" said Sonia.

Uriel asked, "What about the base ten materials . . . we could make fifty-four with those!"

"Money!" said David gleefully. "We could make fifty-four with the coins!"

"I have an idea. You have all of those materials in the shoeboxes in the middle of your tables. In just a moment, I am going to ask each table to make one of these numbers, using the different materials in your shoeboxes. I will call your table to the rug and we can compare what we have built." I assigned each table one of the numbers that was listed, writing a table name next to each listed number. This left fifty-four for us to model together.

"How can I make fifty-four with cubes so that it will be easy for us to see that there are fifty-four?" I asked.

"Make tens!" David replied.

"Will you do that, David?" I asked, and David got busy counting out cubes from one of the shoeboxes that was in the center of the rug.

"How about the money? How can I make fifty-four with coins so that it is easy to see that there is fifty-four cents?" I asked.

"Don't use pennies! That would be too hard!" offered Aaron.

"Yeah . . . use dimes or quarters!" said Kristin.

"Will you and Aaron do that, Kristin?" I asked.

"I'll use dimes," said Kristin. "You use quarters," she said to Aaron, and they got started counting coins from the coin bags that were also in the shoeboxes.

Sonia said, "I can use the base ten materials!"

"That would be great, Sonia. Take a moment to build fifty-four and we will patiently wait to see what you have done." As students finished building the number with materials, they placed it in front of them. Each student then took a turn counting out the materials to show us fifty-four.

"Let's leave these models of fifty-four in the center of the rug. Each table is going to build one of the other listed numbers, in different ways, using the different materials in your shoeboxes. Your table will build your number using cubes, base ten materials, and coins. As you build the number at your table, think about how you can describe what you have built. You need to prove that fifty-four is higher than the number you built. You can use your model and the models of fifty-four we have already built to prove which number is higher. After you have made your model, show the rest of the people at your table." Students were eager to get started, so I dismissed each table group to get to work. It only took a couple of minutes for each group to build their assigned number. I called the students back to the rug so we could compare models.

The visual models allowed students to easily see the magnitude of each number that could be made from the three dice rolls, while also giving students opportunities to compare different numbers.

"Twenty-four only has two dimes, but fifty-four has five," one of the students observed.

"Forty-two looks pretty close. It has four tens and fifty-four has five," another stated.

"Fifty-two is almost as big as fifty-four: it has five dimes, just like fifty-four," said yet another.

"Yeah, but fifty-two has only two pennies and fifty-four has four," someone else added.

"Twenty-five has two trains of ten, just like twenty-four, but twenty-five has five loose cubes and twenty-four has only four," was another comment.

For the next game, I asked students to play. I sent them to their seats and asked them to draw lines on their papers similar to the ones I had drawn on the board, and I began shaking the die in my hand. "Get ready," I announced. "Remember, as I roll, you will write down the number in one of the three spots. Once you write it down, you don't get to change it!" I dropped the die on the table. "First roll! Six!" Students wrote down the numeral on their game board as I wrote it on the board. "Second roll: three!" I paused to write the number on the board while students wrote it down as well. "Third roll: five!" There were some groans, as students recorded the last die roll and I wrote a 5 on the board. I asked, "So, the highest two-digit number you could have written down was . . ."

The students responded "Sixty-five!" I asked for a show of hands to see how many of them had, indeed, written down that number and about half the class had. "I wonder: what are the other possible two-digit numbers? Take a moment. Talk with the people at your table. Make a list of the possible numbers, then build them at your table to prove that sixty-five is, indeed, the highest number possible." Students began discussing, listing, and building with the other students at their tables.

After a few minutes, I asked, "So, how can you prove to me that sixty-five is the highest number you can make with the dice rolls six, three, and five?" Students shared their observations about the possible ways to arrange the three digits and discussed the models that represented these different arrangements.

"Well, we wrote sixty-three and fifty-three. Then we changed the numbers around and made thirty-six and thirty-five," one student said.

"Hey, that's cool!" said a classmate.

"We made fifty-six too!" said another.

"Hey! Last time we made six different numbers! This time we did also!"

"We made them all with money. Sixty-five and sixty-three both had six dimes, but sixty-five had five pennies and sixty-three only had three."

"We used the base ten materials. The most tens used was six."

For the next game, I wanted students to connect with the name of the game. I asked them to draw three new blanks, but this time I asked questions after each roll. I rolled a 3 but asked students to consider the blank on which to write it. I pointed to the left blank and asked, "So, if I wrote the three here, the value of the three would be . . ."

$$\underline{\quad 3 \quad} \quad \underline{\qquad\qquad}$$

$$\underline{\qquad\qquad}$$

Several students answered, "Thirty."

I question my students constantly. I don't want them to think that an answer is sufficient; I want them to know that the reasoning behind the answer is as important as, if not more important than, the answer itself. "What makes you think so?"

Aaron said, "Because it's tens. So it's ten, twenty, thirty." He put up a finger for each number he said.

"Anyone else?" I want students to hear me question them, even if the information they give is correct. I also know that the same information, worded differently, may be more comprehensible to other students.

"Well, that's the tens and the one in the middle is the ones," said Sarah. "So, if the three is there, it's thirty."

"And if it's there," added David, "it's just three." David came up to the board, erased the first 3, and wrote another in the middle blank.

_____   __3__

"What if I write the number here?" I asked, erasing the 3 David had written and writing one in the blank on the right.

_____   _____   __3__

"It doesn't matter!" said Uriel. "You throw it out! It's nothing! Or is it a three . . ."

"Both. It's a three but it doesn't count, because you threw it out," I said. "Let's continue. The next roll," I announced, "is a two." Students wrote down the numeral. Again, I asked the same question, pointing to each blank and asking, "If I wrote two here"— and I pointed to the tens place or ones place—"the value of the two would be . . ." Many students were able to name the quantity—twenty or two—represented by the placement of the numeral. I rolled the die one more time and got a 1. Immediately upon announcing the roll, there were lots of groans. I took advantage of the sudden outcry, because it seemed to represent some knowledge we had yet to discuss.

"You have me so curious!" I said. "What was that sound that came out of many of you?" Some hands went up and students related how they expected a higher number to come up on the die. While I didn't want to have a lengthy or in-depth conversation about probability, this seemed to be a good opportunity to briefly touch on what is possible to role on a conventional six-sided die. "That is so interesting. You must know a lot about dice! What is possible to roll, if you only have one die?" I asked. Students gave me all the numbers, from one to six. While they didn't necessarily report them in order, I wrote them in order on the board, as each was reported. "That might be really important information to have, when playing this game," I offered. After these three rolls, I asked students for the highest possible number we could build with a three, two, and one. Students were able to report that it would be thirty-two. We also

discussed the lowest possible number built from these same digits and they realized it would be twelve. We played one more game with two digits; after each roll, we discussed the value of the roll, depending on which blank the numeral was written in. At the end of each game, we also discussed the highest and lowest possible number. I introduced how to play the same game with three digits and then let the students have about ten minutes to play *The Place-Value Game* with a partner. I asked them to think about how this helped them to better understand place value.

"We began today's mathematics time by discussing 'place value.' I asked you what you thought the phrase meant and then gave you time to play a game. Hopefully, the game helped you develop your understanding of place value. I have a question that I would like you to think about, the same question with which we began today's session: What is 'place value'? Please take a minute or two to think about what new understanding you have and then take some time to write down your thoughts on paper."

The students were remarkably serious about their thinking and writing time. The room became very quiet as students considered what they had done and how this helped them to better understand a difficult concept. I walked around, passing out paper. After a few minutes, students began writing.

When I reviewed the papers, I discovered that Javier had understood the connection between the purpose of the game and the name of the game. (See Figure 12–1.) Beth had been able to recall many different things she learned while playing *The Place-Value Game*. (See Figure 12–2.)

It was clear from their papers that students had enjoyed their math class. This enjoyment is far from trivial: having a positive attitude about mathematics is critical to being a successful mathematician. Their work also demonstrated that knowledge about the

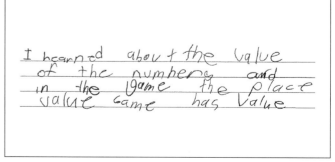

FIGURE 12–1 Javier's work showed an understanding of the term *place value.*

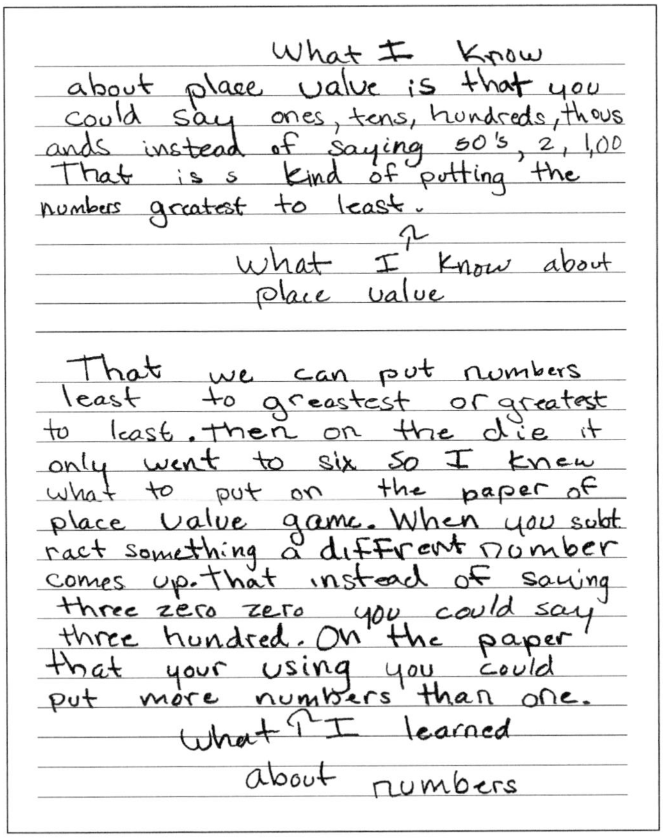

What I Know
about place value is that you
could say ones, tens, hundreds, thous
ands instead of saying 50's, 2, 1,00
That is s kind of putting the
numbers greatest to least.

What I Know about
place value

That we can put numbers
least to greastest or greatest
to least. then on the die it
only went to six so I knew
what to put on the paper of
place value game. When you subt
ract something a diffrent number
comes up. that instead of saying
three zero zero you could say
three hundred. On the paper
that your using you could
put more numbers than one.

What I I learned
about numbers

FIGURE 12–2 Beth's paper demonstrates important understanding of place value.

concept of place value is still forming in the minds of these second-grade students. While this activity broadened their understanding of place value, it is obvious that they will benefit from additional games, activities, and experiences that require them to consider number magnitude based on the placement of a digit.

Linking Assessment and Instruction

As the students work, think about the following:

- Can the students use a variety of models to represent and compare the value of a digit in different positions?
- Are they able to name and compare the value of a digit in the ones place and tens place? Can they explain the value of a digit in the ones or tens position?
- Given a limited number of die rolls, can students use their understanding of probability concepts when deciding where to record the outcome?

Zap It to Zero

OVERVIEW

Zap It to Zero *is an activity that logically follows the* Place-Value Game. *While* The Place-Value Game *requires students to think about the magnitude of a number by considering the arrangement of the digits,* Zap It to Zero *involves using a calculator to "test" understanding of the value of each digit of a multidigit number. Students "zap" a digit to zero by adding or subtracting on the calculator. In order to understand place value, students must understand that the value of a digit depends upon its position in a number. In order to successfully "zap" a digit—by subtracting a number—students must draw on their understanding of this relationship.*

MATERIALS

- ◼ optional: overhead calculator

TIME

- • two to three class periods

Teaching Directions

1. Write a three-digit number on the board. Ask students, who are working in pairs, to enter this number in their calculators.

2. Explain to the students that you want them to "zap" a digit to zero by subtracting one number. Explain to the pairs that they must agree on the number to zap before using the calculator (e.g., if the number is 235 and they are told to zap the 3, students would need to agree to subtract 30 to change the middle digit to 0).

3. Have students enter this number on the calculator and record what they have done. Model this recording on the board.

4. Ask the class to read the new number.

5. Have the students repeat this process until the number on their calculators' display is zero.

Teaching Notes

Understanding place value is fundamental to understanding arithmetic operations. Typically, teachers tell students the value of the digits in multidigit numbers and students are expected to memorize the value associated with the position of the digits. However, that type of experience neglects to develop an important aspect of place value: that the value of a digit (the 4 in 45) represents a quantity (forty), as well as that many groups (four tens). This understanding—knowing how the value of a digit depends on its position in a number—is critical to students' success in playing *Zap It to Zero*. As a result of playing this game, students develop and build on their understanding of a digit's *value*.

The Lesson

I got out the calculators and wrote *Zap It to Zero* on the board. "You have recently had some experience with *The Place-Value Game*," I began. "For each of three die rolls, you had to decide where to place the number in order to build the largest two-digit number. We talked about the value of each digit in those two-digit numbers. We will need to think about the value of each digit in some three-digit numbers today.

Your experience with *The Place-Value Game* will help you in playing this new game: *Zap It to Zero.*"

The students had used calculators before and knew their features and capabilities. They had not used these tools for a while, however, and so I thought it was wise to allow them some "free exploration" time; I knew that this would better enable them to focus on the activity when we began playing the game.

I passed out paper to each table and a calculator to each pair of students, asking the students to let the materials sit on their desktops for a moment. I asked them what the tool I had passed out was called and where they had seen the tool before. Students quickly named the tool and reported that they knew that calculators were used both in the classroom and at home. "What are some of the uses of calculators?" I asked.

"To do hard math," one student said.

"To figure out the math in your checkbook," said another.

I asked the students to take about ten minutes to "find out everything you can" about the calculators. They began pressing the calculator keys and observing the results of their actions. Students eagerly discussed with their partners and with the other students nearby what they noticed. I was surprised by their level of engagement. While students had familiarity with calculators, giving them a simple task on which to focus—"Find out everything you can"—was instrumental in getting them to attend to the features and functions of the calculators.

After this exploratory time I asked the students to put their calculators down and give their attention to their classmates who had observations to share with the class about calculators and their use. Students contributed the following observations:

After you enter a number, you see it on the calculator.
When you press + or −, the number "blinks" but you do not see the + or − signs.
The On/C button makes the number in the "window" go to zero.
You can add and subtract on the calculator.
There were some keys with "funny" pictures on them.

It is not unusual for only a few students to report their observations to the whole class, even though most are involved in partner or small-group discussions. To give more students an opportunity to talk in a less risky setting, I gave the students a chance to share any other observations with those students at their tables before I introduced the next activity.

"*The Place-Value Game* and your exploration of the calculators will really help you to be successful with this next activity," I said. "This is another game that will help you to learn about place value. In *Zap It to Zero*, I am going to put a number on the board. I am going to ask you and your partner to figure out how to 'zap' one of the digits to zero by subtracting. You must discuss how to do this with your partner and you must agree on the number before touching any of the calculator keys."

"I don't get it!" Aaron said at once.

"Me neither," said Dean.

"Let's try it together," I said. "Maybe the directions will make more sense when we go through the steps." On the board, I wrote: *25.*

"Tell me the number I wrote on the board," I said. The students responded as a group. "How will you enter this number into your calculators, so that you have the same number I have written on the board?"

Sarah called out, "First a two, then a five."

"Try that and see," I said. I turned on the overhead and displayed the overhead calculator. Pairs of students entered the digits into their calculators. "Show me a thumbs-up signal when the number displayed on your calculator matches the one that I have written on the board." Most students gave me the signal. I repeated what Sarah had called out, pressing the keys as I named them, "First a two, then a five. You were right! It does display twenty-five!" I went on. "Now, when I say *go!* I want you to talk with your partner about how to 'zap' the five. That means you want to change it into a zero by subtracting. If you zap the five in twenty-five and turn it into a zero, what will you see on the calculator?" I pointed to the digit on the board.

"Twenty!" most responded.

"Talk with your partner. Agree on what you will press on the calculator to zap the five into a zero, so that you will turn twenty-five into twenty. Go!"

Students began discussing their options with their partners. After a few seconds, many students had raised their hands.

"You minus five!" offered Aaron.

"If you have twenty-five and you take away five, you have twenty," added Sarah.

"Zap the five by minusing five," said Ronny.

"Any different ideas?" I asked. When no other student responded, I continued. "So, my calculator has twenty-five displayed and I want to subtract five.

What keys do I press in order to do that, so that I can zap the five to zero?"

Allen suggested, "You touch the minus and the five."

"Then the equals!" added LeAnn.

"Let me try that," I began, pressing the keys as I named them, "minus, five, equals." The overhead calculator display did, indeed, show 20.

"Yeah!" many cheered.

"Yes, it worked!" I said. "Now, you try it."

Pairs of students worked together to press the correct calculator keys.

"Tell me what is displayed on your calculators," I said.

"Twenty!" was the unanimous response.

"Just like mine. Now we want to zap the two in twenty to make it zero. If we zap the two in twenty, what will need to press on the calculator? And what will be displayed once we press those keys? Talk to your partner."

Students talked in pairs and I quickly walked through the room to listen in on their conversations. It seemed as though most students realized that subtracting twenty would result in zero, although some thought subtracting two would. Many thought a zero would be displayed, but some thought two zeros would be displayed (i.e., 00).

"Let's hear what you discussed," I said. "What do we need to do to zap the two in twenty? And what do you think we will see displayed once we do?"

"I think you take away twenty," said LeAnn.

"Me, too," added Allen.

"Does anyone think something different?" I asked.

"I think you minus two," said John.

"So, some of you think we should subtract twenty and some of you think we should subtract two," I said. "Let me think about this . . . I have twenty. If I subtract twenty . . ."

"Uh oh. I changed my mind," said John. "I think you subtract twenty, not two."

"What made you change your mind?" I pressed.

"You want to zap the two in twenty. You want it to be zero, right?" asked John. He went on, "Twenty minus twenty is zero. Twenty minus two is . . ." John softly counted back two from twenty, using his fingers, "Nineteen, eighteen!"

"So you think that, if I have twenty and I subtract twenty, I will have zero. If I have twenty and I subtract two, I will have eighteen. Talk with your partner. Agree on what you think you should do. Try

what you think. I will check back with you in a moment. Go!"

Students became very animated. They were eager to test out what they thought, and quickly displayed smiles and waving hands.

"So what do you think?" I asked.

"Minus, twenty, and equals!" several students called out.

"Let's see." Again, I pressed the overhead calculator keys as I named them: "Minus, twenty, equals."

Again, cheers erupted as the display on the overhead calculator showed a 0.

"Did the display surprise you? Or did you know that there would be a zero?" I asked. Only a few hands went up.

"There was a zero in twenty. If you zap the two, why don't you have zero zero?" asked Aaron.

"I thought there'd be two zeros, too," added Sarah.

"Interesting, isn't it?" I said. "Zero has the same value as zero zero. You don't really need more than one zero. Zero zero zero or zero zero zero zero"—I wrote *000* and *0000* on the board—"still means 'zero.' You just need one zero to mean zero."

I wanted to check and see if students were connecting their knowledge of place value to the activity we were doing together. I said, "I asked you what to do to zap the two in twenty. What is the value of the two in twenty? Talk with the people at your table. See what they think."

I gave students a minute or two to discuss the value of the digit. As they did, I noticed some students take out the Unifix cubes from the plastic shoeboxes in the center of the tables. I asked for the students' attention. "What do you think?"

"The two is not just a two. It's twenty," said LeAnn.

"It's two *tens*," added Dean.

"See?" asked Sarah, pointing to the two sets of cubes lying on her desk. They were snapped together in trains of ten. "You have two tens in twenty. The two means twenty."

Sometimes it is difficult to know if students are reporting what they have heard their classmates or me say or if they are explaining what they truly understand. While it appeared that LeAnn, Dean, and Sarah had some knowledge of place value—that the position of the digit related to a specific quantity, as well as groups of tens—it would take other situations and repeated experiences to convince me that this concept was firmly understood by these students.

"We will try to zap some more zeros in some other numbers. This time, we will do some recording to match what we do on the calculators. Please get a sheet of paper and write *Zap It to Zero* at the top." I gave students a minute to do this. While they did, I wrote these words on an overhead transparency. "Let's start with sixty-three." I began a chart (see below).

Zap It to Zero

63

"Discuss what keys to press to enter sixty-three into your calculators." I gave students a minute and then asked, "Could you help me out? Tell me what I need to do to have sixty-three displayed."

"Six and three," many called out. I pressed these keys on the overhead calculator.

"I want to zap the six in sixty-three. What is the value of that digit? Discuss what keys to press. When you agree, press them and see."

Several hands went up almost immediately. I called on LeAnn.

"Minus sixty equals," reported LeAnn. "The six means sixty."

"It's six tens, so you take away sixty," added Allen.

On the overhead calculator, I did what LeAnn suggested. A 3 appeared. "Hmm . . ." I began. "How come I don't have a zero? What happened? I wanted to zap the six and make it a zero. I don't see a zero. I see a three!" Several hands went up.

Dean said, "I thought it would be zero three!"

Ronny added, "But you don't need zero in front of a number."

"What do you mean?" I asked.

"It's still three. It's like there's zero, but there isn't. It isn't there because you don't need it," he added.

LeAnn spoke up again. "It's like that thing you did with zero zero. You don't need zero zero, you just need a zero. You can put a zero in front of a number and it's like it isn't there. You don't need it. Zero three is still three. You could have zero zero three, too. It would still be three!" I found it interesting that LeAnn was trying to connect the use of zero in the last situation to the use of zero in this one.

"Anyone else?" I asked.

"Sixty-three minus sixty is three. See? Sixty-three is sixty and three. If you have sixty-three and you take away sixty, you have the three," Allen explained.

"You don't have zero three, you just have three." I was relieved to hear that some students were connecting their understanding of the operations to how the calculator was a tool to perform the operations. If they had not, it would be important to have a conversation about zero as a quantity as well as a placeholder.

"I need to remember to record, on paper, what I am doing on the calculator," I continued. "Let me go back to my paper." I placed the previous transparency back on the overhead. "I had sixty-three, but then I pressed some keys to zap the six. I need to record what keys I pressed, and the result."

"You did 'minus sixty equals,'" began John.

"And you got three," added Sarah.

I wrote what John and Sarah said. The transparency now looked like this:

Zap It to Zero

63 − 60 = 3

Students copied what I did on their own papers.

"Now we need to zap the three!" Ronny predicted.

"You are right," I said. "Discuss, agree, then try it," I added. "What is the value of the three?" Students quickly pressed the calculator keys and several hands shot up into the air.

"What do you think I should do? My calculator has three and I need to zap it to zero," I began, showing my overhead calculator.

"Minus three equals!" the class responded.

"What is the value of the three?" I asked.

"Just a three!" said Dean.

"Three ones . . . three!" added Aaron.

I pressed the keys they suggested and the calculator displayed a 0. I placed the transparency back on the overhead.

"Now what?" I asked.

"Three minus three equals zero," several students suggested. I recorded what they told me and my paper now looked like this:

Zap It to Zero

63 − 60 = 3

3 − 3 = 0

"We have tried some two-digit numbers," I said. "I think it is time to graduate." The students giggled at this statement. "Let's try some three-digit numbers," I said.

Students responded with "Uh oh!" and "Easy!" and "Yeah!" On my transparency I wrote *265*. The students wrote down the number on their papers as well. "Which digit should we zap first?" I asked. I called on John.

"Two! It stands for two hundred, so you have to minus two hundred!" he said.

"You think so? Talk with your partners. Discuss what to press on your calculators. Agree and then try it. Talk about the value of the two in two hundred sixty-five. I have a question: if we zap the two, what will be displayed on your calculators? *Go!*"

Students were immediately involved in discussing their ideas with their partners. After a minute or so, many raised their hands to explain their thinking.

"You need to press minus two hundred . . . press 'minus two zero zero,'" began Sarah.

"Then equals," added LeAnn.

"Two is two hundreds. Can I show you?" Aaron asked. He got up and went to the shelves on which the other math materials were stored in plastic shoeboxes. He pulled out the base ten materials. These materials provide a model that some students use to build numbers of various magnitude. They are comprised of "units" (ones), "longs" (tens), and "flats" (hundreds). The units are one square centimeter. The longs are one-by-one-by-ten centimeters, and scored every centimeter. The flats are ten-by-ten-by-one centimeter, scored every centimeter as well. Many students relate to this geometric model and can easily show how ten longs rods equal the size of one flat, how ten units equal one long, or how to find the difference between two quantities. Aaron got out two flats, six longs, and five units and brought them up to the front of the room. As he named a quantity and the part of the model that corresponded to it, he held up the materials.

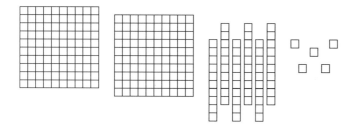

"The two is two hundreds. The six is six tens. The five is five ones. If you want to zap the two, you got to

take away two hundred. This is what's left." Aaron held up the six longs and five units.

"Thanks, Sarah and LeAnn and Aaron. Who else has an idea?" I asked.

Dean said, "We think the same."

Students often admit to having similar ideas and using similar processes as their classmates. I used to discourage students, like Dean, from sharing an idea that had already been discussed, because I wanted to avoid redundancy. Now, I ask students to go ahead and explain their ideas, even if they are similar to ones that have already been expressed. It often benefits a class to hear a similar idea explained through use of slightly different words; some students will better understand a repeated idea or a familiar idea expressed a new way. And all students' understanding deepens through the process of communicating that understanding as well.

"How so?" I asked Dean.

"If you minus two hundred, the two will disappear," he responded. "You'll have sixty-five."

"Thanks, Dean. Let me try that: minus two hundred equals." I pressed the calculator keys. The overhead calculator now displayed 65. "Now I need to record what I did on my paper. Can someone come up and help me? LeAnn?"

LeAnn came up to the overhead and recorded what I had done. As she recorded, her classmates did as well. My paper—the transparency—looked like this when she was done:

Zap It to Zero

$$63 - 60 = 3$$
$$3 - 3 = 0$$

$$265 - 200 = 65$$

"What digit shall we zap next? Ronny?" I asked.

"The five," Ronny answered. "It's five ones, so you take away five. 'Minus five equals.'" I asked Ronny to come up and press the keys on the overhead calculator.

"I wonder what the display on the calculator will be. Voice your prediction to your partner quickly, before Ronny finishes," I said.

I asked Sarah to come up and record what Ronny had done on the overhead transparency. It seemed as though the students understood what to do. I decided to give them one more three-digit number to test out their ability, this time turning over the entire task to them, while I assisted, if necessary. Beginning with

392, I called on students to choose which digit to zap, press the overhead keys, and record, each time reporting why they were making the decisions they did. When we were done with this last example, the overhead looked like this:

Zap It to Zero

$$63 - 60 = 3$$
$$3 - 3 = 0$$

$$265 - 200 = 65$$
$$65 - 5 = 5$$
$$60 - 60 = 0$$

$$392 - 90 = 302$$
$$302 - 2 = 300$$
$$200 - 300 = 0$$

At this point, I decided to let students have about fifteen minutes to practice playing *Zap It to Zero* in pairs. Rather than being a game with a "winner" and "loser," this activity was a cooperative one: students agreed on what digit to "zap," each checking to ensure that calculations on paper and the calculator matched. I asked students to think about place value while playing this game, how this game connects to other games they have played, and how it helped to develop their understanding of place value. At the end of this practice period, I again asked the students to give me their attention.

"We have been discussing 'place value,'" I said. "I have a question for you. What is your understanding of place value after playing this game? Please take a minute or two to think about what new understanding you have and then take some time to write your thoughts down on paper."

The students were remarkably serious about their thinking and writing time. The room became very quiet, as students considered what they had done and how this helped them to better understand a difficult concept. I walked around, passing out paper. After a few minutes, students began writing.

When I reviewed their papers after the lesson, I was pleased at the variety of learning that had taken place. Some students commented on their use of an operation. Allen was impressed by the extent of his own understanding of subtraction. (See Figure 13–1.) John appreciated how use of the calculator helped

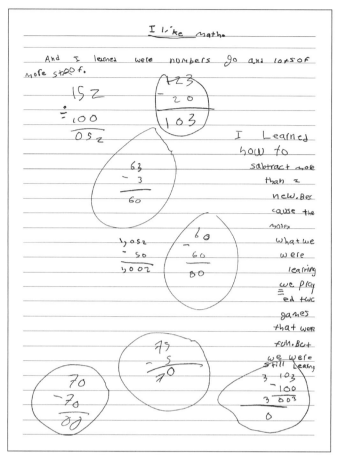

FIGURE 13–1 The game allowed Allen to explore what he knew about subtraction.

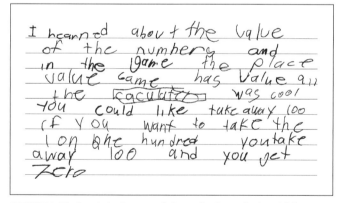

FIGURE 13–2 John's use of the calculator helped him understand place value.

him to understand place value. (See Figure 13–2.) Darren provided an example to demonstrate how he played the game. (See Figure 13–3.) His paper showed that he was a real fan of *Zap It to Zero* and looked forward to more such learning opportunities.

Zap It to Zero had been a big hit with these second graders. While they had clearly enjoyed the

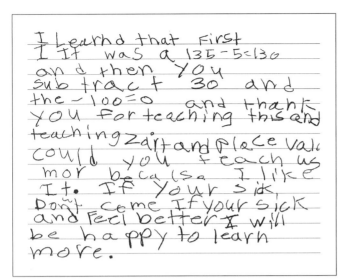

I Learnd that First
I If waS a 135-5<130
and then You
sub tract 30 and
the ~100=0 and thank
you For teaching this and
teaching Zajt and place vale
could you teach us
mor becalse I like
It. IF Your sick,
Don't ceme If your sick
and Feel better I will
be happy to learn
more.

FIGURE 13–3   Darren expressed his enjoyment of the game and desire to play again.

game, their work demonstrated that the activity had enabled them to develop a deeper understanding of place value, a fundamental mathematical concept for this grade level.

Linking Assessment and Instruction

As you observe students work, think about the following:

- Are students comfortable using calculators? Do they regard them as useful, purposeful tools?
- How do students demonstrate their understanding of how subtraction works when working with calculators?
- What place-value understandings do students demonstrate when playing *Zap It to Zero?* What do they say or do that indicates that they understand that changing the ones digit to zero involves subtracting ones, and changing the tens digit to zero involves subtracting tens?
- Can students use manipulatives to represent operations on the calculator?

Make My Number

CHAPTER 14

OVERVIEW

Make My Number *is an activity in which students use a calculator, a list of numbers, and their understanding of place value to make numbers. Students enter a starting number on the calculator and determine which subsequent numbers and operations to enter in order to get to the next number. In order to be successful, students must be able to compare numbers and determine the missing quantity, as well as know the operation on the calculator that will allow them to move from one number to another.*

MATERIALS

- *Make My Number* worksheets, 1 set per pair of students (see Blackline Masters)
- optional: overhead calculator

TIME

- one class period

Teaching Directions

1. Write a starting number on the board, followed by a sequential list of numbers.

2. Ask students, who are working in pairs, to enter the starting number on their calculator. Explain to them that they can enter only one number and operation to get to the next number on the list. Have them discuss potential moves before making their entries on the calculator.

3. Have students keep a written record of their moves.

Teaching Notes

Make My Number presents students with opportunities to use several important mathematical concepts and processes. Students rely on a variety of tools—number lines, the 1–100 chart, manipulatives—and strategies—counting on, counting back, use of known facts—to compare quantities and find the difference between them. They consider how to operate on one number in order for another to result, making a prediction about the effect of an operation and the magnitude of numbers.

Students test their prediction by using the calculator to add on or subtract from a number to make the next number in a series. This immediate feedback, displayed on the calculator, gives students information about the viability of methods and effectiveness of tools. This information leads them to adjust their reasoning in order to successfully "make my number."

The Lesson

The students were excited to find calculators at their desks as they came into the room and sat down at their seats. An overhead calculator was displayed on the screen at the front of the room. While students had had experience with calculators during previous lessons, it seemed important to help them connect today's experiences with what they had already done with these mathematical tools.

"You sound pretty excited to see the calculators," I said. "Let's see if we can recall how to use them. In what ways have you used calculators or seen them used? What do we need to be thinking about when using them?" Various students described their previous experiences with calculators, and some offered ideas about their appropriate use.

"You sound like 'calculator experts,'" I acknowledged. "The information you just shared will be really helpful to you today. Today's activity is called *Make My Number*. I will give you a list of numbers. You and a partner will make the first number on your calculator. You will look at the next number on the list and try to figure out how to get to that number from the first number you entered. Here is the trick: to get from one number to the next, you can only enter one number."

"Huh?" said several students.

"I don't get it . . ." said a few more.

"What do you mean, 'You can only enter one number'?" one student asked.

"Let's try it together. I have the overhead calculator displayed. I am going to list some numbers on the board, next to the screen." I wrote the following list of numbers on the board:

    4
    7
    17
    37
    33
    13
    53
    59
    89

As I touched each listed number, the students helped me read it aloud. "Now I am going to enter in my calculator the first number listed. Remind me what number that is?" I asked.

"Four!" several students responded.

"So, I will press the 'four' key," I said as I entered the number on the calculator. "Now I need to look at the next number on the list. I need to figure out how to get to that number, from the number four. The second number is . . ."

"Seven!" chorused the class.

"Yes," I continued. "How will I get to seven from four?"

"Four plus three is seven," said one student.

"You have to add," said a second.

"Plus three!" said a third.

"Let me try that," I suggested, pressing the + and the 3 on the calculator. The display showed a 3. I looked to the students for some more information, since the display did not yet show me a 7. "Uh oh . . . I don't see 'seven.'"

"Equals! You got to press the equals sign," one student called out.

"Oh, that's right," I said, pressing the = on the calculator. A 7 appeared on the display. "You are

correct. It worked. I have a 'seven' and the next number on my list is 'seventeen.' What can I press on the calculator, to get from seven to seventeen?"

"Hmm," said one student. "You could add three and that would make ten. Then you could add seven and that would make seventeen!"

"How many numbers would that be," I asked the class, "if I added first a three and then a seven?"

"That's easy . . . two!" said one student.

"A three and seven? That's two numbers," said another.

"You said we could only put in one number," said a third.

"That was the tricky part of the directions that I gave in the beginning," I reminded them. "I can only enter one number to get from one number to the next. Talk with your partner: what one number can I enter that will get me from seven to seventeen?"

There was a soft hum of conversation in the classroom and after a few moments, several students had their hands in the air. "So what do you think I should do, if I can only enter one number in the calculator?" I asked.

"There's ten, from seven to seventeen," one student said.

"You got to press 'plus' and 'ten' . . . that will get you to seventeen," said a second.

"Plus ten *equals*," affirmed a third.

Many students nodded in agreement. I explained my moves as I pressed the keys. "Plus, ten, equals," I said. A 17 appeared in the display and the students applauded. "Right, again!" they said.

"What's the next number in the list on the board? Talk with a partner again. Discuss what I need to do in order to get from seventeen to the next number on the list." Again, students conversed with someone at their table and then raised their hands.

"You got to go from seventeen to thirty-seven. You got to add, because the numbers are getting bigger," said one.

"You need to add twenty," said another.

"See? On the hundred chart? If you are on seventeen and you go to thirty-seven, you go down two boxes . . . that's like adding," said yet another.

"So, you press 'plus' and 'twenty' and 'equals,'" one student said.

"You could add ten and add ten again!" said another.

"No, you can't," one student said. "Remember? She said you could only add one number. Ten and ten is *two* numbers."

"It makes twenty though," the first student said.

"Yeah, but you can only use *one*!" the second stated.

Many students nodded in agreement. I waited to see if any other students had something to add. When the students fell quiet, I announced, "I have seventeen on the calculator display. The first key I need to press is . . ."

"Plus!" several students called out.

I followed their directions, saying, "Plus. The next key I press is . . ."

"Twenty! Then the equals sign!" several students said.

I did what they told me. "'Twenty,' 'equals,'" I said, and applause again erupted as 37 appeared on the calculator display. "I am doing a great job, with your help. Now I need to make thirty-three appear. How will I do that? Talk with your partner."

The students and I collaborated in modeling *Make My Number* as we worked our way through the list. Each time we got ready to transform the current number into the next one on the list, I had them discuss with a partner what I should do. We successfully displayed each number on the posted list.

The students seemed to understand the directions for *Make My Number*. Rather than teach them how to do the activity while instructing them in how to do the recording for it, I decided to first model the process, then model the recording of the process. I still needed to model how to keep a written record of what I had done on the calculator. I erased the previous list of numbers and wrote a new list of numbers on the board:

12
32
30
60
57
37
39
89

"I'd like to try this with you again," I said. "This time, I want to remember what keys I pressed on the calculator to go from one number to the next. Jason, could you be my partner this time?" Jason nodded and came up to the front of the classroom. "Let's look at the new list of numbers. Would all of you help Jason and me to read the numbers aloud?" The class said the numbers as I pointed to each one.

"Now, let's look at the first number in this new list of numbers," I said. "What do we need to do?"

Jason said, "Put it into the calculator."

"Could you do that for us, Jason?" I asked.

Jason was eager to use the overhead calculator. He located and pressed the 1 and the 2 to display 12. "That's neat!" he commented.

"Now, if I am going to keep track of what we are doing, I better get busy!" I said. "I need to keep a record of what we are doing on the calculator, and we have already done something. What should I write?"

"He pressed 'twelve' so you should write that down," one student suggested.

Next to the list of numbers, I wrote *12*.

Jason announced our next move. "We have to talk about what to do to get to thirty-two," he said.

"OK, let's talk. The rest of you: talk to a partner about what you think we should do next." I wanted the students to remain engaged in the directions for the activity, even though they were not yet working on it independently. Students talked at their tables while Jason and I agreed that we should add twenty to twelve.

"Jason is going to tell you about our conversation. If it is similar to the conversation you had with a partner, raise your hands," I directed. It was important for students to see how their interpretation of the next move related to that of their peers. Asking them to respond kept them involved as well as accountable.

"We are going to add twenty, so I am going to press 'plus,' then 'twenty,' then 'equals,'" Jason said, pressing the keys as he announced his moves. As he finished, hands went up and students softly clapped.

"We did it!" I said. "Help me decide how to keep track of what we just did on the calculator," I said.

"Next to the twelve write 'plus twenty equals,' then the answer: thirty-two!" Jason explained. I did. It looked like this:

12          $12 + 20 = 32$
32
30
60
57
37
39
89

"I am going to read this aloud. As I do, listen and see if it makes sense and see if it shows what we did on the calculator." I touched the numbers and symbols as I read, "Twelve plus twenty equals thirty-two." Heads nodded in agreement.

"Tell me why you think it is OK," I asked.

"That's what you and Jason did on the calculator," one student said.

"It makes sense because twelve plus twenty equals thirty-two!" said another.

Asking students to explain their reasoning is important, even when answers are correct and make sense. It allows the teacher a chance to assess student understanding, gives students a chance to deepen their own ideas, and provides classmates with additional information that could be helpful.

"Talk at your tables: what do we do next?" I asked. Students discussed the next move, then hands went up in the air.

"Thirty is less than thirty-two. You got to subtract," said one student.

"You have to take away," said another.

"Subtract two. Minus two," said a third.

"Minus two *equals*," asserted another student.

"Don't forget to write down what you did!" one student said.

Jason pressed the keys his classmates had suggested: −, 2, and =. The calculator display now showed 30.

"How will I write down what we did?" I asked.

"Next to the thirty-two, write a minus and a two and an equals and a thirty," one student said.

I recorded what this student had said:

12	12 + 20 = 32 − 2 = 30
32	
30	
60	
57	
37	
39	
89	

I had anticipated this confusion as the class learned about recording calculator moves. The equation that had been recorded gave us an opportunity to address this misconception and the correct way of recording. I explained, "I am going to read this equation aloud. As I do, see if it makes sense." I touched the numbers and symbols as I read the equation aloud. "Twelve plus twenty equals thirty-two minus two equals thirty."

"Huh?" said several students.

"That's not right!" said one.

"That doesn't make any sense," another commented.

"Twelve plus twenty doesn't equal thirty-two minus two!" said yet another.

"Tell me more about why you think so," I prodded.

"Well, twelve plus twenty equals thirty-two and thirty-two minus two equals thirty," said one.

"I get it! Thirty-two doesn't equal thirty!" said another.

A few students were involved in this explanation and nodded in agreement. Some others seemed uncertain. "Anyone else have an idea about this equation?" I asked.

"It's like a lie. Twelve plus twenty equals thirty-two . . . that's the truth. Thirty-two minus two equals thirty . . . that's the truth, too. But twelve plus twenty equals thirty-two minus two . . . that's not true!" one student said.

"One equals thirty-two and the other one equals thirty. They don't equal each other," said another.

"Thirty doesn't equal thirty-two!" said a third.

"So, let me get this straight," I said, talking as I wrote. "I can write, 'twelve plus twenty equals thirty-two' and 'thirty-two minus two equals thirty.' That's OK?" Many of the students nodded in agreement. "So, what should I do with the rest of the equation, the 'minus two equals thirty' part?"

"Get rid of it!" said one student.

"Erase it!" said another.

"Yeah, we don't need it anymore. The other ones are better," said a third.

The board now looked like this:

12	12 + 20 = 32
32	32 − 2 = 30
30	
60	
57	
37	
39	
89	

"Whew! That was some amazing thinking!" I said. "Now, I wonder if you and I can switch jobs, Jason. You can do the writing and I will enter the numbers on the calculator. Would that be OK?"

Jason, the class, and I continued to discuss which calculator keys to press in order to change the displayed number into the next number on the list; each time we kept a written record of what we did on the calculator.

12	12 + 20 = 32
32	32 − 2 = 30
30	30 + 30 = 60
60	60 − 3 = 57
57	57 − 20 = 37
37	37 + 2 = 39
39	39 + 50 = 89
89	

It was now time for the students to pair up and try *Make My Number* on their own. I had made three worksheets, each with a different list of numbers. The first included primarily two-digit numbers that decreased and increased by groups of tens, or "decades." The second list contained numbers that ranged from 9 to 328, most numbers increasing by decades or hundreds. The final list of numbers ranged from 90 to 495, with numbers increasing by decades and hundreds. I put a transparency of the first worksheet on the overhead. "In just a moment, I will be asking you to choose a partner with whom to work and come up front to get a worksheet and calculator. I want you and your partner to look at your list of numbers. Then, just as we have been doing here, enter the first number on the calculator and discuss what you need to do to change it into the next number on your list. Remember that you can only add or subtract *one* number in order to make the next number. Remember to keep a written record of what you have done on the calculator. You will record equations to match your calculator actions, just like we just did together. There are three different lists of numbers for you. If you finish, create your own list of numbers. Find a way to add to or subtract from a number on your list so that you can create the next number on your list." Since none of the students had questions, I called on one student at a time. Each student picked a partner, came up for a calculator and worksheet, and found a place to work in the room.

Students got busy on the task. They understood what to do, but some needed prompting for how to keep both partners involved. Students at this age level often share a task by taking turns and "trading off." Sometimes one student in the pair held both the calculator and worksheet. This student would enter the number and operation on the calculator, check to see if it resulted in the next listed number, and then record the moves on the worksheet, while the other student laid his or her head on the table, flipped through a book, or chatted with someone close by. A quick intervention on my part—"How could you share this task so that both of you are doing something?" remedied these situations and got both students working together, one person entering numbers on the calculator while the other recorded moves on the worksheet.

Students shared common understandings about the relationships between numbers. When comparing two different numbers, they realized that addition makes a number increase in magnitude and subtraction makes a number decrease. Students were resourceful in how to find the difference between one number and the next and used a variety of strategies and tools to successfully do so.

I observed as Valerie and Delia worked together. They were comfortable using the 1–100 chart as a tool to help them figure the difference in two numbers, starting with one number and counting onto or back from another. I watched as they tried to "get to" seventy-nine from twenty-nine. They did not immediately "see" the difference of fifty by looking at the two numbers and thinking about the position of the digits. Instead, Valerie quickly located 29 on the chart, which was in front of her on the desk. She then counted by tens from 29 to 79 by moving down five boxes—fifty—on her chart.

Sometimes students can lose track of the relationships in the 1–100 chart, using the chart without considering these relationships. They can become dependent on the tool and use it without thinking about number values. I was curious about whether Valerie and Delia could wean themselves off of this automatic use of the chart and rely, instead, on the relationships of which they were obviously aware. After observing them for a moment, I asked, "I wonder . . . are you able to count by tens?"

"Sure!" responded Delia. "Ten, twenty, thirty, forty . . . How far?"

"You sure can," I said. "Can you count by tens from twenty-nine?"

"No!" said Delia.

"That's hard!" agreed Valerie.

"I bet you can," I suggested. "Can you go like this? 'Twenty-nine, thirty-nine, forty-nine'? That's counting by tens."

Delia and Valerie counted aloud together, "Twenty-nine, thirty-nine, forty-nine, fifty-nine, sixty-nine, seventy-nine, eighty-nine, ninety-nine!"

"You did it! You counted by tens from twenty-nine!" I acknowledged. "Can you count by tens from twenty-nine to seventy-nine and keep track of how many tens there are?"

They repeated their counting, this time putting up a finger for each ten they counted beyond twenty-nine, ending up with five fingers displayed. "Five! Five tens! That's fifty!"

I wanted them to see that there was a connection between their method of counting by tens from any number on their fingers and counting by tens from any number on the 1–100 chart. I said, "You named each number when you counted by tens. Do you remember the numbers you said?"

"Twenty-nine, thirty-nine, forty-nine, fifty-nine, sixty-nine, seventy-nine," they repeated.

"And when you used the hundred chart, do you remember which numbers you touched when you traveled from twenty-nine to seventy-nine?" I asked.

"The same ones: thirty-nine, forty-nine, fifty-nine, sixty-nine, seventy-nine!" Valerie answered.

"Yeah! That's neat!" said Delia.

"So, I wonder how using the hundred chart is the same as or different from using your fingers?" I said.

"We started on twenty-nine," said Valerie, "and went to seventy-nine."

"We counted . . . on the hundred chart we counted boxes, and on our fingers we counted . . . our fingers!" said Delia.

"We counted by tens!" said Valerie. "Going down a box on the hundred chart is adding ten!"

"I wonder if you can use that information to travel from seventy-nine to the next number: forty-nine," I said.

"Well, we could go backwards on the hundred chart: sixty-nine, fifty-nine, forty-nine," said Valerie.

"We can count backwards on our fingers: sixty-nine, fifty-nine, forty-nine," said Delia, putting up a finger for each ten she used.

"Hmm," I said, smiling as I moved to another table.

Sammy and Joanie had decided to work on the last set of numbers first. When I walked over to see what they were doing, each expressed a great deal of confidence about how easy the task seemed to be. They were working rather quickly through the worksheet and needed coaxing to check their thinking on the calculator.

"We are doing these first," said Joanie, pointing to the list containing numbers of the greatest magnitude. "These others are too easy!"

"Do we have to do these?" Sammy said.

There are times when students mask their aversion for a task by stating that it is "too easy," even when it is at an appropriate level of difficulty. Sammy and Joanie's situation was different: while they clearly appreciated the attention and recognition that came with their ability to easily and readily complete the *Make My Number* worksheet, the speed and facility with which they worked through the list of numbers made their experience and understanding apparent. It seemed unnecessary to have them do the assigned task; another was in order.

"Why don't you come up with your own list of numbers?" I prompted.

"Can we use numbers like a million?" asked Joanie.

"How about if you keep the numbers to four digits? What do you suppose I mean by 'four digits'?" I asked.

"Like this?" asked Sammy, writing down *1,000.* "It has a one and three zeroes . . . that's four digits."

"Yes, that is a four-digit number," I answered. "Make your own list. Tell us the calculator moves needed to move from one number to the next." Sammy and Joanie abandoned the worksheet task and instead worked on choosing their own numbers. I was curious to see what they would create. I moved along to another table.

"Look . . . here's why I think it's one hundred," Troy began explaining to Trevor. He had made a model of fifty-eight with the base ten materials, using five tens rods and eight ones. "Here is fifty-eight, right?" he asked, pointing to the model.

"Yeah," said Trevor.

"And if you add one hundred," Troy went on, adding a flat that represented one hundred, "then it's one hundred and fifty-eight, right?"

"Yeah," said Trevor. While Trevor was agreeing with Troy and was watching and listening to what he was doing and saying, I was not convinced that he really understood what his partner had done.

"You are doing an excellent job of listening to your partner," I said, addressing Trevor. "I wonder if you could tell him what you understood. That might help him to understand how clearly he is explaining." While we have worked very hard in the classroom to make it OK to be confused, it can still be difficult to be the center of attention while you are. Rather than have the focus be on Trevor's understanding, I decided to shift it to Troy's explanation.

"This is fifty-eight," Trevor explained, and then proved it. "Ten, twenty, thirty, forty, fifty, fifty-one, fifty-two, fifty-three, fifty-four, fifty-five, fifty-six, fifty-seven, fifty-eight," he counted, touching each piece of the base ten materials as he counted. "If you take one of these, it's a hundred more." Trevor again counted to demonstrate, by tens from 100 to 150, then by ones to 158. "So, fifty-eight plus one hundred is one hundred fifty-eight," he concluded.

"How will you check that on the calculator?" I asked.

Trevor picked up the calculator and entered *58 + 100 =* and smiled when he saw the display: 158.

"You proved it. Nice explanation, you two," I said.

The students worked for about thirty minutes. Since recording their moves was largely symbolic, it was difficult to get a sense of their thinking about the activity beyond the list of equations. I wrote these questions on the board and then got their attention:

What did you learn?
What was difficult?
What was easy?

"While walking around and looking at your work, I realized that it is not so easy to know your thinking about *Make My Number.* You have a list of equations on your papers but I would like to know a little more. I have written some questions on the board. Let's read those questions together." I touched the words that I had written. As I did, students read along with me. "Take a minute to talk with your partner about what you learned, what was difficult, and what was easy. Then I would like you to do some writing about the talking you did. That will help me to know some more about what you learned playing *Make My Number.*" Students talked for about five minutes, then began writing.

After the lesson I reviewed these papers. It was clear that the students had benefited from their experience with this activity.

Sammy and Joanie, finding the worksheet too easy, had created their own list of numbers. The numbers they chose for their original list were of a greater magnitude than the ones I had given their classmates, but followed a definite pattern. Their number choices did not involve addition or subtraction of tens or hundreds. While the numbers they used were in the thousands, they were definitely "friendly numbers" containing many zeroes. (See Figure 14–1.)

Julie and Rose commented on how both addition and subtraction affected numbers. (See Figure 14–2.)

Valerie and Delia found challenges in remembering what they had done. (See Figure 14–3.) Pedro and Alan saw their progress emerge through the course of the activity. (See Figure 14–4.)

learn: How to make small numbers to big numbers and big numbers

FIGURE 14–2   Julie and Rose commented on how both addition and subtraction affected numbers.

What was hard

We thought that finding out the answer was kind of hard and also reminding each other what were the numbers we used.

FIGURE 14–3   Valerie and Delia found challenges in remembering what they had done.

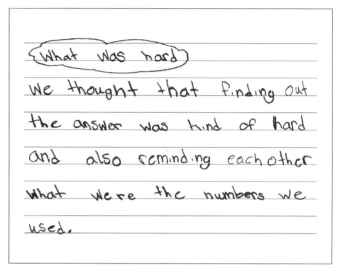

Make My Number

8	4+4=8	58	9+49=58
12	8+4=12	158	58+100=158
22	12+10=22	128	158-40=128
42	22+20=42	328	128+200=328
40	42-2=40	128	328-200=128
20	40-20=20	100	28-28=100
29	20+9=29		
79	29+50=79	165	100+65=165
49	79-30=49	125	165+40=125
45	49-4=45	425	125+300=425
65	45+20=65	495	425+70=495
15	65-50=15	490	495-5=490
9	15-6=9	290	490-200=290
		90	290-200=90

FIGURE 14–4   Pedro and Alan collaborated to successfully record all equations.

$$1,000 \quad 1,000 + 8,000 = 9,000$$
$$9,000 \quad 9,000 + 3,000 = 12,000$$
$$12,000 \quad 12,000 - 4,000$$
$$8,000 \quad 8,000 - 4,000 = 4,000$$
$$4,000 \quad 4,000 -$$
$$1,000$$

FIGURE 14–1   Sammy and Joanie created their own list of numbers.

Make My Number was an appropriate fit for this group of students. The activity allowed students to use models and tools to demonstrate the magnitude of numbers and determine how to change that number into one of greater or lesser magnitude. It gave students opportunities to operate on numbers by first predicting, then checking their predictions through use of the calculators. Students felt safe in dealing with the numbers: they had the support of their peers and were able to use multiple tools, models, and strategies to operate on one number in order to make the next. The activity was easily adapted for students representing a spectrum of experience from those who created models for two-digit numbers to those who came up with their own list of numbers. The activity was accessible to all.

Linking Assessment and Instruction

As you observe students work, think about the following:

- Are students comfortable using calculators? Do they regard them as useful, purposeful tools?
- How do students demonstrate understanding of how subtraction and addition work? Do they realize that adding to a number makes it greater and subtracting from a number makes it lesser than the original?
- What place-value understandings do students use when doing *Make My Number*? Do they associate a change in the ones digit with adding or subtracting ones and a change in the tens digit with adding or subtracting tens? Can students use manipulatives to represent operations on the calculator?

Oh No! 20!

CHAPTER 15

OVERVIEW

Oh No! 20! is a card game for two to four people. Values of zero through five and minus five are given to playing cards. Players take turns using cards and keeping a running total of points. Players strategically use cards to keep from going over twenty on their own turn. Oh No! 20! provides players an engaging context in which to practice addition and subtraction strategies and use logical thinking.

MATERIALS

■ playing cards, 1 deck per pair of students

TIME

● one class period

Teaching Directions

1. Explain to the students that the object of the game is for one player or team to force the opponent past a total of 20.

2. Remove all cards from the deck except the ace, one, two, three, four, and five cards, and the jack, queen, and king of each suit.

3. Explain to the students that aces are worth one point, cards 2–5 are worth the corresponding number of points, jacks are worth − 5, queens are worth 0, and kings are wild (worth the value of any other card used in the game). The suit of the card does not affect its points.

4. Deal four cards to each player. Place the remaining cards in a draw pile in the center of the table, facedown.

5. On each turn, the players discard one card, laying it face up on the table. The value of the card played is noted; and as players continue to take a turn, the new card value is added to or subtracted from the previous card's value. The current total is stated aloud by the player who plays the card. The player then draws a new card from the draw pile.

6. Explain that the first player to add a card forcing his or her opponent past a score of 20 wins the game.

Teaching Notes

Oh No! 20! provides students with numerous and varied experiences in addition and subtraction. Students use mental math strategies to consider possible sums resulting from adding the current total to any one of the four cards they are currently holding in their hand, while also comparing these possible sums to the target number, twenty. They develop strategic thinking while imagining how the card they play in the next hand will affect subsequent moves. Culminating whole-class discussions center on the topics that students naturally encounter during repeated playing of *Oh No! 20!* These include use of negative numbers, addition properties, and the development of game strategies.

The Lesson

The students and I were seated in a circle on the rug. I had a set of playing cards in my hand. I know that children see playing cards as both familiar and engaging. They appreciate the element of chance associated with the cards. I appreciate that the cards will enable us to practice math skills and concepts in the context of a game.

"Tell me what you know about playing cards," I said by way of introduction. Most of the students eagerly raised their hands. Several shared with the class their ideas about the symbols, suits, and names of specific cards.

"So there are 'suits,'" I summed up. "There are two red suits—hearts and diamonds—and two black suits—spades and," I held up the three of clubs, "clubs, like this one. Each suit includes cards from an ace to a ten, and a jack, queen, and king. There are also cards called jokers. You already know a lot about playing cards," I said. "You know a lot about the different kinds of cards there are and how you can use them. Today we will be using some of the cards you mentioned. We will put the rest back in the box for safe keeping. We are going to use the ace through the five, and the jack, queen, and king of each suit." I took the cards out of the box and began sorting through them to retrieve the cards needed for the game. I made a "keep" and a "put away" pile; as I showed each card to the students, they told me in which of the two piles I needed to place the card.

"Each of these cards has a special value," I explained. "The ace card is worth one point, the two is worth two points, and so on. How much do you think a four is worth?"

"Four points!" said several students.

"And a five card?" I asked.

"Five!" said several others.

"How about the three?" I asked again.

"Three!" chimed numerous students.

"Now, these other cards are called 'face cards,'" I said. "Jacks, queens, and kings are special cards with special values. In this game, jacks are worth minus-five points, queens are worth zero, and kings are wild. In card games, 'wild' means that the card can be worth the value of any other card in the game. So a king could be worth . . ." I prompted.

"One, two, three, four, or five points," said one student.

"How about zero? Could a king be worth zero?" another student asked.

"The king is worth whatever you want it to be, as long as it is a value of another card that we are using," I explained. "So, could it be worth zero?"

"Yeah, because we are using queens, and queens are zero!" offered one student.

"A king could be minus five, too!" said another.

"Yes, you are correct. A king could be worth minus-five points," I said.

"What do you mean by 'minus-five' points?" one student asked.

"Let me explain how to play the game and then we can see what 'minus five' means," I said. "But first I am going to write the point value on the board so that I don't forget the value of the cards. I sometimes forget!" On the board, I listed the cards and their values (see below).

card	value
A–5	number on the card
J	−5
Q	0
K	wild

"Let's just make sure that we all agree about the card values," I said. I put my hand where I had written $A - 5$. "We read this as A, or ace, through five." I said. "What does 'ace through five' mean, exactly?"

"It means the ace card, the two card, the three card, the four card, and the five card," said one student.

"It means ace and five and the cards between ace and five," said another.

"OK. What do you suppose I mean by 'number on the card'?" I asked, pointing to the words I had written on the chart.

"A two is two and a three is three . . . like that," said one student.

"Yeah, but A, or the ace, is kind of weird. It's a one," said another.

"Every card—well, the ace and two and three and four and five—is worth the number on the card," another said. "One and two and three and four and five. Like that!"

"How about the 'J,'" I asked. "What card is that?"

"A jack!" said one student.

"Yeah . . . that's the short way of writing 'jack,'" another student said.

"So 'Q' must be . . ." I began.

"Queen!" said several students.

"And 'K'?" I pressed.

"King!" the students chimed.

"Here is how you play the game," I explained. "You use the cards listed on the board. We have already separated out the rest of the cards and I will put them back in the box so that I don't get them mixed up with the ones I need. I am going to play as a team with Aaron, since he is sitting next to me. I am going to ask Cynthia and Steven to play as a team against us. They are sitting across the rug from us and in a place where people can see their moves. I am going to 'stir' the cards to mix them up before I deal them out." I placed the deck in front of me and spread out the cards. With both hands moving in circles at the same time, I quickly shuffled the cards by stirring them, then gathered them back into a deck.

"Each team gets four cards. Instead of holding them in my hand and hiding them from Steven and Cynthia, we are going to lay them down in a row in front of us. We want you to be able to see our cards while you learn how to play the game. I would like Cynthia and Steven to do the same." I alternately gave each team a card, until we each had four cards. We put the cards in a row in front of us. I placed the remaining cards in the center of the rug, between the two teams, telling the students, "The rest of the cards are going in the 'draw pile.' Each time you use a card, you 'draw' a new one from the pile. OK?"

"Each team will take turns putting a card in the middle of the rug, faceup. We are going to add the value of the new card to the total value of the cards. We have to say the new total. Here is the tricky part of the game: the game is called *Oh No! Twenty!*, for a reason: you want to make your opponent go past twenty. So you have to think about what card you need to use to make that happen. It's called *Oh No! Twenty!*, because, when you get to twenty, you will probably think, 'Oh no! I have to do something quick!' If your opponent makes you use a card to push the total over twenty on your turn, you lose the game."

Aaron and I had these cards:

| J | 3 | A | 4 |

Cynthia and Steven had these:

| 5 | 4 | K | 2 |

"We will go first. What card should we use?" I asked Aaron. He took the four and placed it in the center of the rug, next to the draw pile, and said, "Four." I told the students what we needed to do next. "I will replace that card with a card in the draw pile," I said. I took a card and got a queen and put it in our line of cards. Cynthia and Steven discussed their move, and then Steven picked up their four card and placed it, faceup, on top of the four that Aaron and I had played, and then moved to take a card from the draw pile.

"Before you take a card," I said, "let's see if someone can remind us: what do we need to do when we place a new card on the pile?" I wanted to keep the rest of the class involved and avoid putting Cynthia and Steven on the spot under their classmates' watchful eyes.

"You got to add the cards together," one of the students offered.

"Four plus four is eight," said another.

"You have to tell what they equal," said a third.

This was all the support Cynthia and Steven needed. Cynthia said, "Eight," and took a new card from the deck.

We now had:

| J | 3 | A | Q |

Cynthia and Steven had these cards:

| 5 | J | K | 2 |

"It's our turn," I said. "What should we use this time, Aaron?"

"I think the three," he responded.

"OK. We are going to use our three. Touch your knees if you know what we will say, before taking a card from the draw pile," I said. It only took a few seconds for most of the group to rest their hands on their knees. I called on two students to tell the new total, as well as what they did to figure out the new total.

"It's eleven. I put eight in my head and counted on my fingers: nine, ten, eleven!" said the first.

"I know eight and two is ten so eight and three is one more, eleven," said the second.

"Eleven!" I said, then I drew another card. I got a five.

Cynthia reached for the two after talking with Steven. She placed it on the pile of faceup cards and said, "Thirteen." Steven then picked a replacement card.

Our set of cards now looked liked this:

The opposing team's cards looked like this:

"Let's use the five," I suggested, and Aaron nodded. I placed the five on top of the stack. "I would love some help with finding the total," I said.

"You could count on from thirteen: fourteen, fifteen, sixteen, seventeen, eighteen," said one student.

"I know three and five is eight so thirteen and five is eighteen," said another.

"Ooh! It's getting really close to twenty!" one student noticed.

"Uh oh! Eighteen!" said another.

Some of the students giggled. Aaron drew a new card to complete our turn, and then all eyes were on Cynthia and Steven. Steven reached for the jack. I was not sure if he was thinking ahead or if his choice of cards was random. I interrupted him so that we could discuss options at what seemed to be a critical juncture in the game.

"Let's take a minute and talk about what has happened so far and what could happen next. During each move of this game, players have choices to make about cards they could use. Cynthia and Steven were going to use the jack. If they do, what total do you suppose they will have and how do you know?" Students thought for a minute before some hands went up in the air.

"Well, jacks are minus five," one student said. "I think she would have to minus five from eighteen."

"Oh yeah! You'd have to take away," said another.

"Eighteen minus five is . . . thirteen!" another stated.

"Remember? It was thirteen a minute ago! And then she added five. Then it was eighteen. Now it's eighteen minus five so we are back at thirteen!" said yet another.

"Weird!" one student exclaimed.

"So, if Cynthia and Steven used the jack, they would have to subtract five and then they would say . . ." I began.

"Thirteen," said several students.

"Let's say they didn't choose the jack. What other card could they choose? What would happen if they did?" I asked.

"They could choose the five. Eighteen and five is . . ."

"Nineteen, twenty, twenty-one, twenty-two, twenty-three. Twenty-three! That's too much! They'd lose!" said another

"They could choose the four. Eighteen and four . . . that's one less . . . that would be . . . nineteen, twenty, twenty-one, twenty-two . . . That's still too many!" said one student.

"What about the king?" I asked.

"What's the king?" several students asked.

I was impressed by the problem solving that was happening, with little intervention from me. Students were considering various options and the results of using these options. I waited a minute before reminding students about the effect of using a king.

"Let's remember what a king is worth," I said. "It is a wild card. It can take on the value of the ace, the two, the three, the four, the five, the jack, or the queen. We know what would happen if Cynthia and Steven chose a jack, a four, or a five. What if they made the king worth an ace or a two or a three or a queen? What would happen?"

"OK . . . eighteen plus ace . . . I mean plus one is nineteen," one student said.

"If the king was a two . . . eighteen plus two is twenty," said another.

"If we made the king a three, it would be one more . . . twenty-one," said a third.

"But that would be too many!" several students sang out.

"If we made the king a four . . ." one student said.

"Why would we do that? They already have a four . . . and a five!" said another.

"They wouldn't need another four and another five . . ." said yet another.

The group quieted down, seemingly after considering all possible options for our opponent's next move. I summarized what they had said. "They have many choices, don't they? They could use the four or five . . ."

"But they would lose!" several students said.

I continued. "Yes, they would! Or they could use the jack, subtract . . ."

"Five! Then the total would be . . . thirteen," said one student.

I resumed my summarizing. "They could use the king to be the value of any card to get . . . which totals?"

"Nineteen . . . if it was, like . . . an ace . . . a one," said one.

"Twenty! They'd have to use it as a two," said another.

"They could get twenty-one, twenty-two, and twenty-three. But they wouldn't do that! That would be too much!" said yet another.

"If you were on Cynthia and Steven's team, which card would you use and why? Take a minute to think about that question. Touch your knees when you are done thinking." Each turn provided multiple opportunities for "next moves" and these possibilities were important for students to consider. Looking at all possibilities and outcomes for each and every move throughout the game would have been too much for students to attend to while learning how to play the game. Stopping at this point seemed to be a logical place for debate.

"I think they should use a jack. Then they wouldn't go over twenty," one student said.

"But she would be at thirteen. If they used the king, they could get really close to twenty. And Ms. Scharton and Aaron would get stuck, maybe . . ." said another.

"They could make the king a two and then it would be twenty. Ms. Scharton and Aaron would lose, because they would have to play a card and that would make them go over," said another.

"Oh No! Twenty!" said two students together.

The students giggled, then went on discussing Cynthia and Steven's best next move.

"Hey! If Cynthia and Steven used a two—used the king as a two—Ms. Scharton and Aaron could use a jack to subtract! Then they wouldn't go over!" one suggested.

"They could use the queen too. That would be zero. It would still be twenty. Then it would be Cynthia and Aaron's turn," said another.

"What a minute!" one student said.

"I am confused . . ." said another.

"Yeah, my head hurts!" said a third.

"You are doing a lot of thinking about what possible next moves they could make, as well as the possible moves Aaron and I could make after their move. That kind of thinking—looking ahead—is an important part of this game, as well as many other games. Thinking about a strategy to use—what you will do to try and win the game—is really smart. When you play the game, you will be thinking about

a strategy to use. Remember: you get to see all of our cards right now. When you play the game in a few minutes, you and your partner will think about whether you want your cards to be 'on public view' or 'private': do you want to see everybody's cards, or just your own? Now, I am pretty sure that you want to try out this game, so let's give Cynthia and Steven a chance to use your helpful information to make a decision."

After a minute of consulting with Steven, Cynthia told us, "I am going to use the king like a two and make it twenty," she said, placing her card on the pile. Steven took a new card. He got an ace.

I thought aloud before making my next move. "We have a jack, a five, an ace, and a queen. If we use the jack, we could subtract five. Twenty minus five . . ."

"Fifteen!" said several students.

I went on. "If we used the five, we would go over twenty and lose. Do we want to do that?" Aaron shook his head. "We don't want to use the five. If we used the ace, the score would be over twenty and we would lose also." Aaron shook his head again. "We don't want to do that either. If we used the queen . . . hmm . . ."

"It's a zero. Nothing would happen," said Aaron.

"That might be good. It would still be twenty. Do you want to use the queen?" Aaron nodded. "We will do that," I said. Aaron placed the queen on the pile and I took a new card. We now had:

Cynthia and Steven had these cards:

Cynthia and Steven debated quietly and then Steven placed the jack on the pile and said, "That's minus five, so . . . nineteen, eighteen, seventeen, sixteen, fifteen," while he counted backwards, using his fingers. "Fifteen. Your turn!" Cynthia picked a new card from the pile and got a two.

"Hmm. . . it's fifteen. If we use the five . . ."

Aaron quickly interjected, "It will be twenty."

"Uh oh!" I said.

"Oh, no! Twenty!" several students sang out. Again, giggles erupted.

"Cynthia and Steven lost!" one student said.

"What do you mean?" I asked.

"How?" said a few students.

"Oh yeah! If it's twenty, Steven and Cynthia don't have any take-away or zero cards. They lost!" one exclaimed.

Many of the students could see what would happen next. Many were obviously uncertain.

Cynthia and Steven talked for a moment, then acknowledged the inevitable. Cynthia picked up the ace and placed it on the pile. "Twenty-one," Steven said. "We lost."

"You were great sports, you two!" I said. "Thank you for helping us learn how to play the game. We are all going to play now. I will say your name. When I do, I would like you to pick a partner. Look for another pair of students to play with and come up as a group to get a deck of cards. Your team and the opposing team have a decision to make about how you work with the cards. You can display them all in front of you, so that each team can see the other team's cards, or you can keep them private and in your hands. Play until I give a signal. At the end of math time, we will come back together and talk about what you have learned while playing this game." I called students' names. They chose partners, found another pair, got their materials, and spaced themselves throughout the room. I wanted students to play in pairs for the first few games of *Oh No! 20!* While they learned the rules of the game, students would have a partner to eliminate most of the confusion that came while learning how to play. After some experience playing, students would be able to play the game as individuals, with one opponent.

Some groups sat down at tables and others sat on the floor. I circulated the room and observed how students got ready to play the game. The modeling the four of us had done seemed to make the students independent and self-sufficient: any questions that arose were often answered by the members of their group.

"We don't use all the cards," I heard one student remind the group she was playing with.

"Oh yeah!" said her partner.

"Don't forget to mix up the cards," said another student.

"How many do we get?" said yet another.

"Four," was the response.

"Do you want to see each other's cards or hide them?" one teammate asked another.

"Let's try seeing the cards and then hide them later," was the reply.

As I navigated the room, I eventually stopped beside a foursome of players. All of them were looking alternately at the cards they were holding and the pile of cards that lay between them.

"Hi. Tell me where you are at in the game," I said. "What is the score right now?"

"Twenty," said Rosa. "And it's our turn."

I peeked at the four cards that Rosa and Cynthia were holding: an ace, two jacks, and a king. Cynthia reached for the jack and Rosa quickly responded, "No!" Angry looks were exchanged, suggesting an argument might erupt. I intervened to gear the discussion toward consideration of possibilities for a critical move.

"Before you take a card from your hand, remember to discuss your ideas with your partner. What are you thinking? Rosa? Cynthia?" I asked.

"We should put down a jack. Then it will be minus five and the score will be fifteen!" explained Cynthia.

Rosa disagreed. "Yeah, but we could put down a king and say it's a zero. Then the score will be twenty for them. Maybe they don't have a special card to play—like a zero or jack or king . . . only the other cards—and then they'll lose!"

"Well, those are two different things you could do. There are others, too. What do you think is the best one?" I asked.

"Now I think we should use the king as zero," relented Cynthia. "Then they'll be stuck!"

"What do you think?" I asked Rosa. Even though Cynthia had agreed with her idea, it seemed important to model hearing from both people on the team.

"I agree," she said, pulling out the king from their hand, placing it on top of the upturned cards, and stating, "It's a zero, so it's still twenty."

Their opponents' expressions indicated that Rosa's strategy had been a smart one. I moved to take a look at Alisha and Tommy's hand and saw that they were holding two threes, a four, and a five.

I asked, "What will you do?"

"It doesn't matter," admitted Tommy. "We lose whatever we put down." He questioningly looked at Alisha as he reached for the three. She nodded and he placed it on top of the stack, stating, "Twenty-three. You win."

Both teams put their cards in the center and worked together to turn all of the cards facedown. Alisha mixed up the cards and dealt four new cards to each team for the next game.

Martin and Steven had just begun a new game with Aaron and Julia.

A queen lay in the middle of the rug between the two pairs of students. Martin was taking a card from the draw pile and added it to the hand Steven was holding. I thought it was interesting that they had played the queen during the first move of the game, rather than hold onto it until more points had accumulated. Before I could look at the cards that Aaron and Julia were holding, Julia asked her partner, "This one?" She reached for the jack and Aaron nodded. She placed it on top of the queen and then looked at Aaron. I found myself in a familiar predicament. I could intervene and ask questions to get students to think through their strategy. Or I could let them have practice with learning the game. I decided to observe.

"It's minus five," stated Aaron.

I wasn't sure if Aaron was stating the operation associated with the card or the accumulated total. "Minus five" was both the resulting total after playing the jack, and the current total. "So, what is the score right now?" I asked.

"Minus five!" he restated. It would be interesting to see how this group would understand a negative score.

After a brief, whispered discussion, Martin and Steven put a king on top of the jack and stated, "It's a five."

Some groups of students seemed to be quite conservative in the way that they dealt with the current total: several seemed intent on using cards in order to keep the total low, rather than finding the cards that would push their opponents toward a score that was perilously close to 20. I waited a moment to see if Martin and Steven, or the opposing team, would report the total. Julia spoke up after a while.

"The score is zero," she reported.

"Could you let us know what you did to figure that out?" I requested.

"Well, it was minus five. That's like we were five behind. Some video games are like that. You have a minus score and then you get some points and then you get regular points," she explained.

"What kind of points are 'regular' points," I inquired.

Julia explained, "You know . . . points without the minus, like one, two, three . . . you know!"

I pressed further. "So, the score was minus five and then Martin and Steven put down a king, saying it was a five. How does that make zero?"

"See, it's like you owe five cents—a nickel—to your brother. When you give him a nickel, you don't owe him anymore. You owe him zero," attempted Aaron.

"Yeah. In a game, let's say you have a score of minus five and you get five points. Then your score is zero," added Martin.

"Oh! What about the number line!?" Cynthia asked, pointing to the number line on the adding machine tape that was stretched around the classroom. Each day the students were in school, another number was added to the number line. To the left of the 1 was a 0 and negative numbers. These numbers had been added in a previous class discussion, when students had argued whether or not you could subtract a number "larger than itself" from the original number. "You add by going that way and subtract by going that way," Cynthia explained, pointing first to the right, then to the left. "If you are on minus five and you add five, you end up on zero!"

"That's neat!" said Martin.

Students were using their understanding of negative numbers from some varied contexts: owing someone money, playing video games, navigating on the number line. I doubted the students' ability to add and subtract negative and positive numbers symbolically, or outside of the context of this game. I was impressed with their ability to pull in some knowledge to make sense of a situation I had not anticipated happening. I moved along to see how Steven and Alisha were doing. The rest of the classmates were working in teams to play *Oh No! 20!* These two students were left and were willing to play against each other, without the support of another student on their separate teams. I chanced upon a discussion about the associative property: when three or more numbers are added, the sum is the same, regardless of the order of the addends.

"I got the same answer, but I added them differently, see?" said Alisha.

"This sounds like an interesting conversation. Can you tell me a little bit about what you are talking about?" I asked.

"Well, I added them this way," said Steven. He picked up the cards that had been played: two aces, a three, a jack, and another three. He explained how he added the numbers in the order that they were placed on the pile. "An ace plus an ace is two. Two plus the three is five. The jack is minus five, so that's zero. Zero plus three is three!"

"And I added them this way," began Alisha. She picked up the cards, rearranged them so that she was grouping "like" cards together, and said, "I did one and one is two, and three and three is six. Six and two is eight. Eight minus five is three. You get the same answer!"

"So, you added the same numbers together, but in different order, and got the same answer. I wonder if that works with any numbers? What do you think?" I prompted.

"We could try some different cards and see!" offered Steven.

"But let's finish the game first," said Alisha. I couldn't blame her. While this seemed like an opportune moment to discuss this property of addition, Alisha and Steven were still in the middle of the game and their sights were set on finishing what they had set out to do. The seed had been planted and it could easily be revisited at a later time.

The students had been playing the game for about twenty minutes. They were engaged, motivated, and highly interactive. Each group of four students had played about three or four times. This repetition encouraged rich conversations and noteworthy observations that would greatly enrich a whole-class discussion. I rang the bell to get the students' attention and called them back to the rug.

"I really enjoyed spying on your games!" I began. The students chuckled. "I listened to some interesting conversations about best moves to make next and why. I realized that this game can be really tricky. Let me tell you about a tricky situation I saw. The score was twenty," I said, writing this information on the board. "And it was Team One's turn. They were holding an ace, two jacks, and a queen in their hand." I wrote this on the board as well.

Score: 20
Cards: A J J K

"What should Team One do? And why do you think so?" I asked. Students looked at the board and then some hands went up in the air.

"They should put down the jack. They don't want to go past twenty," said one.

"If they used a jack, they would have . . . nineteen, eighteen, seventeen, sixteen, fifteen," said another.

"But if they used the king, they could make it anything. They could say it was zero and then the score would still be twenty," said a third.

"If they used the ace, Team One would lose because they would have twenty-one," one student said.

"Yeah, they shouldn't use the ace," another confirmed.

It seemed that about half of the students understood possible moves and the outcomes; they were participating in the discussion through contributing ideas or nodding in agreement. The other half of the students were fairly quiet; I was not sure if they were confused. To pull everyone back into the conversation, I reminded them of something I had said before they went off to play the game.

"Before you found playing partners, I told you that we would come back together to discuss what you had learned while playing the game. What mathematics did you learn by playing *Oh No! Twenty!* I am going to list your ideas on the board." I said.

Hands went up and students gave me some feedback. Some students identified arithmetic skills they had used, some considered the logical thinking involved, and others pointed to getting familiar with the directions. I listed the following ideas on the chart:

> *I learned about subtracting and adding.*
> *You had to add the cards up to find the total.*
> *You have to try and figure out what the other team is going to do.*
> *You can get different totals, if you use different cards.*
> *You have to try and add the numbers.*
> *You have to remember what the special cards are worth.*
> *You have to use a lot of information. You have to listen to your partner and the other team and you have to do a lot of adding and subtracting.*

I am always interested to hear how children identify and interpret the learning involved in a new game, activity, or experience provided by the teacher. During this first day of playing the game, students were clearly at different places in their understanding of the complexity of *Oh No! 20!* This spectrum of what students learn by playing a new game is typical: some were getting comfortable with remembering how to play the game while others were ready to delve into the mathematics encountered while playing it. This span was to be expected. I was confident that repeated experiences with playing *Oh No! 20!* were necessary, since this is a game that is mathematically "rich." When students are comfortable with the rules and directions, they can turn their focus to the number concepts they come across while playing the game.

Linking Assessment and Instruction

As you observe the students work, think about the following:

- How do students add on to or subtract from the running total? Do they count on or back using their fingers? Do they use known number combinations?

- Do children "think ahead" when deciding which cards to play? Do they save the "special cards" (jacks, queens, and kings) and use them strategically? Or do they play them in a random manner?

- How do students' strategies change with repeated experience?

CHAPTER 16

Capture the Castle

OVERVIEW

Capture the Castle *is a strategy game played by two to four players. Players or teams of players begin the game with a set number of tokens, which they must "spend" wisely in order to move across the board to the opposing side's castle and "capture" it. The first side to land on the opposing side's castle wins. Winning the game requires an understanding of number magnitude, the ability to compare numbers, facility with figuring differences, and a little luck!*

MATERIALS

- *Capture the Castle* game board, 1 per group of 2–4 students (see Blackline Masters)
- tokens, such as beans, pennies, or cubes, 50 per player
- game board playing pieces, such as color tiles, 2 per player or team of players
- optional: *Capture the Castle* recording sheet, 1 per student (see Blackline Masters)

TIME

- one class period, plus additional time for repeat experiences playing the game and follow-up discussions

Teaching Directions

1. Players choose a game piece and put their markers on opposite sides of the game board, in the spaces marked with their "castle."

2. For each round, the opposing sides decide how many of their fifty tokens they are willing to "spend" to advance to the next line. Both sides secretly record their number on a piece of paper, and then reveal the number to their opponent. The side that wrote the larger number advances to the next line. Only one player or team advances, but both sides must deduct from their tokens the number they were willing to spend.

3. If both sides reveal the same amount, it is a tie round and neither advances, nor are any tokens deducted.

4. If a side runs out of tokens before capturing the opposing side's castle, it must record a zero for the amount spent for the remaining rounds.

5. The first player or team to reach the opposite end of the board and land on the castle wins. If neither reaches the opposing castle, it is a tie game.

Teaching Notes

While students at many levels of mathematical understanding can play *Capture the Castle*, this game potentially involves a variety of number concepts and skills. Players must be able to compare two numbers to determine which is greater. On each turn, they subtract from their own bank of tokens but must remember to have enough to pay out over subsequent moves; students who use mental math and think ahead have an advantage over those students that take a more spontaneous approach to making decisions. Paying out tokens throughout the game involves subtraction. Players may perform this operation differently: they may count out tokens (by ones or in groups of any size), utilize mental math strategies, or record symbolically, in order to determine how many tokens they have left for the remaining turns. While it is not necessary that students consider how many tokens the opposing player has at any point in the game, keeping track of the opponent's progress and supply of tokens can be beneficial.

The Lesson

I realized that the directions for *Capture the Castle* are complex and I needed to give some thought to how to keep students engaged while I taught them how to play the game. I called students to the rug and had them sit in a circle. I decided that having the students play with a partner would allow them to check each other's understanding of the directions, as well as the recording involved. To model this arrangement, I chose the student next to me to be my partner and the two students sitting across from us on the rug to be our opponents. In front of me was a blue color tile and red color tile, along with trains of snap cubes with ten cubes in each train. I also had a large sheet of blank white paper and a marker, so that I could model how to construct the game board for today's game.

"I have a new game to teach you today," I began. "It is called *Capture the Castle*. Pretend that you live during the time when kings and queens ruled the land. You and your partner are knights, living under the rule of a very greedy king and queen. Your queen and king want to have more land in their kingdom and it is the job of the knights to get more land. You start the game at the castle of your own king and queen." At one end of the sheet of construction paper, I drew a square.

"The neighboring kingdom also has a king and queen," I continued. "They, too, live in a castle." I drew another square at the opposite end of the piece of paper. "Your job is to capture the castle that belongs to the other kingdom. The goal of the game is simple: you want your team to reach the other side of the game board and capture the castle of your opponent before your partner's team captures yours. That is why the game is called *Capture the Castle*." The students looked eager to play.

"Since Kay is sitting next to me, I have chosen her to be on my team," I explained. "We are going to play against Mark and Ashley's team. Each team needs to have fifty tokens, paper and pencil, and a playing piece. We are going to use color tiles for the playing pieces and snap cubes for the tokens. Let's have each team gather what they need before I go on." Mark

and Ashley selected the blue color tile, so Kay and I took the red one. Each team gathered five trains of cubes, and paper and a pencil.

"What are 'tokens'?" Ashley asked.

"I use them at the arcade!" Larry answered. "They are like coins. You have to buy them and then you use them to play games."

"That is important information," I added. "Tokens are kind of like money. Sometimes you use tokens to travel on a bus or train. Sometimes you put them in machines, like in arcades. I have used them like money to get into public bathrooms or to use a locker at a gym. Sometimes you have to buy tokens and sometimes you get them for free. Today, the snap cubes will be tokens. You will need to use them to travel across the game board. I will show you how when we begin playing."

I showed the students the game board (see below). "Kay and I are going to put our playing piece in our 'castle' at this end of the game board, and Ashley and Mark will do the same on the other side of the board."

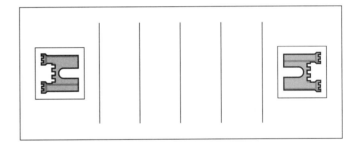

When both teams had their game pieces on the board I went on. "Now we are ready to move and try to capture Ashley and Mark's castle at the opposite end of the game board. We can only travel one space—the next line—on each round. But before we move, partners must decide how many of their fifty tokens they want to spend. Each team writes down the number of tokens they are willing to spend. We show our numbers to the other team and the team that has the largest number gets to move to the next space on the game board. Even though only one team moves, each team has to pay the amount that was written down."

"That's not fair! You both have to spend tokens, even though one team moves?" Thomas said.

"That's right! Pretty tricky rules, aren't they?" I said. "If both players write down the same number, it is a tie round: neither team spends tokens and neither team moves. Watch this demonstration of how the game is played and then we'll see if you have any questions before you go off to play on your own." I didn't want to lose the attention of students that were merely observing the demonstration, so I said to the group, "Whisper to the person next to you: tell them the first thing that teams need to do to begin the game." Students began whispering about how each team needed to agree on the number of tokens they were willing to spend and then write down the number of tokens on a piece of paper. Kay and I talked, as did Mark and Ashley. Kay decided on twenty and she wrote that number down. Mark and Ashley then wrote a number on their paper.

"When it's quiet, each team is going to show their number." The students quickly got quiet. We showed our papers. Ashley and Mark had written down 35.

"Ooh . . . they get to move!" someone said.

"Yeah, but they have used up a lot of their tokens already!" another student commented.

Mark and Ashley counted out three trains of cubes and five single cubes. They set these aside. Kay separated out two trains, making our twenty, and put them with the thirty-five that Mark and Ashley had "spent." They put their color tile on the first line closest to their castle.

"How many tokens does each team have left to spend?" I wondered aloud.

"You and Kay have ten, twenty, thirty."

"Ashley and Mark have ten, eleven, twelve, thirteen, fourteen, fifteen."

"OK. Tell the person next to you what we will do now," I said. The students discussed the directions in pairs.

"They talk about what they want to spend and then write down another number," one student said.

"Yeah . . . and whoever gets the highest gets to move," another stated.

"But they both have to take cubes away. They have to take out the number they wrote down," said a third.

"I think Ms. Scharton's team is going to win. They have more cubes left!" predicted another.

"But Ashley's team is already on the first line!" said yet another.

"I think we are ready to go on with the game," I said. "Talk to your team partner about how many tokens you are willing to spend." Mark and Ashley began whispering to each other and then wrote down a number. Kay and I privately discussed our next move and decided on fifteen. We wrote down this number and then showed our paper to the other team and they showed us their paper. They had written down 10.

I noticed that our paper now had two numbers written on it and that it would be important to differentiate between the number used for this turn and the numbers used for previous ones. I said, "Uh oh. There are two numbers on our paper and that might be confusing. We might not be able to tell which number we want to use for this turn and which number we have already used. How can we show what number we are using for this turn?"

"Cross out the number you have already used," suggested Jeremy.

"Terrific. Let's cross out the numbers we have already used." Both teams did so. To keep the entire class involved in a game between four classmates, I said, "Turn to your partner and tell them what you think will happen on this turn, and how you think the game will turn out. Look at all the information for each team: their papers, their tokens, and their playing pieces."

Students were very interested in what was happening in the game. They predicted the next move easily but had a variety of opinions about how the game would progress.

"I think Ms. Scharton's team is going to win. They are tied with Ashley and Mark, but they have more tokens left to spend," said one student.

"No, they don't! Look!" said a second. "Ms. Scharton and Kay spent twenty the first time and fifteen this time. That's twenty, thirty, thirty-one, thirty-two, thirty-three, thirty-four, thirty-five. That's the same as Mark and Ashley. Mark's team also spent thirty-five."

"Yeah, but Mark and Ashley have to spend ten this time," said the first student. "Then they will only have five left. Ms. Scharton's team will have fifteen left."

"But they will both be on the same line," argued the second.

"I know, but Ms. Scharton's team will have fifteen tokens left to spend," replied the first. "Ashley's team will only have five! That's not enough, if they want to get to the other castle!"

I called the students' attention back to the game. "Let's see how this round turns out. What do you notice about the game right now?"

"Mark and Ashley have to spend ten. They'll have five tokens left," Dana said.

"You will be tied with their team. You will both be on the same line," Thomas added.

Carrie disagreed. "Not really. Kay and Ms. Scharton have to spend fifteen. They will have . . ." She got up to move to the center of the rug, separated out a train of ten and five more cubes and counted, "Ten, eleven, twelve, thirteen, fourteen, fifteen. They will both be on the first line, but Ashley's team will only have five tokens and Ms. Scharton's team will have fifteen."

"You both have five spaces to move to capture the castle. But one team has more tokens to spend than the other," Larry said.

"Kay, will you move our playing piece? Let's take away the cubes we spent for this turn." Kay moved our piece to the first line and removed a train of ten and five more cubes. Ashley counted out ten cubes, one at a time, and set them aside.

"Let's take our next turn. What do you think Kay and I should do and what do you think Ashley and Mark should do?"

"Hey! What if you run out of tokens?" Gary asked.

In an attempt to keep the directions as simple as possible, I had deliberately not covered some of the details of the game when I'd presented it to the class. I had decided to wait until various possibilities presented themselves. This was a good time to discuss one possible challenge of the game. "That is an important question," I said. "You know that you have to spend tokens to travel across the kingdom. What if you have no more tokens?"

"You can't move!" said Jake.

"Exactly," I confirmed. "You are stuck! You cannot travel if you have no tokens."

"So what does the other team do?" Gary inquired.

"What do you think?" I asked the group. "Well . . . if your team still has tokens, you can still spend some to travel. You can still write down a number. The other team can't!" Teri surmised.

"The other team could write down a number! They could write down zero!" Josh said.

Several students giggled at this response. "So if the other team writes down zero and Kay and I write down one . . ." I said.

"Your number is higher, so you get to move!" Gary answered.

"Oh . . ." several students responded.

"So, a minute ago I asked you a question. Let's see what you think now. I asked you to think about what you think Kay and I should do and what you think Ashley and Mark should do. Talk with someone nearby." Students talked to each other. While they did, Mark and Ashley discussed their next move, and so did Kay and I. Each team wrote down a number. We showed each other our numbers. Kay and I had written down 5, and Mark and Ashley had written down 3.

"Uh oh . . ." Teri said.

"Tell us about that 'uh oh,'" I said.

"If they spend three . . ." Teri began, and Mark covered his eyes with his hand.

"We lost!" Mark lamented.

"No, we didn't!" Ashley cried.

"Yes, you did! If you spend three tokens—" Josh began.

"We only have two left," Mark interrupted. "We have one, two, three, four, five spaces to travel to capture their castle! We'll have no more tokens to spend!"

"Ah!" said Ashley.

"Let's finish the game and see what happens. We have to spend five," I began. Kay separated out five cubes and moved our playing piece to the next space. I continued, "And Ashley and Mark have to spend three." Ashley moved three cubes away from their token supply. "Let's write down our numbers for the next turn." Ashley and Mark quickly came to a decision and wrote down a number. Kay and I decided on one token and wrote down this number. We raised our papers to show each other. We had each written down 1.

"What?" Gary said.

"It's a tie!" Josh said.

"Do you remember what happens?" I asked.

"You don't spend any tokens and nobody moves," Josh reminded us.

"That's right," I confirmed.

Play continued. Each team again quietly deliberated, wrote down a number, and showed their paper to the opposing team. Kay and I wrote down 2 and Ashley and Mark wrote down 1. Mark took a cube away from their tokens; Kay removed two from our pile and advanced our color tile to the third and middle line. We had eight cubes left; Mark and Ashley had one.

"How do you think this game will continue?" I asked. "Talk to someone next to you and then we will share out with the whole group." Students talked among themselves and then I asked for their attention. "So what do you think?"

Teri spoke first. "I think that Mark and Ashley will only get to play one more turn. They can only write down *one*, because they only have one cube left. You guys will write down a higher number and you'll get to move."

"You'll win!" said Ashley.

"Why do you think so? How will the game finish?" I pressed her to articulate why she predicted in the way that she did, even though it was pretty clear that the game was nearly over.

"Well, we can only write down *one* next time. After that, we won't have any more cubes so we will have to write down *zero*. We can't move if we don't have any cubes. And we probably won't have any cubes left after the next turn!" Ashley realized that she and Mark would be unable to win at this point, but she was still smiling.

"It doesn't matter what you write down," Josh said. "You and Kay are going to win."

"But they can't write down *eight*. If they did, they'd be out of cubes," said Carrie.

"So, does it matter what number we write down?" I asked. Many students said "yes" and a few said "no."

"I am anxious to hear about your thinking," I said. "Some of you think it matters what we write down. Some of you think it doesn't. What should we do if we want to win the game?"

Larry made a suggestion. "You still have one, two, three spaces to go to capture their castle. You could write down . . . let's see . . . you could write down *two* for the next turn and then . . ." Larry started counting on his fingers. "You could write down *two* the next turn, then *three* the next turn, and then *three* again. Then you'd be at their castle."

I wanted the students to be included in the thinking that Larry had just done. "Could you share with the class what you just did on your fingers, Larry? That might help all of us understand why you just made those suggestions for Kay and me."

"I used eight fingers because you only have eight tokens. I started with two. I know that you want to write down a number that's more than—greater than—Ashley and Mark's. They can only write down *one*. That's all they have left to spend. If you spend two, you get to move. You have six fingers—tokens—left. See?" Larry held up six fingers.

He went on. "So, if you spend two, you get to move. You still have two more spaces to go to land on their castle. You could spend three and then three. Then you will be done and you capture their castle!"

"I wonder if those are the only choices to make," I said. "Do we have to spend two, then three, then three? Or can we spend different amounts of tokens on the remaining turns? What do you think?"

Students began using their fingers to do what Larry had just done. They held up eight fingers and talked about different combinations of three numbers that totaled eight. Students had sat and listened to directions and discussion for some time. I realized that we needed to finish up the demonstration game so that they would have some time to play in pairs.

"Larry did some important thinking about this game. He had to think ahead to figure out how we could best spend our remaining tokens to win the game. Thinking only about the next turn might have kept us from capturing Mark and Ashley's castle. Thinking ahead is important in many different types of games. I appreciate Larry making us realize that it is important in this game, too."

We followed Larry's suggestions for the remaining moves. Kay and I were able to capture Mark and Ashley's castle to win the game. The students clapped when we moved our game piece to the winning spot.

"You listened to some directions and carefully watched our game," I said. "In just a moment, I am going to ask you to choose a team partner and take seats at one of the table groups. Each of them has materials, a game board for each group of players and sheets of paper and a marker for recording. There are cubes and color tile playing pieces at each table. Any questions?"

"Do we play by ourselves, or with partner?" Dana asked.

"Today, you are going to play just like we showed you on the rug: with a partner. There will be two teams at each table: your team and another team. After you learn how to play the game, you can play person against person. This will happen on another day."

Gary inquired, "Who does my team play against?"

"Whoever sits at your table will be playing against your team. I know that you will welcome them to play with you."

"How long do we get to play?" asked Jake.

"Continue playing until I signal for you to stop playing and clean up."

When all the questions had been answered, I told the class, "Enjoy playing the game. Please be thinking about 'thinking ahead' as well as any other strategies that will help you be successful at playing the game. When I give the signal"—and I clapped my hands quickly four times—"I will need you to stop playing and give me your attention. Ready?" As I called their names, the students found a partner and took their seats at the tables.

Students quickly got to work choosing their game pieces and organizing their tokens. Some grouped their cubes into trains of ten, while others made piles of individual cubes.

I stopped at the reading table. Sandra and Tracy were playing against Rick and George. While it didn't seem to bother Rick, I noticed that George would independently decide on the number of tokens to spend on that turn, write down the number, and then show it to Sandra and Tracy, while Rick sat and watched him.

"How's it going?" I inquired.

"Fine," the group unanimously replied.

"There are a lot of directions to this game. Do you remember them?" I asked. The students nodded and said that they did.

"I just want to make sure that I was clear about the directions. Did I let you know what to do before writing down the number of tokens you want to spend on a turn?" I prodded.

"Yeah . . . we have to talk about how many we think," said Sandra.

"We are supposed to agree on a number," Tracy added.

"Great," I confirmed. "I was just wondering. I just wanted to make sure that you realize that both team members make a decision. Have fun!" As I left, George asked Rick what he thought of the number that he had written down and the game continued. I continued my wandering to check in on how well students understood the directions for the game. Gary and Joann were playing against Kay and Zack. As I approached their table, the group was quite animated.

"We're going to win! We're going to win!" chanted Gary.

"Nuh-uh! How do you know?" asked Zack.

"Yes, I am curious, too. How can you tell?" I asked.

"See? Our guy is here," said Gary, pointing to a blue color tile in a position that was two moves away from the opposing team's castle. "And their guy is here," he said, pointing to a yellow tile that was positioned on the middle line. "We have," and he stopped to count, "five, six, seven, eight, nine, *ten* tokens left, but they only have two!"

"Tell me more," I said. "I am not convinced that Zack and Kay are going to lose."

Joann jumped in. "We only have," and Joann counted as she pointed to the remaining moves necessary in order for her team's marker to travel to the opposing castle, "one, two moves left. They have one, two, *three* moves. But they only have two tokens left. They can't win."

I was not certain that Zack and Kay understood what Gary and Joann had explained. "Could you tell us what you two think, Zack and Kay? What did you hear Gary and Joann say?"

"They only have two moves and they have ten tokens. We have three moves and only two tokens," began Kay.

"And we don't have enough tokens to get to their castle. They do!" Zack continued.

"Pretend they spend . . . five tokens next. We can't spend that many," Kay explained.

"Yeah! We can only spend two and then we'd run out!" Zack added.

"Let's see what happens," I prompted.

The game continued. Gary and Joann spent four tokens for the next turn and Kay and Zack spent one, allowing Gary and Joann to advance a space. They repeated the same moves for the remaining turn.

"So, how will this game help you to play the next game?" I asked.

"We won't spend so many tokens at the beginning!" Zack suggested.

"We'll cross our fingers!" added Joann.

"Is it about careful planning, or about luck?" I wondered aloud, before moving on to check on other students.

I came to the table where Thomas and Teri were playing with Carrie and Jeremy.

"Nobody won!" Jeremy announced.

"Really? How come?" I asked.

"We ran out of tokens right here," said Teri, pointing to the playing piece that was on the line two spaces away from the opposing team's castle. I noticed that there were no tokens in front of Thomas and Teri, but Carrie and Jeremy had six left and their playing piece was also on the line that was two spaces away from the opposing castle. I clapped my hands to get the attention of the entire class.

"There is a group that needs some information," I began. "I need to tell you a quick story about what happened in one game." I walked to the chalkboard and drew a diagram of a game board. "One team is here and one is here." I made Xs on the lines where each team's playing piece was lying. "One team is out of tokens and the other team still has some. What should happen?"

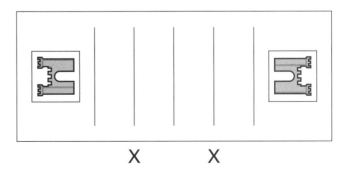

"The game is over!" said George.

"Is it?" I said.

"No, they keep playing!" Sandra stated. "Remember when you guys showed us how to play? You talked about that."

"Could you remind us what to do?" I asked Sandra.

"The team without tokens can't write anything down. They don't have any to spend. The other team does," she explained.

"It's true that they have nothing left to spend," I responded, "but I think both teams can write down a number. What could the team without tokens write down?" Some students looked puzzled and others smiled.

"They can't write down a number. They don't have any more!" said Larry.

"Yes, they can!" smiled Mark.

"They can write down zero!" Ashley added.

"So, the team with no tokens writes down *zero* and the team with tokens writes down . . ." I began.

"Any number! Whatever they write down is going to be greater than zero!" said Josh.

"So, one team writes down *zero* and the other team writes down *one*. What happens? Talk to the people you are playing with." Students discussed in small groups and then I called for their attention. "What do you think? What happens?"

"The team that wrote down *one* gets to move. The other team is stuck," Larry said.

"Then what?" I asked.

"The team that wrote down *one* gets to move," said Sandra.

"Talk in your groups about where the playing pieces would be now," I said. Students debated this for a minute and then I asked for their assistance.

"Can someone come up and show us where each team's marker would be? Joann?" Joann got up, came to the board, and erased the previous position of the team that had tokens. She made an *X* where the new position was, one space away from the opposing team's castle. She announced, pointing to the other team's *X*, "This one is stuck. They don't get to move."

"But the game is not over. What might happen next? Talk in your groups." Again, students predicted what might happen next. After about a minute I again got their attention and asked, "What do you think?"

"The same thing!" said Mark.

"What do you mean?" I asked.

"Teams talk about how many to spend," he explained. "One team still can't move because they don't have any tokens. That team"—he pointed to the drawing—"they can spend anything. One team

writes down *zero* and the other team writes down anything . . . because they are going to be able to move and win, no matter what!" Hearing explanations for what could happen is very different from actually experiencing the situation. I wasn't sure that everyone understood what had just transpired but I realized that repeated experiences playing the game would take care of this initial confusion. Still, it seemed important to review some vital information: if one team uses up tokens and the other team still has some to spend, then the game can still continue.

"You have just listened carefully to some difficult explanations. Remember: if one team has tokens and one team runs out of them, you can still continue the game. Play for a few minutes. When you hear my clap signal, please give me your attention so that I can give you some information about how to clean up."

Students continued to play a while longer. While they were thus engaged, I posted two charts on the board, each titled with a question: *Where is the math in this game?* and *What do you need to think about when playing this game?*

After I'd signaled that time was up, I announced, "Thank you for putting down your tokens and pencils, ending your conversations, and looking my way. The first thing you need to do is clean up. You know where the snap cube 'tokens' go, as well as your pencils. Thumbs up for 'yes' and thumbs down for 'no': can these be used again?" I held up a game board from one of the groups and students gestured with a "thumbs-up" signal. "Let's collect these in a pile on the rug so that we can use them again. How about these; can they be used again?" I held up a piece of paper on which numbers of tokens had been written throughout the course of the games. Students gave the "thumbs-down" signal. "All right. Let's throw these away. After you have taken care of your materials, I have two questions I would like you to talk about in your small groups."

I wanted students to understand that math time could be fun and enjoyable, but I also know that games can disguise learning, unless the learning is made apparent to them. It was important for me to explicitly address how this game involved some important skills and concepts about mathematics. I pointed to the words on the first chart. "Pretend you have to convince your teacher that this was a game that was worthwhile to play during math time, what would you tell your teacher? Where is the math in this game? Why would it be a good game to play during math time? The other question I would like you to think about is this one: What do you need to think about when playing this game?"

An important aspect of *Capture the Castle* is developing a strategy for successfully playing the game. The development of strategic thinking would come from repeated experience in playing the game; at this point, students were only beginning to realize the importance of using a strategy to play and win the game. I pointed to the words on the second chart. "If you were going to play this game tomorrow, what would you be thinking about? How did watching the game on the rug and playing the game at your tables help you to understand how to win the game? If you were going to explain the game to the people in the room next door, what would you tell them? What kinds of things do you need to think about when playing the game? When I say *go!*, the first thing you are going to do is . . ."

"Clean up!" responded most of the students

"And then you are going to . . ." I prompted.

"Talk about the questions!"

"Terrific. Go!" Students began putting the materials away. Cubes went back into the containers at each table, pencils went back in the pencil cups, game boards were stacked in the middle of the rug, and scratch papers were thrown away. Students began talking about the posted questions. Talking in small groups would be a safe way to exchange ideas: students are often more willing to share their ideas in a small, rather than a larger, group. Also, it would be easier for students to attend to explanations offered by members of a small group rather than in a whole-class discussion. After a few minutes, I got the attention of the class and asked each table to come to the rug to help me record some of the content from their conversations.

"You had some lively conversations at your tables. You shared your thinking with a few students and now I hope you will share your ideas with the whole class; that way, we will have more ideas than were possible to hear in your smaller groups. How about this question," I asked, pointing to the question on the first chart. "Where is the math in this game? If you wanted to convince your teacher that this is a game worth playing during math time, what would you tell him or her?" A few hands went up. As I called on students to share their ideas, I wrote them on the class chart. Here are the ideas that the students contributed:

You have to talk and decide on a number.
Each time you write a number, you have to take cubes away so you subtract.

It helps you learn "least to greatest." If one person puts 40 and you put 2, the person that picked 40 would have a little bit of cubes left, and that's least.
You can subtract in the game.

After writing down these ideas, I asked students to turn their attention to the second chart. "Let's take a look at this second question. What do you need to think about when playing this game? If you were playing it again tomorrow, how did today's experience help you to know what to do in order to play and win the game?" Again I wrote down ideas as students contributed them:

Tell your partner to think about the number they are going to pick. Get that number. Count how many you have left.
Think about the least number so you can get to the castle.
You got to think about the numbers and trick the other team. If they put a low number, you put a high number.
Don't use most of your tokens at first. You got to use some each time you move.

Being aware of the mathematics involved in this game and articulating a strategy for winning the game were not easy for students at this point. After repeated experiences playing *Capture the Castle*, students would continue to build on their initial ideas about the mathematics skills and concepts they were using while playing this game. Repeated playing of complex games such as this allows students to turn their focus away from the rules and toward the mathematical ideas and strategies that would enable them to play the game successfully. Further class discussions to bring these ideas and strategies to their awareness would also be helpful. I decided to keep the chart active, and see what ideas students might add at a later time, after more experience with playing *Capture the Castle*.

Note: The *Capture the Castle* recording sheet is best introduced after students have familiarity with how to play the game. Its use was not discussed here because in this lesson, the students were playing the game for only the first time. After playing team against team, students are ready to play student against student. The sheet is intended to help each student focus on number relationships, as well as to allow each student to keep track of his or her moves throughout the game.

Linking Assessment and Instruction

As the students work, think about the following:

- How do the students make decisions about the number of tokens they "spend" on a turn? Do they dole out their tokens in even amounts or do they significantly vary the quantity each turn?
- Do the students consider the quantity of tokens the opposing team has and use this information to make decisions about the number of tokens they will spend on a given turn?
- What strategies do the students use to compare the quantity of tokens they currently have, the number they are considering spending, and the number that will remain? Do they separate out the actual tokens, count on or back from the number of tokens they have, or use their understanding of number combinations to compute the number of tokens before or after a turn? How do the students use the number of remaining turns to decide how many tokens to spend on a turn?
- How effective are the students at communicating about their tentative strategies for successfully playing *Capture the Castle*?

101 and Out!

CHAPTER 17

OVERVIEW

101 and Out! *is a place-value game that involves chance as well as strategic thinking. Students take turns rolling one die. For each roll, students must decide whether they want the roll to represent that number of ones or tens (for example, a 5 could be recorded as 5 or 50). After six rolls, the person who gets closest to one hundred—without going over—is the winner of the game. Knowledge of the place-value system and careful decision-making allow students to develop more effective strategies for winning the game. Students must continually compare their total to the target number to determine which place-value to assign their rolls.*

MATERIALS

- die, 1 per pair of students
- 101 and Out! recording sheet, 1 per student (see Blackline Masters)
- zip-top bag containing 25 dimes and 50 pennies, with label stating bag's contents, 1 per pair of students
- chart paper

TIME

- three class periods, plus additional time for repeat experiences playing the game and for follow-up discussions

Teaching Directions

1. Explain to the students that, in playing the game, partners take turns rolling the die and deciding which place value to assign the numbers rolled; after each roll, a player takes that number of pennies or dimes from the coin bag and records on his or her recording sheet the total coin amount for each roll. The partners each take six turns rolling the die, and then find the total value of their coins. The winner of the game is the student who gets a total closest to one hundred without going over.

2. Have the students play the game in pairs several times.

3. Hold a class discussion about strategies for playing the game.

Teaching Notes

In order to understand the base ten number system, students must understand that the value of a digit is dependent upon its position. A number in the "ones place" represents a quantity of one to nine objects, while a number in the "tens place" represents both a quantity of objects as well as that many groups of ten. In the number 57, the 5 represents fifty, as well as five groups of ten. Students begin to understand the value of digits through experiences in which they count groups of objects. In this game, students have further experience with situations in which they consider how the value of a digit changes depending on its position.

The Lesson

Day 1

As students came in from recess, I asked them to sit in a circle in front of the room. I wanted them to be able to see the game as it was played, so for my partner I chose from those students sitting across from me on the rug. As students sat down, I quietly asked Jimmy if he would like to be my partner in demonstrating the game to the class; he agreed. I had a bag of coins, a die, and a recording sheet next to me. On the board, I had drawn a large representation of the recording sheet that the students would be using to play the game.

"I am really excited to teach a new game to you today," I began. "The game is called *One Hundred One and Out!* because you are 'out' if you go over one hundred. You play this game with a partner and today I am going to play with Jimmy. You also need one die, a bag of coins, and a recording sheet." I put the materials in the middle of the rug, where Jimmy and I could both reach them. I poured out the coins.

"There are two types of coins in this bag." I held up a penny and a dime. "If you can remind us of the name and value of one of these coins, please raise your hand."

"The silver one is a dime. It's worth ten cents," Jacob said.

Donald added, "The other one is a penny. It's one cent."

"Thank you!" I said. "Here is Jimmy's recoding sheet." I showed the sheet to the students and then I passed it to Jimmy. "Mine is drawn on the board so that you can all see it and help me while I am playing the game. I am going to go first so that I can explain the directions to Jimmy along with the rest of you. The recording sheet has a row of seven boxes. The first six are for the six rolls of the die that Jimmy and I will each take. The last box in the row says 'total.' We will use that at the end of the game. We each only get six rolls of the die. At the end of the six rolls, we each will find the total value of all of the coins we have taken. We want to get as close to one hundred as possible, without going over. That's why this game is called *One Hundred One and Out!* Let me show you."

I rolled the die and got a 6. "I have a decision to make each time I roll the die," I explained. "I can take that many dimes or that many pennies. For this roll, I can take six dimes or six pennies. I will take six dimes." I took six dimes from the pile. "Now I need to write the value of the coins from this roll in the first box. The value of my coins for this roll is . . ."

"Sixty cents!" several students answered.

"How did you figure that out?" I asked. "Donald?"

Donald crawled to the center of the rug, and counted aloud as he touched each dime: "Ten, twenty, thirty, forty, fifty, sixty!"

"If you wanted pennies, it would be six cents. But now it's sixty," Marissa added.

"OK. I am going to write 'sixty cents' in this first box." I got up and wrote in the first box of the recording sheet I had drawn on the board:

Total

"Now it's Jimmy's turn. He will roll and follow the same steps I did."

Jimmy rolled a 3. "What decision must Jimmy make?" I asked.

Jacob had an idea. "He can take that many dimes or that many pennies."

"I think he should take dimes!" said Stacy. "Then he will be close to Ms. Scharton!"

"I wonder how close he would be," I said, hoping that my question would prompt a comparison between our two current totals. Some students softly counted aloud, beginning with thirty and counting on to sixty. Some began counting by ones, while others counted by tens.

"I am going to take dimes," said Jimmy. Jimmy reached for three dimes and then passed the die to me. "Your turn," he said. I wondered if he was thinking ahead, or just copying what I had done, taking dimes instead of pennies.

"You need to write something down!" Linda reminded him.

Jimmy smiled shyly and said, "Oops! I forgot." He wrote *10¢* in the first box on his recording sheet.

"You know how I explained what I wrote down?" I asked. "Can you tell us what you wrote on your paper?"

"I have to write down how much I have," Jimmy said. "I have thirty cents, so I wrote . . . Uh oh! It should be thirty cents, not ten cents!" Jimmy erased what he had written first and wrote the correct amount. "*Now* it's your turn," he said. He passed the die.

I rolled a 3 on my second turn. To involve all of the students in the game, I asked them to think about my strategy. "Please talk to the person next to you. Tell them what decision you think I should make and why you think so." Students quickly talked among themselves, then quieted down and looked to see what I would do. I knew that I could bring my total very close to one hundred if I took dimes. I was also hoping that Jimmy would win with a lower score, so that students could see that a *lower* score can win this game. "I am going to take three dimes. What would happen if I took three pennies?"

"You'd have . . . sixty-three cents," said Marissa.

"And you figured that out by . . ." I prodded.

"The dimes are ten," Marissa answered, "twenty, thirty, forty, fifty, sixty. . . . If you had three pennies, it would be sixty-one, sixty-two, sixty-three." She counted the last three numbers on her fingers.

"So, what would I have if I took three dimes?" I wondered aloud.

"You'd have sixty," began Jimmy, while raising one finger at a time, "seventy, eighty, ninety. Ninety cents!"

"You're going to win," said Stacy.

"Tell us why you think so," I pressed.

"You want to get to one hundred one . . . I mean one hundred. You have ninety. That's pretty close!" she said.

Sarah added, "But she still has four more rolls. I think she should take pennies!"

"Why do you think I should take three pennies?" I asked Sarah.

"If you take three pennies, you will have sixty-three cents. That's still a pretty good number. But it's not really high. Ninety is really high. See," and she walked over to the 1–100 chart posted by the board. "Here's ninety and here's one hundred. They are really close together."

While our discussion about careful decision making was valuable and informative, I didn't want students to lose interest in the game. After they learned the rules and had played the game several times, a discussion about strategies for playing and winning the game would be more meaningful.

"Sarah brought up a good point," I said, "but I'm going to take a chance and take three dimes. Remind me what I need to write on my paper." Some students said, "Thirty cents," while others said, "Ninety cents."

"Uh oh. Which is it, thirty cents or ninety cents? What do you think?"

Linda said, "I think it's ninety cents. You put how much you have."

"I think it's thirty cents. You write down how much for that roll," Donald said.

"I can see why you would say 'ninety cents' and why you would say 'thirty cents.' It's true that I do have ninety cents so far. But, remember: each box tells the value of the coins for that roll. Does that help?"

"Thirty cents!" most responded. I wrote the amount from my roll in the second box (see below).

I passed the die to Jimmy. He rolled a 6. I said, "What did Jimmy roll? What do you think he will take? What will he write in the second box of his recording sheet?" I wanted the students to notice the steps that Jimmy was using to play the game and my questions were ways of making his behavior explicit. Jimmy took six pennies, wrote *6¢* in the second box on his recording sheet, and then gave me the die.

My next roll was a 3. There was a murmur of "Uh ohs" from some of the students. I was tempted to ask the students about this response, but I pressed on with modeling the directions. Again, I had the students turn to someone next to them and explain what decision I should make and why. After a minute, I said, "I am going to take three pennies." Students reminded me to write *3¢* in the third box.

Sarah volunteered to count my current total; she first counted the dimes by tens and then counted on for the pennies to get a total of ninety-three cents. I noticed that Jimmy and I had different methods for organizing our coins and thought that this might be an interesting observation to share with the students.

"I think our way of organizing coins is really interesting," I said. "Jimmy has grouped all of his dimes together and all of his pennies together. I have my coins from each turn grouped together."

With a running total of thirty-six cents so far, Jimmy rolled a 4 for his third turn. He took four dimes and wrote *40¢* in the third box of his recording sheet. After he passed the die to me, I rolled a 5. I again asked the students to talk among themselves about whether I should take dimes or pennies. Many students immediately realized that I would lose if I took dimes, although many had difficulty determining what I would have if I added fifty cents to my current total: ninety-three cents.

"So, what decision do you think I should make?" I asked.

Most students quickly responded, "Pennies!"

"Why do you think so?" I inquired.

Richard answered, "If you take pennies, you could still win. If you take dimes, you will lose . . . *definitely*!"

"Does anyone else have an idea to share?" I wanted to hear students' strategies for adding the possible amounts to find the potential totals.

"If you take pennies, you'd have"—Stacy softly counted on her fingers—"ninety-four, ninety-five, ninety-six, ninety-seven, ninety-eight. Ninety-eight cents. You could still win. You'd have to roll . . ." She got quiet.

"Ones. You'd have to roll ones on both turns left. I don't think so!" said Jose.

The students had some experience with dice games as well as vocabulary associated with probability. "Is it possible to get two ones in a row?" I asked. Some students thought it was, while others did not think so or were unsure. "What do you think and why do you think so?"

Jose came over and picked up the die. He turned it until the face with one dot was faceup. "You could roll a one and then roll a one," he said.

"So, it's *possible* to roll two ones in a row," I said. Some students nodded and some were still unsure.

"Is it *likely* for me to roll two ones in a row?" I asked.

"No way!" said Richard.

"Uh-uh," responded Jacob. "I think you'll roll a five or a three . . . maybe a one . . . but not both times!"

"Maybe . . ." suggested Jimmy.

"We'll just have to see," I said teasingly. "I wonder what I would have if I took dimes. Talk to someone next to you and explain your thinking." It was difficult for many students to figure this out. I had previously observed that most students were able to start with a multiple of ten and count on by tens up to and past one hundred. From studying patterns on the 1–100 chart, many students could count by tens starting with any number as long as the starting number was less than one hundred. Once the starting number went past one hundred, students became confused and frustrated. Many resorted to counting by ones. But because the number to be counted on was fifty ones, this quickly became an overwhelmingly difficult task.

"I have asked you a really challenging question," I acknowledged. I talked slowly, so that students could keep up with my explanation. "Imagine you are at your desk. You are playing this game. You have ninety-three cents and you have rolled a five. You want to know what you would have if you took five dimes. What could you do?"

"You could use the cubes!" Sarah said. She pointed to the plastic shoeboxes that were placed at each group of desks. These shoeboxes contained two colors of snap cubes: one color was grouped into "trains" of ten cubes each and the others were single cubes.

"How so?" I asked.

"You could take five trains. Those could be the dimes. You could count them. You could count on . . . ?"

I gave her some time to think, and then suggested, "Go get five trains. Let's see."

Sarah quickly got up, got five trains of snap cubes and a handful of single cubes, and returned. She started with 93 and began counting by ones aloud; each time she touched a cube, she said the next number in sequence. I stopped and asked her if the class could help, hoping to keep the other students engaged and involved while also giving them practice with counting past 100. The students joined in. It took a while, but eventually we were successful at counting all the way to 143. The students sighed, some with big smiles of accomplishment, others feigning fatigue.

"I know something about this game," I said. "I don't want to go past one hundred, and one hundred and forty-three is way past one hundred! I am going to take pennies." I got five pennies and put them in the fourth pile in front of me on the rug. I wrote 5¢ in the fourth box on the board. I explained my counting aloud. "I had ninety-three cents and I just got five more cents." I touched the piles already counted and said, "Ninety-three," and then counted by ones, using five of my fingers, saying, "Ninety-four, ninety-five, ninety-six, ninety-seven, ninety-eight. I have ninety-eight cents." I passed the die to Jimmy for his fourth turn.

60¢	30¢	3¢	5¢			
						Total

He rolled a 2 and took two pennies. He wrote the amount in the appropriate box on his paper and handed the die to me. He had seventy-eight cents in front of him.

For my fifth roll, I rolled a 4. Many students groaned and many students stifled giggles.

"You made some very interesting sounds after I rolled! How come?" I asked.

"You lost the game, Ms. Scharton!" several students said.

"But how could you tell?"

"Look," said Jacob. He took four pennies. "See. If you have ninety-eight and you take four, you have ninety-nine, one hundred, one hundred and one, one hundred and two. It's too many! It's one hundred *one* and out! You have one hundred *two*!"

"I guess I don't want to take dimes," I joked. "The game isn't over, even though I lost. I still have to continue." I took the four pennies Jacob had counted, wrote the amount from the roll in the fifth box, and handed the die to Jimmy.

60¢	30¢	3¢	5¢	4¢		
						Total

Jimmy rolled a 6 for his fifth roll and took pennies. We finished the game, rolling the die for the sixth round. Jimmy had 89 cents for a total and I had 107 cents. My record looked like this:

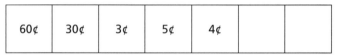

60¢	30¢	3¢	5¢	4¢	5¢	107¢
						Total

"Now it's time for you to play the game with a partner," I said. "When someone taps you on the shoulder, I know you will thank them for choosing you to be your partner. When you see me wink at you, get up and tap a partner on the shoulder. Come up for a bag of coins, a die, and two recording sheets. Find a place to play the game. We will play for a while and then we will need to clean up. When we clean up, I want you to carefully count the coins before you put them back in the bag. Notice that the bags are labeled with the number of pennies and the number of dimes that should be inside. Bring the bags and the dice up front. Any questions?"

While students played, I roamed the room to observe. My experiences with using games in the mathematics classroom helped me to see certain patterns of behavior. Students appeared intent on winning the game. But during the initial period of playing any game, students' learning seems to focus primarily on

remembering the directions for playing the game and accurately recording, rather than on thinking mathematically. For that reason, my observations at this time were focused on the technical aspects of playing the game. I wanted to see if the students were utilizing math strategies, but I was also curious about whether or not they were able to keep track of their current totals and how they counted the coins at any given time.

I stopped by the table at which Marissa and Stacy were playing. "How's it going?" I said.

"Good!" they said, smiling back at me.

"What is your total right now?" I asked them. Marissa began counting the pennies, "One, two, three . . ." When she got to the two dimes, she started counting by ones on her fingers, "Four, five, six," all the way to twenty-three. Stacy, on the other hand, started counting her dimes by tens first, and then counted her pennies by ones: "Ten, twenty, thirty, thirty-one, thirty-two. I have thirty-two cents." This seemed like a good opportunity for Stacy to explain a more efficient way of counting to Marissa. I said, "Marissa, I noticed that you counted your pennies first. And Stacy, you counted your dimes first. I wonder which way is faster, or if it matters?"

Stacy said, "You still get the same number. But my way is quicker. See?" She began counting Marissa's coins, beginning with the dimes, and then counting the pennies: "Ten, twenty, twenty-one, twenty-two, twenty-three!"

Marissa exclaimed, "Oh! Let me try!" She was less experienced than her partner was, but was still able to use the method that Stacy had explained. She counted her coins, beginning with the dimes. To make sure that she understood what she was doing, I asked her to recount Stacy's coins as well. She was successful at doing so, and proud of her newfound skill. I would have to check back later in the game and during the week, to ask her to count coins again. I would be interested to see if she would continue this method or go back to her previous way.

I walked by Timothy and Donald's table. "He won't let me use the die!" Timothy said angrily.

"You already had a turn!" Donald corrected.

"No, I didn't! You took two turns in a row!" Timothy complained.

When I looked at their recording sheets, I noticed that Donald had three boxes filled in on his paper, while Timothy only had one. "How could your paper help you figure out whose turn it is?" I asked. They both looked at their own papers and then at each other's.

"Look!" Timothy said. "I only took one turn!" He pointed to the one box he had filled in with *4¢*, and then pointed to the three boxes filled in on Donald's paper. "You rolled three times!"

"Oops . . ." Donald said sheepishly.

Both students fell silent. "So, what could you do now?" I asked.

Donald said, "He could take another turn and then another. And then it will be my turn again."

I asked, "Will that solve your problem?" Both nodded in agreement.

"What could you do so that you can make sure that both of you take an equal number of turns?"

"How about if I keep the die by me until I am done. I'll be done when I roll the die, take some coins, and write down how much the coins are worth. And then I can give you the die. And then you will know that I am done with my turn," Timothy suggested.

"How does that sound, Donald?" I asked.

"OK. Sorry, Timothy," Donald added.

"That's OK," Timothy offered. They continued to play.

I stopped to listen to Sarah and Richard. Sarah had the die and was saying, "Five! Five! Five!" and Richard was shaking his head, saying, "I lost!"

"How do you know?" I questioned.

"I have too much money," he explained. He counted the dimes, then the pennies, all the way to 107 cents. "See?" he said.

"I have ninety-five cents," said Sarah. She proved her total to me by counting the coins. "If I get a five, I will have exactly one hundred and I'll win!" she exclaimed.

"You already won!" said Richard.

"What do you mean?" I asked.

"I went over. She didn't," he explained.

"But I'm not done. I can still lose!" said Sarah.

"Explain to Richard how you could lose," I said.

"If I get higher than a five . . . if I get a six or seven," said Sarah.

"You can't get a seven!" Richard exclaimed. "The die only goes up to six!"

"But if I get a six, I will have ninety-six, ninety-seven, ninety-eight, ninety-nine, one hundred, one hundred one. If I get one hundred and one, I'm out!" said Sarah.

"So you'd lose, too?!" Richard looked at me questioningly.

"Well, the rules of the game say that the winner of the game is the person that gets closest to one hundred without going over. If you get one hundred one . . . what do you think should happen?" I questioned.

"Cat's game!" said Sarah.

"Cat's game?" said Richard. "What does *that* mean?"

"That means we tie. Is that right, Ms. Scharton?"

This question provided a good opportunity for all of us to revisit the rules of the game and confirm what could possibly happen. I agreed with Sarah's logic, saying, "That sounds right to me, Sarah. What do you think, Richard?"

"I guess so," said Richard.

"Let's see!" Sarah was eager to determine the game's outcome. She rolled the die and got a 3.

"Yeah!" she cried.

It was time for the lesson to end. I got the students' attention and asked them to count the coins before putting them back in the bags. I reminded them to bring the bags and dice to the front of the room, and hand their recording sheets in to me. The class continued to play *101 and Out!* throughout the week. It was a featured activity during math time for the next couple of days and an optional activity during other parts of the day as well. Everyone got a chance to play it three or four times before our next Friday math period.

Day 2

On Friday, I called all of the students to the rug at the beginning of math time. "You have all practiced *One Hundred One and Out!* during the week," I began. "You have become experts at playing the game. Today we are going to play again. But this time, I want you to do something a little different. Today I want you to pay close attention to your thinking while you play the game. Think about the 'strategy' that you use to win the game."

"What's a strategy?" a few students asked.

"Remember?" asked Jimmy. "How you win the game . . . that's your strategy."

"That's right," I confirmed. "A strategy is all the things you do in order to win the game. So, you have two jobs today. One is to play the game. The other is to think about your strategy for winning . . . what you do to win the game. We will play for a while, and then I will ask you to give me your attention."

I had the students play the game with a partner for about twenty minutes. At that point, I got the students' attention and I asked them to do a "Think-Pair-Share": think about their strategy, pair up with their partner and tell their strategy, then listen to their partner's strategy. I wanted them to rehearse their ideas aloud so that they would have some ideas to put down on paper. Explaining their ideas to another person helps them to more clearly understand their own ideas, and listening to the ideas of others exposes them to ideas they may not have otherwise considered. The students were happily engaged in explaining their ideas to their partners. As they did, I wandered around the room and listened in on many of their conversations. I wanted to get an idea of the kinds of things students were considering in their development of a strategy. Students were talking about what they would do if they got certain numbers when rolling the die, as well as their actions at critical points in the game. After they had been engaged in dialogue for a few minutes, I asked the students for their attention once again.

"You have thought about your strategy, explained it to another person, and heard your partner's strategy. I have listened to many of your conversations and heard you mention many different things. Some of you talked about what to do if you rolled a one or two and what to do if you rolled a five or six. Some of you talked about what coins you would take at the beginning of the game and what coins you would take at the end. Now I'd like you to turn over the recording sheet you used during the game and explain your strategy on the back. Explain what you would do in order to win the game. We will then come together and share our ideas."

Students began writing. Some filled up the page, while others wrote a simple sentence after much encouragement from me. After about fifteen minutes, I asked students to bring their papers to the rug so that we could share our ideas with one another. I posted a piece of chart paper on the board. At the top of the chart, I had written, *Strategies for 101 and Out!* I wanted to have a record of their strategies that we could continue to adapt and revise through continued experience with the game.

"You were really busy at your seats," I began. "You got many ideas down on your papers. I would like to give you a chance to share some of these ideas with each other. We will have time to share a few ideas."

Donald raised his hand. "At the beginning, if you roll a five," he said, "you take dimes."

I wrote these words on the chart. I wanted the students to begin to connect the ideas together or see how they were related, so I asked, "Does someone else have an idea about rolling certain numbers or what to do with a roll at the beginning of the game?"

"I think if you roll any high number at the beginning you should take dimes," added Stacy.

"What is a 'high number,' Stacy?" I asked.

"Like a five or a six. Those are high numbers," Stacy explained.

"What is possible, when you roll a die?" I questioned.

Students called out all of the possibilities, from one to six. I wrote the numbers in order on the board. "So, Stacy says that five and six are 'high numbers' when you roll a die. And if you get a high number at the beginning of a game, you should take dimes." On the chart, I wrote, *If you roll a 5 or 6 at the beginning of the game, you should take dimes.* Again, to prompt students to make connections between strategies, I asked, "Does someone else have a strategy that involves high numbers or a strategy that involves something to do at the beginning of *One Hundred One and Out!?*"

I called on Richard. "I think the opposite of Stacy. If you roll a high number any time, you should take pennies. If you roll a low number, take dimes." I would later see how Richard explained this strategy in writing. (See Figure 17–1.)

"Tell us what you mean by low numbers," I said.

"A low number is like one or two," Richard said.

"So, no matter when you roll, if you roll a high number, you should take pennies. If you roll a low number, take dimes." I added Richard's strategy to the class chart, writing, *If you roll a 1 or 2, take dimes. If you roll a 5 or 6, take pennies.*

"My idea is like Richard's," said Sarah. On her own, she had connected her strategy to a previous one. "I think that, no matter when you roll the die, if

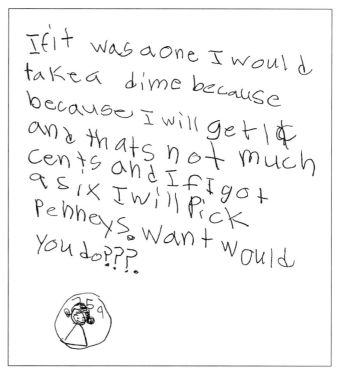

FIGURE 17–1 Richard explained what he would do, depending upon the roll of the die.

you get a low number like one, two, or three, you take dimes. If you roll a high number like six, five, or four, you take pennies."

"Tell us how your idea is different than, or similar to, Richard's," I said.

"Richard said a low number was one or two and I said it is a one, two, or three. He said a high number was six or five and I said it is a six or a five or a four. Besides that, it's the same."

I added Sarah's idea to the chart: *If you roll a 6, 5, or 4, take pennies. If you roll 1, 2, or 3, take dimes.*

It was time to end our math period for the day. I told the students, "We have some strategies on our class chart. Let's leave these up for a few days and try some of them out while we continue to play *One Hundred and One and Out!* We will have a class discussion in a few more days. We will see if we need to change any of these strategies or add some others to the chart. Please pass your papers forward. I am anxious to read through your papers and get an idea of the strategies that you have come up with!"

When I reviewed their papers, I saw that students had various ideas about strategies. Some thought specific rolls should determine whether a player took dimes or pennies, regardless of whether it was the beginning or end of the game. (See Figure 17–2.)

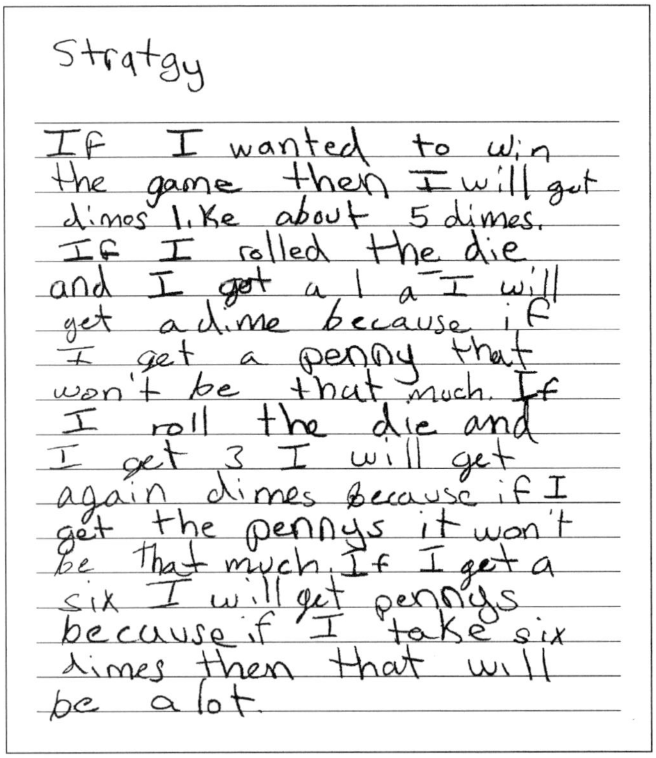
Stratgy

If I wanted to win the game then I will get dimes like about 5 dimes. If I rolled the die and I got a 1 a I will get a dime because if I get a penny that won't be that much. If I roll the die and I get 3 I will get again dimes because if I get the pennys it won't be that much. If I get a six I will get pennys because if I take six dimes then that will be a lot.

FIGURE 17–2 Sarah's work demonstrates a belief that certain die rolls should determine what coins to take.

Other students thought a good decision depended upon when the die was rolled. (See Figure 17–3.) Still others realized that it was possible to win by accumulating coins of a lesser value. (See Figure 17–4.)

Playing *101 and Out!* was an option for "Choice Time" for the next two weeks. Typically, games and activities become Choice Time activities after they are introduced in whole-class lessons. Introducing activities in this way helps students to learn the rules and directions for a game so that they can eventually play it independently, increasing their understanding, through repeated experiences, of the mathematics involved. Once the students were comfortable with how to play the game and the strategies involved, I would offer them a challenge with a second version of the game.

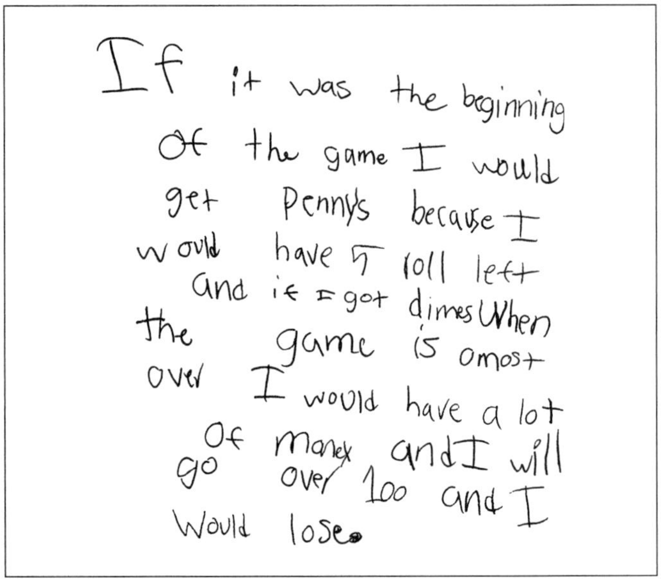
If it was the beginning of the game I would get pennys because I would have 5 roll left and if I got dimes When the game is omost over I would have a lot of maney and I will go over 100 and I would lose.

FIGURE 17–3 Rick's decision about which coins to take depends upon when the die is rolled.

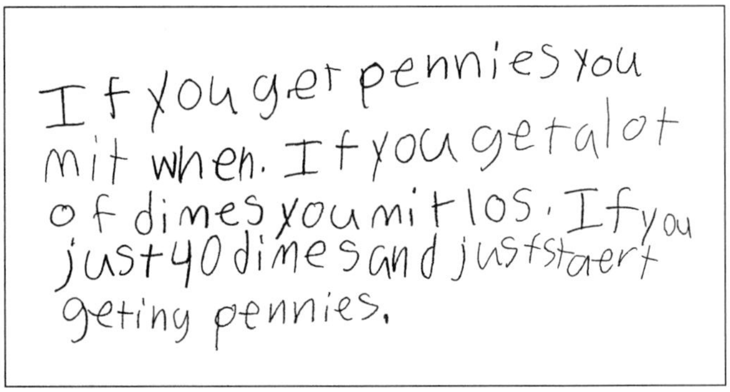
If you get pennies you mit when. If you get a lot of dimes you mit los. If you just 40 dimes and just staert geting pennies.

FIGURE 17–4 Marissa realized that is possible to win the game by having coins of a lesser value.

Version 2

A few weeks later, I asked the students to take a seat in a circle on the rug after recess. I had posted some chart paper and in my hand was a die.

"Good morning!" I said. "I am really excited to share a new game with you today. I have two challenges for you. One is to listen carefully to the directions of the new game I am going to explain. The second is to think about how this game might be similar to or different from another game you might know. Listen carefully."

Again, I asked a student sitting across from me on the rug to be my partner. "I am going to play with Leon, because he is sitting right across from me and you can all see him. I am going to write my recording sheet, as well as Leon's recording sheet, on the board."

I got up from my chair to draw two rows of seven connected boxes on the board, one for Leon and one for me. Under the seventh box in both rows, I wrote the word *Total*.

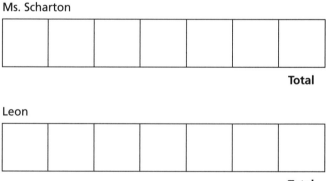

Students began smiling, wiggling, and raising their hands when they realized that the illustration on the board was familiar to them.

"Does this look like something you have seen?" I asked. "Don't tell me! Watch and see if your guess is true after I continue explaining! We are going to take turns rolling the die. We will each take six turns." The students kept smiling and some were nodding their heads knowingly. "I am going to roll first," I continued.

My first roll was a 5. This is where the previous version of *101 and Out!* was different from this one. I continued explaining. "Now I have a decision to make. I can use this roll for the total numbers of ones I can have, or I can use it for the total number of tens I can have. If I decided to use ones, how many would I have?"

Donald said, "Five cents!"

Unsurprisingly, Donald had connected his understanding of the familiar game with the new one. "Why do you think so, Donald?" I asked.

"Pennies are one cent. You got a five. So, you got five cents!" Donald explained.

"That's right," I said, "but in this game, you will notice that I have no pennies! If I did, I could take pennies. But instead, I have to figure out what I would have if I had five ones. Does anyone else have an idea?"

"If you had blocks, you could take five blocks," Marissa said.

"Go get them and show us what you mean," I said.

Marissa went to the math corner and brought back a plastic shoebox that had base ten materials inside: single units (ones), "rods" (tens), and "flats" (hundreds). She took out five single units, laid them on the rug, and said, "See? One, two, three, four, five!"

"Yes, if I had the blocks, I could use them. What else could I use? Any other ideas?" I asked.

"You could have five books, or five chairs, or five anything!" Jose said.

"Yes, I could. What if I decided to use tens, instead of ones? If I wanted tens for my roll of five, what would I have?" Some students raised their hands, while others counted softly by tens on five fingers. "Stacy? What do you think?"

"It would be fifty." She extended five fingers, one at time, counting by tens, saying, "Ten, twenty, thirty, forty, fifty!"

"What is another way to figure out how much five tens is?" I asked.

"You could use the hundred chart!" said Richard.

"How might you use the hundred chart?" I prodded.

He got up and walked to the chart posted behind me. He picked up the pointer on the ledge of the board and pointed to 10. "There's one ten," he said, "and there's two tens, three tens, four tens, five tens!" Each time, Richard pointed to the corresponding number on the chart.

"So, we could use fingers, the hundred chart . . . what else?" I inquired.

Sarah pointed to the snap cubes at each group of student desks and said, "You could use those!"

"Come show us," I encouraged.

Sarah went to a table and returned with a shoebox. She pulled out five trains of ten cubes each, laid them out side by side, and said, "See? Ten, twenty, thirty, forty, fifty!"

"So, you have lots of tools you could use to figure out your total for the round. I have to decide: do I want five ones—five—or five tens—fifty. Hmmm . . . I think I will take five ones—five. Now I have to do something with that number. Would you like to take a guess and see where I would write 'five'?"

"In the first box!" was the overwhelming response. I wrote down the number.

Ms. Scharton

5						

Total

I passed the die to Leon and he rolled a 3.

"Remind Leon what he needs to do," I said.

"Decide!" was the group response.

"I'm going to take tens," Leon told us. "That's . . ." He stopped to softly count by tens, extending three fingers, "Ten, twenty, thirty."

"I am going to write 'thirty' in the first of Leon's boxes," I said.

Leon

30						

Total

"Uh oh! I forgot to tell you the object of this game!" I said.

"I know! I know!" said several students as they quickly raised their hands.

"How would you know?" I said with mock astonishment. "Sarah?"

"You want to get close to one hundred!" said Sarah.

"Yeah . . . but you can't go over!" added Donald.

"You read my mind! You are right! So, Leon and I need to be thinking ahead in this game. In the end, when we total up our rounds, we want to be as close as we can be to one hundred, without going over."

Leon and I continued to play the rest of the game in front of the circle of students. After each roll, we talked about what was possible. We also talked about the current total: I asked volunteers to explain how they came up with the total and individual students would explain how they combined the numbers. At the end of the game, we collaborated to find the total for both Leon and me. I was nervous about this step. In the first version of *101 and Out!*, students could count the money to find the total. In this version, they did not have the same support. I was curious to see

what students would do. "How will we figure the total, to see who has won the game?" I asked.

"Add the numbers!" the students replied.

"How might the numbers be added?" I asked.

Students added the numbers in different ways. Many students combined all of the tens, then all of the ones; when they were left with two numbers to combine, they either counted on from the larger number or they decomposed the smaller number (e.g., 12) into tens and ones (10 and 2) and then recombined the tens and the ones to get a total. When they told me how they added the numbers, I recorded their method on the board. For example, my six numbers were 5, 30, 10, 40, 4, and 3. Here are two ways students added these numbers:

$$30 + 10 = 40$$
$$4 + 4 = 8 \text{ so } 40 + 40 = 80$$
$$5 + 4 = 9$$
$$9 + 3 = 12$$
$$12 = 10 + 2$$
$$80 + 10 = 90$$
$$90 + 2 = 92$$

$$30 + 10 + 40 = 80$$
$$80 + 5 = 85$$
$$85 + 4 = 89$$
$$89 + 3 = 92$$

Other students added the numbers in a string, beginning with the first number, counting on to the second number, then the third, and so on. Sometimes they used their fingers, and other times, when counting on was too cumbersome (e.g., + 40), they resorted to using the 1–100 chart.

$$5 + 30 = 35$$
$$35 + 10 = 45$$
$$45 + 40 = 85$$
$$85 + 4 = 89$$
$$89 + 3 = 92$$

This method was more time consuming and a few students commented that "looking for tens" was easier. However, it was important for students to notice that it didn't matter the order in which the numbers were combined; the total was still the same.

"I see you have lots of ways of finding the total," I said. "Use a way that makes sense to you. Find the total and see who has won the game." We spent a few minutes figuring Leon's total; I then asked the students to think about my earlier challenges.

"There were two challenges I gave you at the beginning of our math period. One was to listen carefully to the rules of the new game. Help me quickly write the steps on the chart paper." As they voiced suggestions, I wrote:

1. *Get a partner.*

2. *Take turns rolling the die. Roll six times.*

3. *Decide: tens? Or ones?*

4. *Record your roll.*

5. *Find the total.*

"The second challenge I gave you was to see how today's game is similar to or different from another game you might know. What do you think?" It was clear, from the students' responses, that they were comparing what I had intended: the two versions of *101 and Out!* I recorded their ideas on the chart paper (see below).

Different

old game	new game
¢	no sign
used coins	used our brains

Similar

old game	new game
pennies and dimes	ones and tens

"You have begun to compare these two games," I said. "These are two different ways of playing, or two 'versions' of the same game, *One Hundred One and Out!* Today you are going to play this new way. I am going to ask you to play for a few days and then I am going to ask you to write some ideas about what you think you have learned from playing this game." Students were dismissed to try out this new version of *101 and Out!*

I was apprehensive about what would happen. It seemed as though this version would be quite a leap for students to make: they would have to find the total from the six rounds without the support of coins. I was surprised to find that this extension of the game was less challenging than I had anticipated. Most students had little difficulty playing the new version and were actually excited by playing what seemed to be a new game. This version pushed them to compute rather than count money. They were able to use various methods to find the total. Although students were allowed to use manipulatives to help them combine the rolls for each round, most students chose to find the totals by relying on the numbers, rather than the use of manipulatives, and were successful at doing so.

Students played this new version of *101 and Out!* for a few days before I asked them to reflect on the game. I wanted them to have some time to get comfortable with rules and differences of the game before considering the concepts involved in playing it. Near the end of a math period during which they had played the game, I wrote on the board, *What I learned from playing the game is . . .* I asked the students to spend about ten minutes writing down some feedback on a separate sheet of paper. Some students referred to the earlier version of the game, as did Sarah. She wrote, *This game is the same as* 101 and Out. *What I learned about this game is that we don't have to put the cents sign. This game is a good game too.* Marissa compared this game to the earlier one as well, writing, *I learned that it's different from* 101 and Out *because in* 101 and Out, *you used dimes and pennies but in this game you don't. They look kind of the same game but they kind of don't.*

Robert and Donald responded to the type of thinking involved in playing this game. Robert wrote, *There is no pennies and no dimes. You need to think in your head.* Donald referred to the thinking involved, as well as some understanding of place value, depending on the decision made when rolling a particular number, stating, *If you roll a 5, you haf to thingk if your going to get 50 or 5. It is omost the same as* 101 and Out*!!!*

Other students referred to ways of adding numbers or the use of strategic thinking. Robert and Timothy provided information about strategies used during the course of the game that were based more on wishful thinking than an understanding of the probability of getting a particular roll. Robert wrote, *I will get high numbers then I will get low numbers so I will win,* and Timothy wrote, *When you are like at 70 or 80 get little nummers so you can win.* Fernando referred to some of the operations involved and also made an attempt at a strategy, explaining, *What I learn from playing this game is to add big numbers and to use big numbers.* Stacy helped me to understand some benchmark numbers that were comfortable for her to use when adding, as well as her flexibility in combining numbers in different ways, recording, *I can count by fives and 10s adding and I can count to 100 any way I want to. This game is just like* 101 and Out *with cents but you just think in your head.*

Linking Assessment and Instruction

As the students work, think about the following:

- What strategies do the students use while playing the game? Can they communicate their strategies while playing the game? Does their strategy for a particular die roll change depending on whether it is the beginning/middle/end of the game? Do students' strategies change with more experience?

- While playing the game, do students compare their running total to one hundred? How do they find the difference between their running total and this benchmark? Do students count on from their running total by tens, then ones, or solely by ones? Can they count back from one hundred by tens, then ones? Do students use other tools and/or materials to compare their running and/or final totals to one hundred?

- When playing the coin version of the game, how do students find the value of their coins during the game? Do they group like coins together, then count by dimes, then pennies? Do they count by tens, then ones, or do they count only by ones?

- When playing the coin version of *101 and Out!*, how do students find the total at the end of the game? Do they rely solely on the coins they have collected, on the numbers they have written down, or do they use both sets of information?

- When playing the variation of the game without coins, what strategies do students use to find the total at the end of the game? Do they combine the tens, then the ones, or do they combine numbers in the order in which they are written?

- When comparing the different versions of *101 and Out!*, what connections do students make?

Blackline Masters

Lengths of Yarn

Yarn Name	Estimate	Measurement	Difference

The Missing Piece

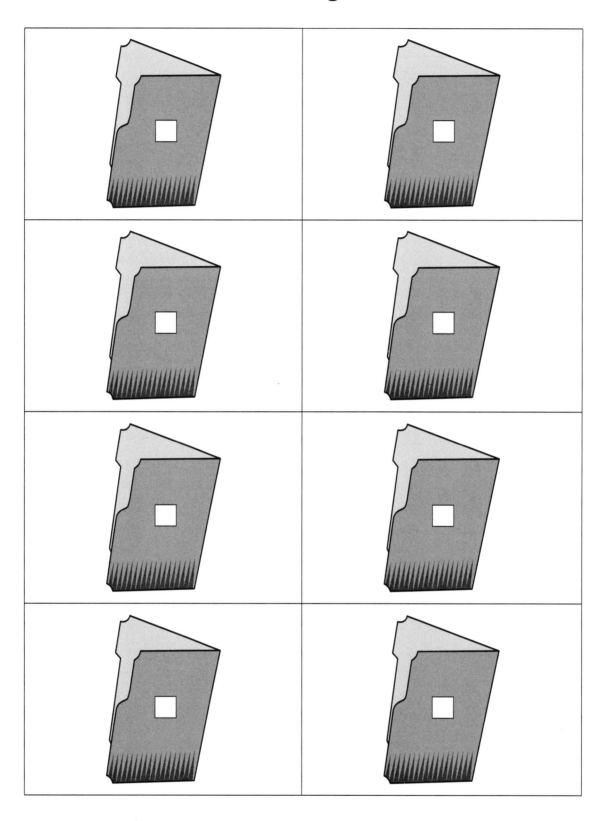

From *Teaching Number Sense, Grade 2* by Susan Scharton. © 2005 Math Solutions Publications.

Tile Riddles

Riddle 1

1. I have 12 tiles.

2. I used 3 colors.

3. There are no red tiles.

4. There are the same number of green tiles and blue tiles.

5. I have 4 yellow tiles.

Riddle 2

1. There are fewer than 10 tiles.

2. I used 2 colors.

3. I have no green or red tiles.

4. I have twice as many blue tiles as yellow tiles.

5. I have 2 yellow tiles.

Writing Riddles

1. Work in pairs.
2. Choose less than 15 tiles.
3. Write clues about what you have chosen.
4. Think about the order of your clues and if you have enough clues or too many.
5. Try out your clues with someone else.

From *Teaching Number Sense, Grade 2* by Susan Scharton. © 2005 Math Solutions Publications.

Numbers and Me

- Think of some numbers that are special to you.
- Record them.
- Write a sentence about each of your numbers.

My number	A sentence about my number

From *Teaching Number Sense, Grade 2* by Susan Scharton. © 2005 Math Solutions Publications.

Ten-Frames

From *Teaching Number Sense, Grade 2* by Susan Scharton. © 2005 Math Solutions Publications.

Ten-Frames Models

From *Teaching Number Sense, Grade 2* by Susan Scharton. © 2005 Math Solutions Publications.

Ten-Frames Models

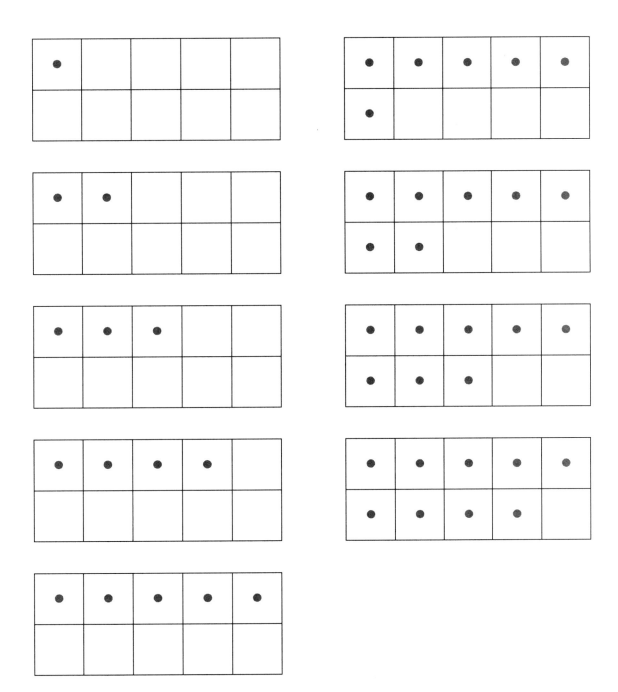

Story Problems

Your teacher had _____ pencils. She collected _____ more pencils. How many pencils did she have then?

(38, 30)   (47, 23)   (57, 25)

From *Teaching Number Sense, Grade 2* by Susan Scharton. © 2005 Math Solutions Publications.

Story Problems

_____ children were playing soccer.

_____ were boys and the rest were girls.

How many girls were playing soccer?

(45, 20)   (50, 26)   (63, 28)

Story Problems

_____ children were on the playground.

Some children went inside their classrooms.

_____ were still on the playground.

How many children went inside their classrooms?

(50, 24) (89, 46) (93, 58)

From *Teaching Number Sense, Grade 2* by Susan Scharton. © 2005 Math Solutions Publications.

Story Problems

There were _____ children on the playground.

_____ more came to join them.

How many children were on the playground then?

(48, 26)   (138, 134)

Make My Number

8

12

22

42

40

20

29

79

49

45

From *Teaching Number Sense, Grade 2* by Susan Scharron. © 2005 Math Solutions Publications.

Make My Number

65

15

9

58

158

128

328

128

100

From *Teaching Number Sense, Grade 2* by Susan Scharton. © 2005 Math Solutions Publications.

Make My Number

165

125

425

495

490

290

90

From *Teaching Number Sense, Grade 2* by Susan Scharton. © 2005 Math Solutions Publications.

Capture the Castle Game Board

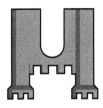

Capture the Castle Recording Sheet

Secret #	Tokens I Have	Tokens I Have Spent	Tokens I Have Left

From *Teaching Number Sense, Grade 2* by Susan Scharton. © 2005 Math Solutions Publications.

101 and Out!

<table>
<tr><td></td><td></td><td></td><td></td><td></td><td></td><td></td></tr>
</table>

Total

<table>
<tr><td></td><td></td><td></td><td></td><td></td><td></td><td></td></tr>
</table>

Total

<table>
<tr><td></td><td></td><td></td><td></td><td></td><td></td><td></td></tr>
</table>

Total

<table>
<tr><td></td><td></td><td></td><td></td><td></td><td></td><td></td></tr>
</table>

Total

<table>
<tr><td></td><td></td><td></td><td></td><td></td><td></td><td></td></tr>
</table>

Total

<table>
<tr><td></td><td></td><td></td><td></td><td></td><td></td><td></td></tr>
</table>

Total

Index